A Voice of Warning

and

Key to the Science of Theology

(First Edition – 1855)

By Parley P. Pratt

Designed as an Introduction to the first principles of spiritual philosophy; religion; law and government; as delivered by the ancients, and as restored in this age, for the final development of universal peace, truth and knowledge.

PANTIANOS
CLASSICS

Published by Pantianos Classics

ISBN-13: 978-1-78987-008-4

A Voice of Warning was first published in 1837

Key to the Science of Theology was first published in 1855

Contents

Preface to the Second European Edition

When the following Work was first published in America, in 1837, it was but little known, and seemed to meet with little or no encouragement. Months passed away, and very few copies were sold or read. But, to the astonishment of the author, it worked itself into notice more and more, by the blessing of God, and by virtue of its own real merits; till, in two years, the first edition, consisting of three thousand copies, was all sold, and many more were called for. A new edition was published in 1839, consisting of two thousand five hundred copies; these were also disposed of. Other three editions have since been published, making in all thirteen thousand copies now disposed of, and the demand is still increasing both in America and Europe.

It has already found its way into most of the American States, and into the provinces of the Canadas, as well as many parts of England, Scotland, Ireland, and Wales. It has visited the cottages of the humble, and the parlors of the great; and from the best information we have on the subject, very few have risen from its perusal without a deep and settled conviction of the truth of its principles.

The author has now in his possession the testimony of hundreds of people, from different states and nations, all bearing witness that this Work has been a means, in the hands of God, of saving them from infidelity, from sectarian error and delusion, and of guiding them into the light of TRUTH.

All these considerations, and an intense desire to impart the truth to mankind as widely as possible, have induced the author to send forth this new edition; which he greatly desires may prove a blessing to thousands who are yet grovelling in darkness and superstition, and lead them to the true fold of God.

If there be anything to admire, or anything praiseworthy in this Work, the author has no claim to the honor or the praise; it is justly due to Him who is the Source and Fountain of all TRUTH. The author was a husbandman, inured to the plow—unpolished by education, untaught in the schools of modern Sectarianism, (falsely called "Divinity")— reared in the wilds of America, with a mind independent, untrammelled and free. He drank of the pure fountain of Truth, unsullied and unmixed, as it unfolded in majesty of light and splendor from the opening heavens in all the simplicity of its nature. As such it has flowed from his pen in the following volume; not veiled in mystery; not dressed in the pomp of high-sounding names, and titles, and learned terms; not adorned in the gay attire of eloquence flowing from the imagination and the passions; but standing forth in the undress of its own native modesty, as if conscious of the purity and innocence of its nature.

He is indebted not only to the Spirit of Truth for the principles contained in this Work, but also to several men, who have been made the instruments in the hands of God, to reveal the knowledge of God to this generation, and to be the founders and leaders of the Church of Jesus Christ of Latter-day Saints.

Among the foremost of these, he would make honorable mention of President Joseph Smith, by whose instrumentality most of these glorious truths (so well known to the ancients) have been restored to the knowledge of the world—and whose zeal, labors, sufferings, and subsequent murder, will stand forth as a bright memorial to all succeeding ages, and be celebrated by happy millions yet unborn.

With an assurance that the principles of this Work will yet prevail over the whole earth, this new edition of the VOICE OF WARNING is now sent forth; and should the author be called to sacrifice his life for the cause of Truth, he will have the consolation that it will be said of him, as it was said of Abel, viz: "HE, BEING DEAD, YET SPEAKETH."

Parley P. Pratt.
Manchester, England,
Dec. 4, 1846.

Preface to the First American Edition

During the last nine years, the public mind has been constantly agitated, more or less, through all parts of our country, with the cry of "Mormonism, Mormonism, Delusion, Imposture, Fanaticism," etc., chiefly through the instrumentality of the press. Many of the newspapers of the day have been constantly teeming with misrepresentations and slanders of the foulest kind, in order to destroy the influence and character of an innocent society in its very infancy; a society of whose real principles many of them know nothing at all. Every species of wickedness has been resorted to, and all manner of evil has been spoken against them falsely; insomuch, that in many places, houses and ears are closed against them, without the possibility of being heard for a moment.

Were this the only evil, we might have less cause of complaint; but in consequence of this we have been assaulted by mobs, some of our houses have been torn down or burned, our goods destroyed, and fields of grain laid waste. Yea, more—some of us have been stoned, whipped, and shot; our blood has been caused to flow, and still smokes to heaven, because of our religious principles, in this our native land, the boasted land of liberty and equal law! while we have sought in vain for redress. Officers of state have been deaf to the voice of Innocence, imploring at their feet for justice and protection in the enjoyment of rights as American citizens.

Under these circumstances, what could be done? How were we to correct the public mind? We were few in number, and our means of giving information very limited; the columns of most of the papers were closed against us, their popularity being at stake the moment our principles were admitted. It is true we published a monthly paper, in which our principles were clearly set forth; but its circulation was limited to a few thousands. Under these circumstances, had we the tongue of angels, and the zeal of Apostles, with our hearts expanded wide as eternity, with the intelligence of heaven, and the love of God burning in our bosoms; and commissioned to bear as joyful tidings as ever were borne by Michael, the Archangel, from the regions of glory; yet, it would have been as impossible for us to have communicated the same to the public, as it was for Paul, when he stood in the midst of Ephesus, to declare the glad tidings of a crucified and risen Redeemer, when his voice was lost amid the universal cry of "Great is Diana of the Ephesians!"

Go, lift your voice to the tumultuous waves of the ocean, or try to reason amid the roar of cannon while the tumult of war is gathering thick around, or speak to the howling tempest while it pours a deluge over the plains; let your voice be heard amid the roar of chariots rushing suddenly over the pavements; or, what is still less useful, converse with a man who is lost in slumbers, or reason with a drunkard while he reels to and fro under the influence of the intoxicating poison, and those will convince you of the impossibility of communicating truth to that soul who is willing to make up his judgment upon popular rumor, or to be wafted gently down the current of public opinion, without stopping for a moment to listen, to weigh, to hear both sides of the question, and judge for himself.

One of the greatest obstacles in the way of the spread of truth, in every age, is the tide of public opinion. Let one ray of light burst upon the world in any age, and it is sure to come in contact with the traditions and long-established usages of men, and their opinions; or with some religious craft, so that, like the Ephesians, they counsel together what shall be done; their great goddess will be spoken against, her magnificence despised, her temple deserted; or, what is still worse, their craft is in danger, for by this they have their wealth. Call to mind the Apostles in contact with the Jewish Rabbis, or with Gentile superstitions; in short, at war with every religious establishment on the earth. Witness the popular clamor: "If we let them thus alone, all men will believe on them, and the Romans will come and take away our place and nation." "These men that turn the world upside down have come hither also." "What new doctrine is this, for thou bringest certain strange things to our ears?" "These men do exceedingly trouble our city, and teach customs which are not lawful for us to receive, being Romans." "What will this babbler say, he seems to be a setter forth of strange gods?" And many other such like sayings.

Or, let us for a moment contemplate the events of later date; for instance, the Mother Church against the reformers of various ages; see them belied, slandered, degraded, whipped, stoned, imprisoned, burned, and destroyed in various ways, while the ignorant multitude were made to believe they were the very worst of men.

Again, think for a moment of the struggles of Columbus, an obscure individual of limited education, but blessed with a largeness of heart, a noble genius, a mind which disdained to confine itself to the old beaten track; accustomed to think for itself, it burst the chains which, in ages past, had held in bondage the nations of the earth; it soared aloft, as it were on eagle's wings;

it outstripped and left far behind the boasted genius of Greece and Rome; it penetrated the dark mysteries which lay concealed amid the western waters. Behold him struggling for eight years against the learned ignorance of the courts and councils of Europe, while the sneer of contempt, the finger of scorn, and the hiss of derision, were the solid arguments opposed to his theory.

But what was the result when, after many a fruitless struggle, an expedition was fitted out, consisting of three small vessels? A new world presented itself to the wondering nations of the East, destined, at no distant period, to become the theatre of the most glorious and astonishing events of the last days. This fact was no sooner demonstrated than their philosophical, geographical, and religious objections vanished in a moment; haughty ignorance and bigotry were for once constrained to cast their honors in the dust, and bow their reverend heads at the feet of real worth, and learn, in humble silence, that one fact, clearly demonstrated, was worth ten thousand theories and opinions of men.

Having said so much to impress upon the human mind the necessity of hearing, and then judging, I would only add, that the object of this publication is to give the public correct information concerning a religious system, which has penetrated every State from Maine to Missouri, as well as the Canadas, in the short space of nine years; organizing Churches and Conferences in every region, and gathering in its progress from fifty to a hundred thousand disciples; having, at the same time, to sustain the shock of an overwhelming, religious influence, opposed to it by the combined powers of every sect in America. What but the arm of Omnipotence could have moved it forward amid the rage of mobs? having to contend with the prejudice of the ignorant and the pen of the learned; at war with every creed and craft in Christendom; while the combined powers of earth and hell were hurling a storm of persecution, unparalleled in the history of our country.

This Work is also intended as a warning voice, or proclamation of truth, to all people into whose hands it may fall, that they may understand, and be prepared for the great day of the Lord. Opinion and guesswork in the things of God are worse than useless; facts, well demonstrated, can alone be of service to mankind. And as the Holy Ghost can alone guide us into all truth, we pray God the Eternal Father, in the name of Jesus Christ His Son, that the Spirit of Truth may inspire our hearts in inditing this matter; that we may be able to write the truth in demonstration of the Spirit and of power, that it may be the word of God, the everlasting Gospel, the power of God unto salvation, to the Gentile first, and also to the Jew.

A Voice of Warning and Instruction to All People

Chapter One - On Prophecy Already Fulfilled

We have also a more sure word of prophecy, whereunto ye do well that ye take heed as unto a light that shineth in a dark place, until the day dawn, and the day-star arise in your hearts: knowing this first, that no prophecy of the Scripture is of any private interpretation; for the prophecy came not in old time by the will of man, but holy men of God spake as they were moved upon by the Holy Ghost.

—PETER.

In order to prove anything from Scripture, it is highly necessary in the first place to lay down some certain, definite, infallible rule of interpretation, without which the mind is lost in uncertainty and doubt, ever learning, and never able to come to the knowledge of the truth.

The neglect of such a rule has thrown mankind into the utmost confusion and uncertainty in all their biblical researches. Indeed, while mankind are left at liberty to transform, spiritualize, or give any uncertain or private interpretation to the word of God, all is uncertainty.

"Whatsoever was written aforetime, was written for our profit and learning, that we through patience and comfort of the Scriptures, might have hope." Now, suppose a friend from a distance should write us a letter, making certain promises to us on certain conditions, which, if we obtained, would be greatly to our profit and advantage: of course it might be said the letter was written for our profit and learning, that through patience and comfort of the letter we might have hope to obtain the things promised. Now if we clearly understood the letter, and knew what to expect, then it would afford us comfort and hope; whereas, if there was any doubt or uncertainty on our minds in the understanding of the same, then could we derive no certain comfort or hope from the things written, not knowing what to hope for; consequently the letter would not profit us at all. And so it is with the Scriptures. No prophecy or promise will profit the reader, or produce patience, comfort, or hope in his mind until clearly understood, that he may know precisely what to hope for. Now, the predictions of the Prophets can be clearly understood, as much so as the almanac when it foretells an eclipse; or else the Bible of all books is of most doubtful usefulness. Far better would it have been for mankind, if the great Author of our existence had revealed nothing to His fallen creatures, than to have revealed a book which would leave them in doubt and uncertainty, to contend with one another, from age to age, respecting the meaning of its contents. That such uncertainty and contention have existed for ages, none will deny. The wise and learned have differed, and do still widely differ, from each other, in the understanding of prophecy. Whence then this difference? Either Revelation itself is deficient, or else the fault is in mankind. But to say Revelation is deficient, would be to charge God foolishly; God forbid: the fault must be in man. There are two great causes for this blindness, which I will now show:

First, mankind have supposed that direct inspiration by the Holy Ghost was not intended for all ages of the Church, but was confined to primitive times; the "Canon of Scripture being full," and all things necessary being revealed; the Spirit which guides into all truth was no longer for the people: therefore they sought to understand, by their own wisdom, and by their own learning, what could never be clearly understood, except by the Spirit of Truth: for the things of God knoweth no man, except by the Spirit of God.

Secondly, having lost the Spirit of Inspiration, they began to institute their own opinions, traditions, and commandments; giving constructions and private interpretations to the written word, instead of believing the things written. And the moment they departed from its literal meaning, one man's opinion, or interpretation, was just as good as another's; all were clothed with equal authority, and from thence arose all the darkness and misunderstanding on these points, which have agitated the world for the last seventeen hundred years.

Among the variety of commodities which attract the attention of mankind, there is one thing of more value than all others. A principle which, if once possessed, will greatly assist in obtaining all other things worth possessing, whether it were power, wealth, riches, honors, thrones, or dominions. Comparatively few have ever possessed it, although it was within the reach of many others, but they were either not aware of it, or did not know its value. It has worked wonders for the few who have possessed it. Some it enabled to

12

escape from drowning, while every soul who did not possess it was lost in the mighty deep. Others it saved from famine, while thousands perished all around them; by it men have often been raised to dignity in the state; yea, more, some have been raised to the throne of empires. The possession of it has sometimes raised men from a dungeon to a palace; and there are instances in which those that possessed it were delivered from the flames, while cities were consumed, and every soul, themselves excepted, perished. Frequently, when a famine or the sword has destroyed a city or nation, they alone who possessed it escaped unhurt. By this time the reader inquires, What can this be? Inform me, and I will purchase it, even at the sacrifice of all I possess on earth. Well, kind reader, this treasure is FOREKNOWLEDGE! a knowledge of things future! Let a book be published, entitled, "A Knowledge of the Future," and let mankind be really convinced that it did give a certain, definite knowledge of future events, so that its pages unfold the future history of the nations, and of many great events, as the history of Greece or Rome does unfold the past, and a large edition would immediately sell at a great sum per copy; indeed, they would be above all price. Now, kind reader, the books of the Prophets, and the Spirit of Prophecy were intended for this very purpose. Well did the Apostle say, "Covet earnestly the best gifts; but rather that ye prophesy."

Having said so much, we will now enter into the wide expanded field which lies before us, and search out the treasures of wisdom and knowledge which have been shining for ages like a light in a dark place. We will explore regions unknown to many; we will gaze upon the opening glories which present themselves on every side, and feast our souls with knowledge which is calculated in its nature to enlarge the heart, to exalt the mind, and to raise the affections above the little, mean, grovelling things of the world, and to make one wise unto salvation.

But, first, for the definite rule of interpretation. For this we will not depend on any man or commentary, for the Holy Ghost has given it by the mouth of Peter: "Knowing this first, that no prophecy of the Scripture is of any private interpretation." 2 Peter i, 20.

There is one grand division to be kept constantly, in view in the study of prophecy; namely, the distinction between the past and the future. The reader should be careful to ascertain what portion has been fulfilled, and what remains to be fulfilled: always remembering Peter's rule of interpretation will apply to both. Now, if we should find in our researches that every prophecy which has been fulfilled to the present year, has been literally fulfilled, then it follows of necessity that every prophecy which is yet future will not fail of a literal fulfilment. Let us commence with the days of Noah. Gen. vi, 17: "And behold I, even I, do bring a flood of waters upon the earth, to destroy all flesh, wherein is the breath of life, from under heaven; and every thing that is in the earth shall die."

In the verses which follow the above the Lord commands Noah to enter the Ark, and take with him animals of every kind, etc. And in the 22d verse it is written, "Thus did Noah, according to all that God commanded him, so did he." It was well for Noah that he was not well versed in the spiritualizing systems of modern divinity; for, under their benighted influence, he would never have believed that so marvelous a prophecy would have had a literal meaning and accomplishment. No, he would have been told that the flood meant a spiritual flood, and the Ark a spiritual Ark, and, the moment he thought otherwise, he would have been set down for a fanatic, knave, or fool; but it was so, that he was just simple enough to believe the prophecy literally. Here then is a fair sample of foreknowledge; for all the world, who did not possess it, perished by the flood.

The next prediction we will notice is Gen. xv, 13-16. "And he said unto Abraham. Know of a surety that thy seed shall be a stranger in a land that is not theirs, and shall serve them, and they shall afflict them four hundred years. And also that nation, whom they shall serve, will I judge; and afterwards shall they come out with great substance. And thou shalt go to thy fathers in peace; thou shalt be buried in a good old age; but in the fourth generation they shall come hither again, for the iniquity of the Amorites is not yet full."

The evil entreating of the children of Israel four hundred years, together with their coming out with great substance, and the judgment of God upon Egypt, as well as the death of Abraham in a good old age, are all facts too well known to need comment here; suffice it to say, that it is a striking example of the exact fulfilment of prophecy, uttered more than four hundred years before it had its accomplishment. From this we gather that none of those ancient men knew anything of the modern system of spiritualizing.

Our next is Gen. xix, 12, 13: "And the men said unto Lot, Hast thou here any besides? son-in-law, and thy sons, and thy daughters, and whatsoever thou hast in the city, bring them out of this place: for we will destroy this place, because the cry of them is waxed great before the face of the Lord; and the Lord hath sent us to destroy it." Now, Lot being simple enough to believe the thing in its literal sense, took as many of his family as would follow, and escaped for his life; to the great amusement, no doubt, of the Sodomites, who probably stood gazing after, crying "Delusion, delusion!" they thinking all the while that the prophecy was only a figure. Here is an example of a man escaping from the flames by foreknowledge imparted to him, while the whole city perished. O! what a blessing that Lot had no knowledge of the modern manner of interpreting prophecy. If it had once entered his heart that he must come out of Sodom spiritually, instead of literally, it would have cost him his life.

Let us examine a prophecy of Joseph in the land of Egypt. Gen. xli, 29-31: "Behold, there come seven years of great plenty throughout all the land of Egypt: and there shall arise after them seven years of famine; and all the plenty shall be forgotten in the land of Egypt; and the famine shall consume the land: and the plenty shall not be known in the land by reason of that famine following; for it shall be very grievous." Joseph then proceeds to give directions for corn to be laid up in great abundance during the seven plenteous years, in order to provide against the famine. And Pharaoh, being no better versed in the school of modern divinity than his predecessors, never once thought of any other interpretation but the most literal, And thus he was the means, together with Joseph, in the hand of God, of saving, not only their nation, but the house of Israel, from famine. This is another striking example of the power of foreknowledge. It not only saved from famine, but it exalted Joseph from a dungeon to a palace; from the lowest degradation to the highest honor; so that they cried before him, "Bow the knee!" But, O! what death and mourning would have followed had they dreamed only of spiritual famine and spiritual corn.

Having given a few plain examples of early ages, we will lightly touch upon some of the most remarkable events of prophecy, and its fulfilment, until we come down to the Jewish Prophets, where the field opens wide, touching in its progress the most remarkable events of all ages, and terminating in a full development of the opening glories of the last days.

One remarkable instance, concerning Elijah the Prophet, was, that he prophesied to Ahab that it should not rain for three years and upwards, which came to pass according to his word. There is also a remarkable instance of Hazael, the Syrian, who came to Elisha to inquire of the Lord concerning the king of Syria, his master, who was sick. The Prophet, earnestly beholding him, burst into tears: and Hazael asked him, saying, "Why weepest thou?" and he, answering, said, "The Lord hath showed me that thou shalt be king over Syria." And he then proceeded to unfold unto him the cruelties which he would afterwards exercise towards Israel, which are too horrible to mention here, lest in so doing I might offend the delicate ear. But Hazael, astonished to hear these things predicted concerning himself, which at that time filled him with horror, exclaimed with surprise, "But what? is thy serv- ant a dog, that he should do this great thing?" Yet astonishing to tell, all was afterwards fulfilled to the very letter.

In the 21st chapter, 2 Chron., it is written that there came a writing to Je- horam from Elijah, which, after stating the great wickedness of which he had been guilty, in turning to idolatry, and also murdering his brethren of his fa- ther's house, who were better than himself, proceeds thus: "Behold, with a great plague will the Lord smite thy people, and thy children, and thy wives, and all thy goods; and thou shalt have great sickness by disease of the bow- els, until thy bowels fall out, by reason of thy sickness, day by day." In the same chapter it is written, that the Philistines and Arabians came against him, and took his wives, and children, and goods captive; and after all this, the Lord smote him in his bowels with an incurable disease, and his bowels fell out by reason of his sickness, so he died of sore disease.

In the 6th chapter of Joshua, 26th verse, there is a wonderful prediction concerning Jericho: "Cursed be the man before the Lord, that riseth up and buildeth this city Jericho. He shall lay the foundation thereof in his first-born, and in his youngest son shall he set up the gates of it."

After this curse the city of Jericho lay waste for ages, none daring to re- build it at the expense of their first-born and of their youngest son; until after a long succession of judges and kings, when hundreds of years had passed, Hiel the Bethelite, who lived in the days of Ahab, probably supposing that the Lord had forgotten the curse pronounced upon it by Joshua, ventured to re- build the city: but no sooner had he laid the foundation thereof than Abiram his first-born died, and, still persevering in the hardness of his heart, he set up the gates thereof, with the loss of his youngest son, Segub, according to the word of the Lord by Joshua; see 1 Kings, xvi, 34. We might fill a volume with instances of a similar kind, dispersed through the historical part of the Scriptures; but we forbear, in order to hasten to a more full examination of the books of the Jewish Prophets. We shall trace them in their fulfilment up- on Jerusalem, Babylon, Tyre, Egypt, and various other nations.

Babylon, the most ancient and renowned city of the world, was pleasantly situated on the banks of a majestic river, that flowed through the plains of Shinar, near to which the tower of Babel once stood. It was laid out four square, and surrounded with a wall upwards of three hundred feet high, and sixty miles in circumference; having a hundred gates of brass with bars of iron; twenty-five gates on each side, which opened to streets running through the city, a distance of fifteen miles; thus forming the whole city into exact squares of equal size. In the midst of these squares were beautiful gardens, adorned with trees and walks, diversified with flowers of varied hue; while the houses were built upon the borders of the squares, directly fronting on the streets. In the midst of this city sat Nebuchadnezzar, enthroned in royal splendor and magnificence, and swaying his sceptre over all the kingdoms of the world, when it pleased God, in a vision of the night, to unveil the dark curtain of the future, and to present before him, at one view, the history of the world, even down to the consummation of all things. Behold, a great image stood before him, whose head was of fine gold, his breast and arms of silver, his belly and thighs of brass, his legs of iron, his feet and toes part of iron and part of miry clay. He beheld, till a stone was cut out of the mountain without hands, which smote the image upon the feet, which were part of iron and part of clay, and brake them in pieces; then was the iron, the brass, the silver, and the gold, broken to pieces together, and became as the chaff of the summer threshing-floors; and the wind carried them away, and there was no place found for them; but the stone which smote the image became a great mountain, and filled the whole earth. When Daniel was brought in before the king, to tell the dream and the interpretation, he exclaimed, "There is a God in heaven that revealeth secrets, and maketh known to the king, Nebuchadnezzar, what shall be in the latter days." Then, after telling the dream, he continues thus: "Thou, O king, art a king of kings; for the God of heaven hath given thee a kingdom, power, and strength, and glory. And wheresoever the children of men dwell, the beasts of the field and the fowls of the heaven hath he given into thine hand, and hath made thee ruler over them all. Thou art this head of gold. And after thee shall arise another kingdom inferior to thee, and another third kingdom of brass, which shall bear rule over all the earth. And the fourth kingdom shall be strong as iron: forasmuch as iron breaketh in pieces and subdueth all things; and as iron that breaketh all these, shall it break in pieces and bruise. And whereas thou sawest the feet and toes, part of potters' clay, and part of iron, the kingdom shall be divided: but there shall be in it of the strength of the iron, forasmuch as thou sawest the iron mixed with miry clay. And as the toes of the feet were part of iron, and part of clay, so the kingdom shall be partly strong, and partly broken. And whereas thou sawest iron mixed with miry clay, they shall mingle themselves with the seed of men: but they shall not cleave one to another, even as iron is not mixed with clay. And in the days of these kings shall the God of heaven set up a kingdom, which shall never be destroyed: and the kingdom shall not be left to other people, but it shall break in pieces and consume all these kingdoms, and it shall stand forever. Forasmuch as thou sawest that the stone was cut out of the mountain without hands, and that it brake in pieces the iron, the brass, the clay, the silver, and the gold; the great God hath made known to the king what shall come to pass hereafter; and the dream is certain, and the interpretation thereof sure."

In this great view of the subject we have presented before us, in succession, first, the kingdom of Nebuchadnezzar; second, the Medes and Persians, who took Babylon from Belshazzar, and reigned over all the earth; third, the Greeks under Alexander, who conquered the world, and reigned in the midst of Babylon; and fourth, the Roman empire, which subdued all things; fifth, its division into eastern and western empires, and its final breaking up or subdivision into the various kingdoms of modern Europe, represented by the feet and toes, part of iron and part of clay. And, lastly, we have presented before us an entirely new kingdom, organized by the God of heaven in the last days, or during the reign of these kings, represented by the feet and toes. This last kingdom was never to change masters, like all the kingdoms which had gone before it. It was never to be left to another people. It was to break in pieces all these kingdoms, and stand forever. Many suppose that this last kingdom alluded to was the kingdom of God which was organized in the days of Christ, or his Apostles. But a greater blunder could not exist; the kingdom of God set up in the days of Christ, or his Apostles, did not break in pieces any of the kingdoms of the world: it was itself warred against and overcome, in fulfilment of the words of Daniel, chapter vii, 21; "I beheld, and the same horn made war with the saints, and prevailed against them;" also 22d verse, "Until the Ancient of Days came, and judgment was given to the saints of the Most High; and the time came that the saints possessed the kingdom;" also verse 27th, "And the kingdom and dominion, and the greatness of the kingdom, under the whole heaven, shall be given to the people of the saints of the Most High, whose kingdom is an everlasting kingdom; and all dominions shall serve and obey him."

John records, Rev. xiii. 7, "And it was given unto him to make war with the saints, and to overcome them; and power was given him over all kindreds, and tongues, and nations." In fulfilment of these sayings, power has been given, to the authorities of the earth to kill the Apostles and inspired men, until, if any remained, they were banished from among men, or forced to retire to the desolate islands, or the dens and caves of the mountains of the earth, being men of whom the world was not worthy; while at the same time, many false prophets and teachers were introduced in their place, whom men heaped to themselves, because they would not endure sound doctrine. In this way the kingdom of God became disorganized, and lost from among men, and the doctrines and churches of men instituted in its place. But we design to speak more fully on this subject when we come to treat on the subject of the kingdom of God. Suffice it to say, that the kingdom spoken of by Daniel is something to be organized in the last days, by the God of heaven Himself, without the aid of human institutions or the precepts of men. And, when once organized, it will never cease to roll; all the powers of earth and hell will not impede its progress, until at length the Ancient of Days shall sit, and the Lord Jesus will come in the clouds of heaven, with power and great glory, as the King of kings, and Lord of lords, and destroy all these kingdoms, and give the kingdom and the greatness of the kingdom, under the whole heaven, to the Saints. Then there will be but one Lord, and His name one, and He shall be King over all the earth.

We will now return to Nebuchadnezzar, whom the Lord, by the mouth of Jeremiah, calls His servant, to execute His judgment upon the nations. It seems that the Lord exalted this great man, and made him a king of kings, and lord of lords, arming him with His own sword, and clothing him with power and authority, for the express purpose of executing His judgments, and scourging and humbling all the nations of the earth. Jeremiah, chapter xxv, says that the Lord purposed to bring Nebuchadnezzar and his army against Jerusalem, and against all the nations round about, that he might bring them to desolation and captivity for seventy years; and after seventy years, He would turn and punish the king of Babylon and that nation for their iniquity. Now, who can trace the history of the fulfilment of these great events, so exactly pointed out by Jeremiah, Isaiah, and Ezekiel, and not be struck with astonishment and wonder at the marvellous gift of prophecy enabling men in those days to read the history of the future as they read the history of the past? Indeed, the reader of history in the nineteenth century, holding in his hand the history of the Babylonians, Medes and Persians, Greeks, Romans and Egyptians, together with that of the Jews, will hardly render himself more familiar with the events which transpired among those nations, than the Prophets were seventy years previous to their accomplishment.

The Jews were reduced to subjection by Nebuchadnezzar; their city, Jerusalem, was burned, together with their temple; their princes, nobles, and people were carried to Babylon, together with all their holy things. All the particulars of this destruction and captivity were distinctly foretold by Jeremiah, and the time of its continuance, viz., seventy years. After subduing the Jews, the king of Babylon marched his army against Tyre, the city of merchants, situated at the haven of the sea, surrounded not only by the sea, but by a strong wall. A hold so strong required the utmost skill and perseverance of Nebuchadnezzar and his whole army, who labored incessantly for a long time, and at length succeeded in taking Tyre, and bringing it into captivity for seventy years. After which they returned and established their city, for Jeremiah had previously foretold the reduction of Tyre, its captivity for seventy years, and its restoration at the expiration of that time. After the restoration of Tyre, the city flourished for a time, but was afterwards reduced to an entire desolation. Its ruined fragments are seen to this day in the bottom of the sea; its site has become a barren rock, only occupied by poor fishermen. All this desolation, and even its present appearance of desolation and perpetual waste, were clearly pointed out by the Prophets.

But when the king of Babylon had succeeded in taking Tyre, after many a bald head and peeled shoulder, caused by the hard service of his army in the siege, the Lord, by the mouth of Ezekiel, promised to give the spoils of Egypt unto him, for wages for his army, in order to pay him for the great service, wherewith he had served God, against Tyre. Next, witness his war in the taking of Egypt, and bringing it into captivity, until the seventy years were accomplished.

And, finally, trace him executing the Lord's vengeance and anger against Uz, upon the kings of the Philistines, and Askelon, Azaah; Ekrom, Edom, Moab, Ammon; Dedan, Tema, and Buz; and upon the kings of Arabia, Zimri and Elam; and upon all the kings of the Medes; and upon all the kings of the north, far and near; and finally upon all the kingdoms of the world, who were to be drunken, and spew, and fall to rise no more, because of the sword which He would send among them. But, when the Lord had accomplished all his mind on these nations, He purposed, in turn, to punish this great monarch, and those who succeeded him; and also the city and nation over which he reigned; and finally to make it perpetual desolations. And all this for their pride and haughtiness. The Lord exclaims: "Shall the ax boast itself against him that heweth therewith, or shall the saw boast itself against him that shaketh it?" etc. But, in order to trace the events of the return of the Jews, and the other nations, from their seventy years' captivity and bondage, and the punishment of Babylon, another and very different character from that of Nebuchadnezzar is introduced by the Prophets—one who is in Scripture termed the Lord's anointed. He may be considered one of the most extraordinary characters that ever the heathen world produced: his mildness, courage, perseverance, success, and, above all, his strict obedience to the command of that God which neither he nor his fathers had known, all go to prove that Isaiah was not mistaken when he called him by name, as the Lord's anointed, to deliver the nations from bondage, to scourge and subdue the greatest city and monarchy that have at any time existed on the earth, and to restore the Jews, and rebuild their city and temple. Indeed, he was one of those few whom the world never produces except for extraordinary purposes. But let us hear the Prophet's own description of him, Isaiah, chapter xlv: "Thus saith the Lord to his anointed, to Cyrus, whose right hand I have holden to subdue nations before him: and I will loose the loins of kings, to open before him the two-leaved gates, and the gates shall not be shut. I will go before thee, and make the crooked places straight: I will break in pieces the gates of brass, and cut in sunder the bars of iron. And I will give thee the treasures of darkness, and hidden riches of secret places, that thou mayest know that I, the Lord, which call thee by thy name, am the God of Israel. For Jacob my servant's sake, and Israel mine elect, I have even called thee by thy name: I have surnamed thee, though thou hast not known me. I am the Lord, and there is none else, there is no God beside me: I girded thee, though thou hast not known me: that they may know from the rising of the sun, and from the west, that there is none besides me." In the 13th verse, he says: "I have raised him up in righteousness, and I will direct all his ways: he shall build my city, and he shall let go my captives, not for price nor reward, saith the Lord of hosts." The reader will bear in mind that Isaiah lived about one hundred years before the Jewish captivity, and one hundred and seventy years before Cyrus caused their return.

Here I would pause and inquire, What power but the power of the great God could enable one man to call another by name, a century before his birth, and also to foretell correctly the history of his life? What must have been his wonder and astonishment, when, after many years of wars and commotions, during which he marched forth, conquering and to conquer, gathering as a nest the riches of the nations, he at last pitched his camp near the walls of the strongest hold in all the earth? He gazed upon its walls of upwards of three hundred feet in height, with its gates of brass and its bars of iron: the people

21

within feeling perfectly safe, with provisions enough to last the inhabitants of the city for several years. How could he think of taking that city? Who would not have shrunk from such an undertaking, unless inspired by the great Jehovah? But, turning the river Euphrates from its course, and marching under the walls of the city, in the dried bed of the river, he found himself in possession of the city, without any difficulty; for Belshazzar, the king, was drinking himself drunk, with his nobles and concubines, and that, too, from the vessels of the House of the Lord which his father had taken from Jerusalem, and his knees had already smote together with horror, from the handwriting on the wall, which Daniel had just been called in to interpret, giving his kingdom to the Medes and Persians. Having subdued this great monarchy, he seated himself upon the throne of kingdoms; and, becoming familiar with Daniel, he was, no doubt, introduced to an acquaintance with the Jewish records, and then the mystery was unfolded: he could then see that God had called him by name, that the Almighty hand girded him for the battle, and directed all his work; he could then understand why the treasures of the earth poured themselves into his bosom, and why the loins of kings had been unloosed before him, and why the gates of brass had been opened, and the bars of iron burst asunder. It was that he might know that there was a God in Israel, and none else, and that all idols were as nothing; that he might also restore the Jews, and rebuild their city and temple, and fulfil God's purposes upon Babylon. He accordingly issued his proclamation to the Jews to return, and for the nations to assist them in rebuilding, "for," said he, "God hath commanded me to build him an house at Jerusalem." Ezra, chapter i, 2, 3, says: "Thus saith Cyrus, king of Persia, The Lord God of heaven hath given me all the kingdoms of the earth; and he hath charged me to build him an house at Jerusalem, which is in Judea. Who is there among you of all his people? his God be with him, and let him go up to Jerusalem, which is in Judea, and build the house of the Lord God of Israel, he is the God which is in Jerusalem."

What powerful argument, what mighty influence was it which caused Cyrus to be convinced that it was the God of heaven who dwelt at Jerusalem, who alone was God, and who had done all these things? He had not been traditioned in the belief of the true God, nor of the holy Scriptures. Nay, he had ever been very zealous in the worship of idols; it was to idols he looked for assistance in the former part of his life. I reply, it was the power of God, made manifest by prophecy and its fulfilment; not in a spiritualized sense, not in some obscure, uncertain, or dark, mysterious way, which was difficult to be understood; but in positive, literal, plain demonstration, which none could

22

gainsay or resist. Isaiah says that this was the object the Lord had in view when he revealed such plainness. And Cyrus manifested that it had the desired effect.

I would here remark that when we come to treat of that part of prophecy which yet remains to be fulfilled, we shall bring proof positive that the heathen nations of the latter days are to be convinced in the same way that Cyrus was; that is, there are certain events plainly predicted in the Prophets, yet future, which, when fulfilled, will convince all the heathen nations of the true God, and they shall know that he hath spoken and performed it. And all the great and learned men of Christendom, and all societies, who put any other than a literal construction on the word of prophecy, shall stand confounded, and be constrained to acknowledge that all has come to pass even as it is written.

But to return to our research of prophecy and its fulfilment. The Prophets had not only predicted the reduction of Babylon by Cyrus, but they had denounced its fate through all ages, until reduced to entire desolation, never to be inhabited, not even as a temporary residence for the wandering Arab: "And the Arabian shall not pitch tent there." See Isaiah, xiii, 19-22.

Mr. Joseph Wolfe, the celebrated Jewish missionary, while traveling in Chaldea, inquired of the Arabs whether they pitched their tents among the ruins of Babylon, to which they replied in the negative, declaring their fears that, should they do so, Nimrod's ghost would haunt them. Thus all the predictions of the Prophets concerning that mighty city have been fulfilled.

Edom also presents a striking fulfilment of plain and pointed predictions in the Prophets. These predictions were pronounced upon Edom at a time when its soil was very productive and well cultivated, and everywhere abounding in flourishing towns and cities. But now its cities have become heaps of desolate ruins, only inhabited by the cormorant, bittern, and by wild beasts, serpents, etc., and its soil has become barren; the Lord has cast upon it the line of confusion, and the stones of emptiness, and it has been waste from generation to generation, in express fulfilment of the word of prophecy.

We will now give a passing notice of the vision of Daniel, recorded in the eighth chapter of his prophecies, concerning the ram and the goat. The reader would do well to turn and read the whole chapter; but we will more particularly notice the interpretation, as it was given him by Gabriel, recorded from the nineteenth to the twenty-fifth verses. And he said: "I will make thee know what shall be in the last end of the indignation, for at the time appointed the end shall be. The ram which thou sawest having two horns, are the kings of Media and Persia: and the rough goat is the king of Grecia; and the great horn that is between the eyes is the first king. Now that being broken, whereas four stood up for it, four kingdoms shall stand up out of the nation, but not in his power. And in the latter time of their kingdom, when the transgressors are come to the full, a king of fierce countenance, and understanding dark sentences, shall stand up; and his power shall be mighty, but not by his own power; and he shall destroy wonderfully, and shall prosper, and practise, and shall destroy the mighty and the holy people; and through his policy also he shall cause craft to prosper in his hand, and he shall magnify himself in his heart, and by peace shall destroy many; he shall also stand up against the Prince of princes; but he shall be broken without hand." In this vision we have first presented the Medes and Persians, as they were to exist until they were conquered by Alexander the Great. Now, it is a fact well known that this empire waxed exceedingly great for some time after the death of Daniel, pushing its conquests westward, northward, and southward, so that none could stand before it; until Alexander, the king of Grecia, came from the west, with a small army of chosen men, and attacked the Persians upon the banks of the river, and plunging his horse in, and his army following, they crossed, and attacked the Persians, who stood to oppose them on the bank with many times their number; but, notwithstanding their number, and their advantage of the ground, they were totally routed, and the Grecians proceeded to overrun and subdue the country, beating the Persians in a number of pitched battles, until they were entirely subdued. It is also well known that Alexander, the king of Greece, went forth from nation to nation, subduing the world before him, until, having conquered the world, he died at Babylon, at the age of thirty-two years. And thus, when he had waxed strong, the great horn was broken, and for it came up four notable ones towards the four winds of heaven. His kingdom was divided among four of his generals, who never attained unto his power. Now, in the latter time of their kingdom, when the transgression of the Jewish nation was come to the full, the Roman power destroyed the Jewish nation, took Jerusalem, caused the daily sacrifice to cease, and not only that, bat afterwards destroyed the mighty and holy people, that is, the Apostles and primitive Christians, who were slain by the authorities at Rome.

Now, let me inquire, Does the history of these United States give a plainer account of past events than Daniel's wisdom did of events which were then future, and some of them reaching down the stream of time for several hundred years, unfolding events which no human sagacity could possibly have foreseen? Man, by his own sagacity, may accomplish many things; he may plough the trackless ocean without wind or tide in his favor; he may soar aloft amid the clouds without the aid of wings; he may traverse the land with astonishing velocity without the aid of beasts; or he may convey his thoughts to his fellows by the aid of letters. But there is a principle which he can never attain to; no, not even by the wisdom of ages combined; money will not purchase it; it comes from God only, and is bestowed upon man as a free gift. Says the Prophet to the idols, "Tell us what shall be, thai we may know that ye are gods."

We will now proceed to show how exactly the prophecies were fulfilled literally in the person of Jesus Christ. "Behold," said the Prophet, "a virgin shall conceive and bear a son." Again, Bethlehem should be the place of his birth, and Egypt, where he sojourned with his parents, the place out of which he was to be called. He turned aside to Nazareth, for it was written, "He shall be called a Nazarene." He rode into Jerusalem upon a colt, the foal of an ass, because the Prophet had said, "Behold thy King cometh, meek and lowly, riding upon a colt," etc. And again, saith the Prophet: "He shall be afflicted and despised; he shall be a man of sorrows, and acquainted with grief; he shall be led as a lamb to the slaughter, and, like a sheep dumb before his shearers, so he opened not his mouth; in his humiliation his judgment was taken away; and who shall declare his generation, for his life is taken from the earth. He was wounded for our transgressions, and by his stripes we are healed; he was numbered with the transgressors; he made his grave with the rich." Not a bone of him is broken; they divide his raiment; cast lots for his vesture; give him gall and vinegar to drink; betray him for thirty pieces of silver; and finally, when it was finished, he rested in the tomb until the third day, and then rose triumphant, without seeing corruption. Now, kind reader, had you walked up and down with our dear Redeemer during his whole sojourn in the flesh, and had you taken pains to record the particular circumstances of his life and death, as they occurred from time to time, your history would not be a plainer one than the Prophets gave of him hundreds of years before he was born. There is one thing we would do well to notice concerning the manner in which the Apostles interpreted prophecy, and that is this—they simply quoted it, and recorded its literal fulfilment. By pursuing this course, they were enabled to bring it home to the hearts of the people in the Jewish synagogues, with such convincing proof that they were constrained to believe the supposed impostor whom they had crucified was the Messiah. But had they once dreamed of rendering a spiritualizing or uncertain application, like the teachers of the present day, all would have been uncertainty and doubt, and demonstration would have vanished from the earth.

Having taken a view of the Old Testament Prophets, concerning prophecy and its fulfilment, and having shown clearly that nothing but a literal fulfilment was intended, the objector may inquire whether the same mode will apply to the predictions contained in the New Testament. We will therefore bring a few important instances of prophecy, and its fulfilment, from the New Testament; after which we shall be prepared to enter the vast field which is still future. One of the most remarkable prophecies in sacred writ is recorded by Luke, chap, xxi, 20-24: "And when ye shall see Jerusalem compassed with armies, then know that the desolation thereof is nigh. Then let them which are in Judea flee to the mountains, and let them which are in the midst of it depart out; and let not them that are in the countries enter thereinto; for these be the days of vengeance, that all things which are written may be fulfilled. But woe unto them that are with child, and to them that give suck in those days; for there shall be great distress in the land, and wrath upon this people; and they shall fall by the edge of the sword, and shall be led away captive into all nations; and Jerusalem shall be trodden down of the Gentiles, until the times of the Gentiles be fulfilled." This prophecy involves the fate of Jerusalem and the temple, and the whole Jewish nation, for at least eighteen hundred years. About the year seventy, the Roman army compassed Jerusalem. The disciples remembered the warning which had been given them by their Lord and Master forty years before, and fled to the mountains. The city of Jerusalem was taken, after a long and tedious siege, in which the Jews suffered the extreme of famine, pestilence and the sword; filling houses with the dead, for want of a place to bury them, while women ate their own children, for want of all things. In this struggle there perished, in Judea, near one million and a half of Jews, besides those taken captive. Their country was laid waste, their city burned, their temple destroyed, and the miserable remnant dispersed abroad into all the nations of the earth; in which situation they have continued ever since, being driven from one nation to another, often falsely accused of the worst of crimes, for which they have been banished and their goods confiscated. Indeed, they have been mostly accounted as outlaws among the various nations; the soles of their feet have found no rest, and they have been a hiss and a byword; and people have said, "These are the people of the Lord, and are gone forth out of his land."

During all this time the Gentiles have possessed the land of Canaan, and trodden under foot the holy city where their forefathers worshipped the

Lord. Now, in this long captivity, the Jews have never lost sight of the promises respecting their return. Their eyes have watched and failed with longing for the day, when they might possess again that blessed inheritance bequeathed to their forefathers; when they might again rear their city and temple, and re-establish their priesthood, and worship as in days of old. Indeed they have made several attempts to return, but were always frustrated in all their attempts; for it was an unalterable decree, that Jerusalem should be trodden down of the Gentiles, until the times of the Gentiles should be fulfilled. On the subject of this long dispersion, Moses and the Prophets have written very plainly; indeed, Moses even mentioned the particulars of their eating their children secretly in the siege and in the straitness, wherewith their enemies should besiege them in all their gates. Whoever will read the twenty-eighth of Deuteronomy, will read the history of what has befallen the Jews, foretold by Moses with all the clearness that characterizes the history of past events, and all this thousands of years before its accomplishment.

Our next is found in Acts xxi, 10, 11, where a Prophet named Agabus took Paul's girdle and bound his own hands and feet, and said: "Thus saith the Holy Ghost, So shall the Jews at Jerusalem bind the man that owneth this girdle, and shall deliver him into the hands of the Gentiles." The fulfilment of this prediction is too well known to need any description. We therefore proceed to notice a prophecy of Paul, recorded in 2 Tim. iv, 3, 4: "For the time will come, when they will not endure sound doctrine, but, after their own lusts, shall they heap to themselves teachers, having itching ears; and they shall turn away their ears from the truth, and shall be turned unto fables." This prophecy has been fulfilled to the very letter; for it applies to every religious teacher who has arisen from that day unto the present, except those commissioned by direct revelation and inspired by the Holy Ghost. But, to convince the reader of its full accomplishment, we need only point to the numberless priests of the day who preach for hire, and divine for money, and who receive their authority from their fellow man; and as to the fables to which they are turned, we need only to mention the spiritualizings and private interpretations which salute our ears from almost every religious press and pulpit.

But there is another prophecy of Paul well worth our attention, as illustrative of the times in which we live; it is found in the first five verses of the third chapter of 2 Timothy: "This know also that in the last days perilous times shall come; for men shall be lovers of their own selves, covetous, boasters, proud, blasphemers, disobedient to parents, unthankful, unholy,

27

without natural affection, truce breakers, false accusers, incontinent, fierce, despisers of those that are good, traitors, heady, high minded, lovers of pleasures more than lovers of God, having a form of godliness, but denying the power thereof: from such turn away." From the last verse of this quotation we learn to our astonishment that this sum of awful wickedness applies to professors of religion ONLY; that is, this would be the character of the (so called) Christian part of the community in the last days. Do not startle, kind reader; we do not make the application without proof positive to the point, for, remember, non-professors have no form of godliness, but those ungodly characters spoken of were to have a form of godliness, denying the power thereof. But, if you doubt Paul's testimony on the subject, look around you, examine for yourselves. "By their fruits ye shall know them." My heart is pained while I write. Alas, has it come to this; has the Spirit of Truth removed the veil of obscurity from the last days, only to present us with the vision of a fallen people; an apostate church, full of all manner of abominations, and even despising those who are good; while they themselves have nothing left but the form of godliness, denying the power of God; that is, setting aside the direct inspiration and supernatural gifts of the Spirit, which ever characterize the Church of Christ? Was it for this only that the Holy Spirit opened to the view of holy men the events of unborn time, enabling them to gaze upon the opening glories of the latter days? O ye Prophets and Apostles, ye holy men of old, what have you done if you stop here; if your prophetic vision only extended down the stream of time to the present year? Alas! you have filled our minds with sorrow and despair: the Jews you have left wandering in sorrow and darkness, far from all their hearts hold most dear on earth; their land a desolation, their city and temple in ruins, and they, without the knowledge of the true Messiah. The Gentiles, after partaking of the root and fatness of the tame olive tree, having fallen, after the same example of unbelief, are left without fruit, dead, plucked up by the roots, with naught but a form of godliness; while the powers that characterized the ancient church have fled from among men. Is this the consummation of all your labors? Was it for this you searched, toiled, bled, and died? I pause for a reply; if you have a word of comfort yet in store, concerning the future, let it quickly speak, lest our souls should linger in the dark valley of sorrow and despair!

Chapter Two - On the Fulfilment of Prophecy Yet Future

What is Prophecy but History reversed?

Having made the discovery and produced sufficient proof that the prophecies, thus far, have been LITERALLY fulfilled—to the very letter—we hope the reader will never lose sight of the same rule with regard to those yet future. And, while we stand upon the threshold of futurity, with the wonders of unborn time about to open upon our view, presenting before our astonished vision the most mighty and majestic scenes, the most astonishing revolutions, the most extraordinary destructions, as well as the most miraculous displays of the power and majesty of Jehovah, in His great restoration of His long dispersed covenant people from the four quarters of the earth: I say, as these scenes are about to open to our view, let us bow before the great I AM, in the name of Jesus, and pray in faith for His Spirit to enlarge our hearts and enlighten our minds, that we may understand and believe all that is written, however miraculous it may be. But, O! kind reader, whoever you are, if you are not prepared for persecution, if you are unprepared to have your name cast out as evil, if you cannot bear to be called a knave, an impostor, or madman, or one that hath a devil; or if you are bound by the creeds of men to believe just so much and no more, you had better stop here; for if you were to believe the things written in the Bible that are yet to come, you will be under the necessity of believing miracles, signs and wonders, revelations, and manifestations of the power of God, even beyond anything that any former generation has witnessed; yes, you will believe that the waters will be divided and Israel go through dryshod, as they journey to their own land, as they did in the days of Moses; for no man ever yet believed the Bible without believing and expecting such glorious events in the latter days. And I will now venture to say that a believer in the Bible would be something that very few men have ever seen in this generation, with all its boasted religion: for there is a great difference between believing the book to be true when shut, and believing the things therein written. It is now considered in Christendom a great disgrace not to believe the Bible when shut: but whosoever tries the experiment will find it a greater disgrace to believe that the things therein written will surely come to pass. Indeed, it is our firm belief in the things written in the Bible, and careful teaching of them, that is one great cause of the persecution we suffer. For let the prophecies be understood by the people, and let them roll on in their fulfilment, and this will blow to the four winds every religious craft in Christendom, and cause the kingdom of Christ to rise upon their ruins, while the actual knowledge of the truth will cover the earth as the waters do the sea.

Having said so much by way of caution, if there are any of my readers so bold, and regardless of consequences, as to dare with me to gaze upon the future, we will commence with Isaiah xi, 11, 12, 15, 16: "And it shall come to pass in that day, that the Lord shall set his hand again the second time to recover the remnant of his people, which shall be left, from Assyria, and from Egypt, and from Pathros, and from Cush, and from Elam, and from Shinar, and from Hamath, and from the islands of the sea. And he shall set up an ensign for the nations, and shall assemble the outcasts of Israel, and gather together the dispersed of Judah from the four corners of the earth. And the LORD shall utterly destroy the tongue of the Egyptian Sea; and with his mighty wind shall he shake his hand over the river, and shall smite it in the seven streams, and make men go over dryshod. And there shall be an highway for the remnant of his people, which shall be left from Assyria; like as it was to Israel in the day that he came up out of the land of Egypt."

Here you behold an ensign to be reared for the nations; not only for the dispersed of Judah, but the outcasts of Israel. The Jews are called dispersed, because they are scattered among the nations; but the ten tribes are called outcasts, because they are cast out from the knowledge of the nations, into a land by themselves. Now, the reader will bear in mind that the ten tribes have not dwelt in the land of Canaan since they were led captive by Shalmaneser, king of Assyria. We have also presented before us, in the fifteenth verse, the marvelous power of God, which will be displayed in the destruction of a small branch of the Red Sea, called the tongue of the Egyptian Sea; and also the dividing of the seven streams of some river, and causing men to go over dryshod; and, lest any should not understand it literally, the fifteenth verse says: "There shall be a highway for the remnant of his people, which shall be left from Assyria, like as it was to Israel when he came up out of the land of Egypt." Now, we have only to ask whether, in the days of Moses, the Red Sea was literally divided, or whether it was only a figure? For as it was then so shall it be again. And yet we are told by modern divines that the days of miracles have gone forever; and those who believe in miracles, in our day, are counted as impostors, or, at least, poor ignorant fanatics, and the public are warned against them, as false teachers who would, if possible, deceive

30

the very elect. On the subject of this restoration the Prophets have spoken so fully and repeatedly, that we can only notice a few of the most striking instances, which will go to show the particular circumstances and incidents attending it, and the manner and means of its accomplishment. The sixteenth chapter of Jeremiah, fourteenth, fifteenth and sixteenth verses, says: "Therefore, behold, the days come, saith the Lord, that it shall no more be said, the Lord liveth that brought up the children of Israel out of the land of Egypt; but, the Lord liveth that brought up the children of Israel from the land of the north, and from all the lands whither he had driven them: and I will bring them again into their land that I gave unto their fathers. Behold, I will send for many fishers, saith the Lord, and they shall fish them; and after will I send for many hunters, and they shall hunt them from every mountain, and from every hill, and out of the holes of the rocks." Now it has ever been the case with Israel, when they wished to express the greatness of their God, to say, The Lord liveth, which brought up our fathers out of the land of Egypt. This saying at once called to mind the power and miracles of that memorable event, and associated with it all that was great and grand, and was calculated to strike the mind with awe, under a lively sense of the power of Israel's God. But, to our astonishment, something is yet to transpire which will cast into momentary forgetfulness all the great events of that day, and the children of Israel shall know that their God liveth, by casting their minds upon events of recent date, which shall have transpired, still more glorious and wonderful than their coming out of Egypt. They will exclaim, The Lord liveth, which recently brought the children of Israel from the north, and from all lands whither He had driven them, and hath planted them in the land of Canaan, which He gave our fathers. With this idea will be associated every display of grandeur and sublimity, of wonder and amazement; while they call to mind the revelations, manifestations, miracles and mercies displayed in bringing about this great event, in the eyes of all the nations. In view of this, Jeremiah exclaims, in the last verse of this chapter: "Therefore, behold, I will this once cause them to know, I will cause them to know mine hand and my might; and they shall know that my name is the Lord."

But the means made use of to bring about this glorious event are, not only the raising of a standard, the lifting up of an ensign, so that we may know when the time is fulfilled, but fishers and hunters are to be employed to fish and hunt them from every mountain, from every hill, and out of the holes of the rocks. Let the reader mark here: men were not to send missionaries, who were not inspired, to go and teach Israel several hundred different doctrines, and opinions of men, and to tell them they supposed the time had about arrived for them to gather; but the God of heaven is to call men by actual revelation, direct from heaven, and to tell them who Israel is; who the Indians of America are, if they should be of Israel; and also where the ten tribes are, and all the scattered remnants of that long lost people. He it is who is to give them their errand and mission, and to clothe them with power from on high to execute the great work, in defiance of opposing elements, and all the opposition of earth and hell combined. But do you ask: "Why is the Lord to commission men by actual revelation?" I reply, because He has no other way of sending men in any age. "No man," says the Apostle, "taketh this honor upon himself, but he that is called of God, as was Aaron." Now, we all acknowledge that Aaron was called by revelation.

Now the great Jehovah never did, nor never will, acknowledge the priesthood or ministry of any man who is not called by revelation, and inspired, as in days of old. But, "O!" says the reader, "you startle me, for the whole train of modern divines profess no revelation later than the Bible, and no direct inspiration or supernatural gift of the Spirit. Do you cast them all off, and say that they have no authority?" I reply, No, for the Bible does it, and I only humbly acquiesce in the decision, as they are nowhere known in the Scripture, except as teachers whom the people have heaped to themselves (the word heap does not mean a few, but many). But to prove more fully that God will give revelations in order to bring about this glorious work, we will refer you to Ezekiel xx, 33-38. It reads: "As I live, saith the Lord God, surely with a mighty hand, and with a stretched out arm, and with fury poured out, will I rule over you; and I will bring you out from the people, and will gather you out of the countries wherein ye are scattered, with a mighty hand, and with a stretched out arm, and with fury poured out. And I will bring you into the wilderness of the people, and there will I plead with you face to face. Like as I pleaded with your fathers in the wilderness of the land of Egypt, so will I plead with you, saith the Lord God, And I will cause you to pass under the rod, and I will bring you into the bond of the covenant, and I will purge out from among you the rebels, and them that transgress against me; I will bring them forth out of the country where they sojourn, and they shall not enter into the land of Israel; and ye shall know that I am the Lord."

You discover that this promise begins with a double assurance: first, with an oath, as I live; second, with an assurance, surely, with a mighty hand, etc. And, in the close of the same chapter, lest the people should possibly misunderstand him, he exclaims: "O Lord, they say of me, doth he not speak in parables?" Here we have the children of Israel brought from among all nations, with a mighty hand and a stretched out arm, and with fury poured out (O ye nations who oppose these things, beware, remember Pharaoh, and learn wisdom), we see them brought into the wilderness of the people; and there the Lord is to plead with them, face to face, just as he did with their fathers in the wilderness of Egypt. This pleading face to face can never be done without revelation, and a personal manifestation, as much so as in old times. Now I ask, were all His manifestations to Israel in the wilderness mere fables not to be understood literally? If so, this will be so too; for one will be precisely like the other, no parable, but a glorious reality. He will cause them to pass under the rod, and bring them into the bond of the covenant.

This brings to mind the new covenant so often promised in the Scriptures, to be made with the house of Israel and with the house of Judah, just in time to gather them from their long dispersion. Some may suppose that the new covenant which was to gather Israel made its appearance in the days of Christ and his Apostles. But Paul tells us it was yet future in his day. So, in his eleventh chapter to the Romans, he says, "that blindness in part is happened to Israel, until the fulness of the Gentiles be come in, and so all Israel shall be saved; as it is written, There shall come out of Sion the Deliverer, and shall turn away ungodliness from Jacob, for this is my covenant unto them, when I shall take away their sins." From this we learn that Paul placed that covenant in the future, even down to the restoration of Israel, in the last days, when the times of the Gentiles should be fulfilled. Then there should come a Deliverer for Israel, and not before, seeing that they had rejected the first coming of that Deliverer. And he himself said to the Jews: "Behold, your house is left unto you desolate; for I say unto you, ye shall not see me henceforth till ye shall say, Blessed is he that cometh in the name of the Lord." Then, and not until then, should the covenant be renewed with Israel. And even when the Apostles inquired, saying, "Wilt thou at this time restore again the kingdom to Israel?" the Savior made answer, that it was not for them to know the times and seasons which the Father had put in His own power; but they were to receive power, and bear witness of Him, etc.; as much as to say, that work is not for you Apostles to accomplish, but shall be done in the Lord's own time, by whom He will; but go ye and do the work I have commanded you.

Again, Isaiah, lxi, 8, 9, in speaking of this covenant, tells us that it should make their seed known among the Gentiles, and their offspring among the people; and should cause all that see them to acknowledge them that they are the seed that the Lord hath blessed. Now, we know that it is a question which can only be decided by revelation, whether the aborigines of America are the seed of Jacob or not. Again, it is a matter of uncertainty where the ten tribes are, or who they are; but the new covenant, whenever it makes its appearance, will reveal these things, and will leave the matter no longer in suspense; we shall then know their seed among the Gentiles, and their offspring among the people. But, O! how different was the effect of the covenant made eighteen hundred years ago in its effects upon Israel; it cast them off in unbelief, and caused all that have seen them or heard of them ever since to acknowledge that they are the seed that the Lord hath cursed. When the covenant is renewed in the last days, the Lord will bring them into the bond of the covenant, by manifesting Himself to them face to face. Let me inquire, How does God make a covenant with the people in any age? The answer is, By communicating His will to them by actual revelation; for, without this, it would be impossible to make a covenant between two parties. In order to illustrate this subject, let us bring an example. We see how we make covenants with each other. For instance, a young man wishes to enter into a covenant of matrimony with a young lady; but deprive him of the privilege of revealing his mind to her, cut off all direct communication between them, and a covenant could never be made; and so it is with the Almighty. He never did enter into a covenant with His creatures, without revelations; and He never can do it. In short, whenever He made a covenant with the people, where a whole people were concerned, He included in the covenant the priesthood, offices, and authorities, together with the ordinances and blessings which pertain to His covenant; and so will He do at this time. Whenever the new covenant is established, it will organize the kingdom of God with all its offices, ordinances, gifts, and blessings as in the days of old; but more of this when we come to treat of the kingdom of God.

"But," says the inquirer, "what need have we of the renewal of a covenant which has never been broken? If the Lord made a covenant in the days of the Apostles, called a new covenant, why should that covenant still be renewed again, seeing it is in full force, until it is broken by one party or the other?" This is an important inquiry, involving the fate of all Christendom in its decision; we must therefore be very careful to make the decision perfectly plain, and the proof easy to be understood. That there was a covenant made between God and the people in the days of Christ and His Apostles, none will attempt to deny, and if that covenant never has been broken, it must be of force to the present day, and consequently there is no need of a new one. It therefore remains for us to prove that that covenant has been broken, completely broken, so that it is not in force, either among Jews or Gentiles, having lost its offices, authorities, powers, and blessings, insomuch that they are nowhere to be found among men. In order to do this, we must examine what were its offices, authorities, powers, and blessings, and then see whether they are still known among men.

We read that its offices consisted of Apostles, Prophets, Evangelists, Pastors, and Teachers, all inspired and set in the Church, by the Lord Himself, for the edifying of the saints, for the work of the ministry, etc. And they were to continue in the Church, wherever it was found, until they all came to the unity of the faith, and unto the measure of the stature of a man in Christ.

Secondly, the gifts of the Spirit, which some call supernatural, were the powers and blessings which pertained to that covenant, wherever it existed, among the Jews or the Gentiles, so long as the covenant was of force. Now, I would ask the world of Christendom, or either of its sects or parties, if they have Apostles, Prophets, Evangelists, Pastors and Teachers inspired from on high, together with all the gifts and blessings of the Holy Spirit, which pertained to the Gospel covenant? If not, then the offices and powers of that covenant have been lost. And it must be through the breaking of that covenant that they were lost, for in this way the Jews lost these privileges, when they were handed to the Gentiles. And Paul told the Gentiles, in his eleventh chapter to the Romans, that if they did not abide in the goodness of God, they would fall, as the Jews had done before them.

But in order to prove, by further demonstration, that the Gospel covenant has been broken, by Jew and Gentile, and all people, so as to be no longer in force, I shall quote Isaiah, xxiv, 1-6: "Behold, the Lord maketh the earth empty, and maketh it waste, and turneth it upside down, and scattereth abroad the inhabitants thereof. And it shall be, as with the people, so with the priest; as with the servant, so with his master; as with the maid, so with her mistress; as with the buyer, so with the seller; as with the lender, so with the borrower; as with the taker of usury, so with the giver of usury to him. The land shall be utterly emptied, and utterly spoiled: for the Lord hath spoken this word. The earth mourneth and fadeth away, the world languisheth and fadeth away, the haughty people of the earth do languish. The earth also is defiled under the inhabitants thereof; BECAUSE THEY HAVE TRANSGRESSED THE LAWS, CHANGED THE ORDINANCE, BROKEN THE EVERLASTING COVENANT. Therefore hath the curse devoured the earth, and they that dwell therein are desolate: therefore the inhabitants of the earth are burned, and few men left." In these few verses, we discover a like calamity awaiting priests and people, rich and poor, bond and free, insomuch that they are all to be burned up but a few; and the complaint is that the earth is defiled under the inhabitants thereof, because they have transgressed the laws, changed the ordinance, and broken the everlasting covenant. Now this could not be speaking of any other than the covenant, ordinance, and laws of the Gospel, made with the people in the days of the Apostles; because, however any former covenant may have been broken, yet the inhabitants of the earth have never been destroyed by fire, all but a few, for having broken any previous covenant. But this destruction is to come by fire, as literally as the flood in the days of Noah; and it will consume both priests and people from the earth, and that, too, for having broken the covenant of the Gospel, with its laws and its ordinances; or else we must get a new edition of the Bible, leaving out the twenty-fourth of Isaiah.

Now, having settled this question, I trust the reader will see the need of a new covenant, in order to save the few that are not to be burned. We will therefore drop this subject for the present, and turn again to the subject of the gathering of Israel. You will please turn and read the thirty-sixth, thirty-seventh, thirty-eighth, and thirty-ninth chapters of Ezekiel. In the thirty-sixth chapter you will discover a promise that Israel are to return from all the nations whither they have been scattered, and to be brought again to the land which God gave to their fathers; Jerusalem is to be filled with flocks of men, and all the desolate cities of Judea are to be rebuilt, fenced and inhabited; the land is to be fenced, tilled and sown, insomuch that they shall say: "This land that was desolate is become like the garden of Eden." "I the Lord have spoken it, and I will do it; and the heathen shall know that I the Lord build the ruined places, and plant that that was desolate." "So shall the waste cities be filled with flocks of men, and they shall know that I am the Lord." In the thirty-seventh chapter you will find, after the vision of the resurrection of the dead, the Prophet goes on to speak of the two nations becoming one nation upon the mountains of Israel, and one king being king to them all; and when this takes place, they are no more to be divided into two kingdoms. Moreover, the Lord's tabernacle is to be with them, and His sanctuary in the midst of them forevermore. He will forever be their God, and they shall be His people. "And the heathen shall know that I the Lord do sanctify Israel, when my sanctuary shall be in the midst of them forevermore." Now, it is a fact well known, that Judah and the ten tribes have never been one nation, upon the mountains of Israel, since the day they were first divided into two nations.

But, when this does take place, even the very heathen are to know it, and are to be convinced of the true God, as was Cyrus. Now if the missionaries should convert the world, before the Lord does this great work, then it will save the Lord the trouble of doing it in His own way, and it will save the trouble of fulfilling the Prophets, and the word of the Lord will fail, and all the world lay hold of infidelity. Well did the Lord say: "My ways are not as your ways, nor my thoughts as your thoughts." Chapters xxxviii and xxxix present us with a view of many nations united under one great head, whom the Lord is pleased to call Gog; and being mounted on horseback, and armed with all sorts of armor, they come up against the mountains of Israel, as a cloud to cover the land; their object is to take a prey, to take away silver and gold, and cattle, and goods in great abundance.

This is an event which is to transpire after the return of the Jews, and the rebuilding of Jerusalem; while the towns and the land of Judea are without walls, having neither bars nor gates. But while they are at the point to swallow up the Jews, and lay waste their country, behold the Lord's fury comes up in His face, a mighty earthquake is the result, insomuch that the fishes of the sea, and the fowls of the air, and all the creeping things, and all men upon the face of the earth, shall shake at His presence, and every wall shall fall to the ground, and every man's sword shall be turned against his neighbor in this army, and the Lord shall rain upon Gog, and upon his bands, and upon the many people that are with him, an overflowing rain, great hailstones, fire and brimstone. And thus He will magnify Himself, and sanctify Himself, in the eyes of many nations, and they shall know that He is the Lord; thus they shall fall upon the open field, upon the mountains of Israel, even Gog and all his army, horses and horsemen; and the Jews shall go forth and gather the weapons of war, such as handstaves, spears, shields, bows and arrows; and these weapons shall last the cities of Israel seven years for fuel, so that they shall cut no wood out of the forest, for they shall burn the weapons with the fire; and they shall spoil those that spoiled them, and rob those that robbed them, and they shall gather gold and silver, and apparel, in great abundance.

At this time the fowls of the air, and the beasts of the field shall have a great feast; yea, they are to eat fat until they be full, and drink blood until they be drunken. They are to eat the flesh of captains, and kings, and mighty men, and all men of war. But the Jews will have a very serious duty to perform, which will take no less than seven months; namely, the burying of their enemies. They will select a place on the east side of the sea, called the Valley of the Passengers, and there shall they bury Gog and all his multitude, and they shall call it the Valley of Hamon Gog. And the scent shall go forth, insomuch that it shall stop the noses of the passengers; thus shall they cleanse the land. "And I will set my glory among the heathen, and all the heathen shall see my judgment that I have executed, and my hand that I have laid upon them: so the house of Israel shall know that I am the Lord their God from that day and forward. And the heathen shall know that the house of Israel went into captivity for their iniquity; because they trespassed against me, therefore hid I my face from them, and gave them into the hand of their enemies; so fell they all by the sword. According to their uncleanness, and according to their transgressions, have I done unto them, and hid myself from them. Therefore thus saith the Lord God, Now will I bring again the captivity of Jacob, and have mercy upon the whole house of Israel, and will be jealous for my holy name: after that they have borne their shame, and all their trespasses whereby they have trespassed against me, when they dwelt safely in their own land, and none made them afraid. When I have brought them again from the people, and gathered them out of their enemy's lands, and am sanctified in them in the sight of many nations; then shall they know that I am the Lord their God, which caused them to be led into captivity among the heathen; but I have gathered them into their own land, and have left none of them any more there. Neither will I hide my face any more from them; for I have poured out my Spirit upon the house of Israel, saith the Lord God."

In the foregoing, we discover that the heathen are to know that the house of Israel went into captivity for their iniquity, and are gathered again by the hand of God, after having borne their shame for all their trespasses: and the house of Israel will know that it was the Lord their God who caused them to be led into captivity among the heathen, and that He it was that gathered and defended them, and He will hide His face no more from them, but will pour out His Spirit upon them.

O ye blind, ye stiffnecked, ye hardhearted generation, with the Bible circulated among all nations, will whole nations be so blind as to fulfil this prophecy, and not know it until it brings destruction upon their own heads? Why all this blindness? Alas! it is because of false teachers, who will tell them the Bible must be spiritualized. Others declare that these prophecies can never be understood until they are fulfilled. If this be the case, then we can never escape the judgments predicted in them, but must continue the children of darkness, until they come upon us unawares and sweep us from the earth. Then, where will be the consolation of looking back and seeing them fulfilled? But blessed be God, He has told us by the mouth of Daniel that many shall run to and fro, and knowledge shall be increased, and that the wise shall understand, but none of the wicked shall understand. And now, I would ask, who are more wicked than the wilfully blind leaders of the blind, who tell us we cannot understand the Scriptures?

Zachariah, in his fourteenth chapter, has told us much concerning the great battle and overthrow of the nations who fight against Jerusalem; and he has said, in plain words, that the Lord shall come at the very time of the overthrow of that army; yes, in fact, even while they are in the act of taking Jerusalem, and have already succeeded in taking one half the city, and spoiling their houses, and ravishing their women. Then, behold their long expected Messiah, suddenly appearing, shall stand upon the Mount of Olives, a little east of Jerusalem, to fight against those nations and deliver the Jews. Zachariah says, The Mount of Olives shall cleave in twain, from east to west, and one half of the mountain shall remove to the north, while the other half falls off to the south, suddenly forming a very great valley, into which the Jews shall flee for protection from their enemies, as they fled from the earthquake in the days of Uzziah, king of Judah; while the Lord cometh and all the saints with him. Then will the Jews behold that long, long expected Messiah, coming in power to their deliverance, as they always looked for Him. He will destroy their enemies, and deliver them from trouble at the very time they are in the utmost consternation, and about to be swallowed up by their enemies.

But what will be their astonishment, when they are about to fall at the feet of their Deliverer, and acknowledge him their Messiah! They discover the wounds which were once made in his hands, feet, and side; and, on inquiry, at once recognize Jesus of Nazareth, the king of the Jews, the man so long rejected. Well did the Prophet say, they should mourn and weep, every family apart, and their wives apart. But, thank heaven, there will be an end to their mourning; for He will forgive their iniquities, and cleanse them from all uncleanness. Jerusalem shall be a holy city from that time forth, and all the land shall be turned as a plain from Geba to Rimmon, and she shall be lifted up and inhabited in her place, and men shall dwell there, and there shall be no more utter destruction of Jerusalem; "and in that day there shall be one Lord, and His name one, and He shall be King over all the earth."

John, in his eleventh chapter of Revelations, gives us many more particulars concerning this same event. He informs us that, after the city and temple are rebuilt by the Jews, the Gentiles will tread it underfoot forty and two months, during which time there will be two Prophets continually prophesying and working mighty miracles. And it seems that the Gentile army shall be hindered from utterly destroying and overthrowing the city, while these two Prophets continue. But, after a struggle of three years and a half, they at length succeed in destroying these two Prophets, and then overrunning much of the city; they send gifts to each other because of the death of the two Prophets, and in the mean time will not allow their dead bodies to be put in graves, but suffer them to lie in the streets of Jerusalem three days and a half; during which the armies of the Gentiles, consisting of many kindreds, tongues, and nations, passing through the city, plundering the Jews, see their dead bodies lying in the street. But, after three days and a half, on a sudden, the spirit of life from God enters them, and they will arise and stand upon their feet, and great fear will fall upon them that see them. And then they shall hear a voice from heaven, saying, "Come up hither," and they will ascend up to heaven in a cloud, their enemies beholding them. And, having described all these things, then come the shaking, spoken of by Ezekiel, and the rending of the Mount of Olives, spoken of by Zachariah. John says: "The same hour there was a great earthquake, and the tenth part of the city fell; and in the earthquake were slain of men seven thousand." And then one of the next scenes that follow is the sound of voices, saying: "The kingdoms of this world are become the kingdoms of our Lord and of His Christ, and He shall reign forever and ever."

Now, having summed up the description of these great events spoken of by these Prophets, I would just remark, there is no difficulty in understanding them all to be perfectly plain and literal in their fulfilment.

Suffice it to say, the Jews gather home, and rebuild Jerusalem. The nations gather against them to battle. Their armies encompass the city, and have more or less power over it for three years and a half. A couple of Jewish Prophets, by their mighty miracles, keep them from utterly overcoming the Jews; until at length they are slain, and the city is left in a great measure to the mercy of their enemies for three days and a half; the two Prophets rise from the dead and ascend up into heaven. The Messiah comes, convulses the earth, overthrows the army of the Gentiles, delivers the Jews, cleanses Jerusalem, cuts off all wickedness from the earth, raises the saints from the dead, brings them with Him, and commences His reign for a thousand years; during which time His Spirit will be poured out upon all flesh; men and beasts, birds and serpents, will be perfectly harmless, and peace and the knowledge and glory of God shall cover the earth as the waters cover the sea; and the kingdom, and the greatness of the kingdom under the whole heaven, shall be given to the saints of the Most High.

During this thousand years, Satan will be bound, and have no power to tempt the children of men. And the earth itself will be delivered from the curse, which came by reason of the Fall. The rough places will become smooth, the barren deserts fruitful; the mountains leveled; the valleys exalted; the thorn and thistle shall no more be found, but all the earth shall yield her increase in abundance to the saints of God. But, after the thousand years are ended, then shall Satan be loosed, and shall go out to deceive the nations which dwell in the four quarters of the earth, to gather them to battle, and to bring them up to battle against the camp of the saints. Then the great and last struggle shall take place between God and Satan, for the empire of the earth. Satan and his army shall be overthrown. And after these great things, come the end of the earth, the resurrection of the wicked, and the last judgment. And there shall be a new earth and a new heaven, for the former earth and the former heaven shall have passed away, that is, they will be changed from temporal to eternal, and made fit for the abode of immortals. Then cometh Jerusalem down from God, out of heaven, having been renewed as well as the heavens and the earth. "For," says He, "behold, I make all things new."

This new city, placed upon the new earth, with the Lord God and the Lamb in the midst, seems to be man's eternal abode, insomuch that, after all our longings for a place beyond the bounds of time and space, as saith the poet, we are at last brought to our proper senses, and given to understand that man is destined forever to inherit this selfsame planet, upon which he was first created, which shall be redeemed, sanctified, renewed, purified, and prepared as an eternal inheritance for immortality and eternal life; with the holy city for its capital, the throne of God in the midst, for its seat of government; and watered with a stream, clear as crystal, called the Waters of Life, issuing from the throne of Jehovah; while either side is adorned with trees of never fading beauty. "Blessed are they that do his commandments, that they may have a right to the tree of life, and may enter in through the gates into the city." By this time we begin to understand the words of the Savior: "Blessed are the meek, for they shall inherit the earth." And also the song which John heard in heaven, which ended thus: "We shall reign on the EARTH."

Reader, do not be startled; suppose you were to be caught up into heaven, there to stand with the redeemed of every nation, kindred, tongue, and people, and join them in singing, and to your astonishment, all heaven is filled with joy, while they tune the immortal lyre, in joyful anticipation of one day reigning on the earth—a planet now under the dominion of Satan, the abode of wretchedness and misery, from which your glad spirit had taken its flight, and, as you supposed, an everlasting farewell. You might perhaps be startled for a moment, and inquire within yourself: "Why have I never heard this theme sung among the churches on earth?" Well, my friend, the answer would be—"Because you lived in a day when people did not understand the Scriptures."

Abraham would tell you, you should have read the promise of God to him, Gen. xvii, 8, where God not only promised the land of Canaan to his seed for an everlasting possession, but also to him. Then you should have read the testimony of Stephen, Acts, vii, 5, by which you would have ascertained that Abraham never had inherited the things promised, but was still expecting to rise from the dead and be brought into the land of Canaan, to inherit them. "Yes," says Ezekiel, "if you had read the thirty-seventh chapter of my prophecies, you would have found a positive promise, that God would open the graves of the whole house of Israel, who were dead, and gather up their dry bones, and put them together, each to its own proper place, and even clothe them again with flesh, sinews, and skin, and put His Spirit in them, and they should live; and then, instead of being caught up to heaven, they should be brought into the land of Canaan, which the Lord gave them, and they should inherit it."

But, still astonished, you might turn to Job; and he, surprised to find one unacquainted with so plain a subject, would exclaim: "Did you never read my nineteenth chapter, from the twenty-third to the twenty-seventh verses, where I declare, I wish my words were written in a book, saying, that my Redeemer would stand on the earth in the latter-day; and that I should see Him in the flesh, for myself, and not another; though worms should destroy this body?" Even David, the sweet singer of Israel, would call to your mind the thirty-seventh Psalm, where he repeatedly declares that the meek shall inherit the earth forever, after the wicked are cut off from the face thereof.

And last of all, to set the matter forever at rest, the voice of the Savior would mildly fall upon your ear, in his sermon on the mount, declaring emphatically: "Blessed are the meek, for they shall inherit the earth." To these things you would answer: "I have read these passages, to be sure, but was always taught to believe that they did not mean so, therefore, I never understood them until now. Let me go and tell the people what wonders have opened to my view, since my arrival in heaven, merely from having heard one short song. It is true, I have heard much of the glories of heaven described, while on earth, but never once thought of their rejoicing in anticipation of returning to the earth." Says the Savior: "They have Moses and the Prophets; if they will not believe them, neither would they believe although one should rise from the dead."

We will now return to the subject of the coming of Messiah, and the ushering in of that glorious day, called the Millennium, or rest of a thousand years. We gather from the field of prophecy, through which we have passed: first, that that glorious day will be ushered in by the personal coming of Christ, and the resurrection of all the saints; second, that all the wicked will be destroyed from the earth, by overwhelming judgments of God, and by fire, at the time of His coming, insomuch that the earth will be cleansed by fire from its wicked inhabitants, as it once was by water; and this burning will include priests as well as people: all but a few shall be burned. This burning more especially applies to the fallen church, rather than to the heathen or Jews, whom they are now trying to convert. Woe unto you, Gentiles, who call yourselves the people of the Lord, but have made void the law of God by your traditions; for in vain do you call Lord, Lord, and do not the things which Jesus commands; in vain do ye worship Him, teaching for doctrines the commandments of men. Behold, the sword of vengeance hangs over you, and except you repent, it will soon fall upon you; and it will be more tolerable in that day for the Jews and heathen than for you. Behold, ye flatter yourselves that the glorious day spoken of by the Prophets will be ushered in by your modern inventions and moneyed plans, which are got up in order to convert the Jews and heathen to the various sectarian principles now existing among yourselves; and you expect, when this is done, to behold a millennium after your own heart. But the Jews and heathen never will be converted, as a people, to any other plan than that laid down in the Bible for the great restoration of Israel. And you yourselves are laboring under a broken covenant, and ripening for the fire as fast as possible. But do not count me your enemy because I tell you the truth, for God is my witness that I love your souls too well to keep back any truth from you, however severe it may seem. The wounds of a friend are better than the kisses of an enemy. Now, concerning the signs of the times, the inquiry often arises: "When shall these things be, and what signs shall there be when these things shall come to pass?" I am often asked the question, whether it is near at hand; I will therefore tell you all, whereby you may know for yourselves when it is nigh, even at the doors, and not be dependent on the knowledge of others.

Now, you behold the apple tree, and all the trees, when they begin to shoot forth their leaves, ye know of your own selves that summer is nigh at hand; and so likewise when ye shall see great earthquakes, famines, pestilence, and plagues of every kind; the sea breaking beyond its bounds, and all things in commotion; the nations distressed with perplexity; men's hearts failing them for fear, and for looking for the things which are coming on the earth; when you see signs in the heaven above, and in the earth beneath, blood, and fire, and vapor of smoke, the sun turned to darkness, the moon to blood, and stars hurled from their courses; when you see the Jews gathering to Jerusalem, and the armies of the nations gathering against them to battle, you may know, with a perfect knowledge, that Christ's coming is near, even at the doors. "Verily, I say unto you, this generation shall not pass till all these things be fulfilled." Heaven and earth shall pass away, but not one word of all that the Lord has spoken by the mouth of His holy Prophets and Apostles shall fail.

Whoever will look to the word of the Prophets, and to the sayings of Jesus Christ, on this subject, the same will be convinced that all the signs of which I have spoken are clearly pointed out as the signs of His coming. But, notwithstanding all these things are written, His coming will overtake the world unawares, as the flood did the people in the days of Noah. The reason is, they will not understand the Prophets. They will not endure sound doctrine; their ears are turned away from the truth, and turned to fables, because of false teachers, and the precepts of men; and what is still worse, when God sends men with the New and Everlasting Covenant, and clothes them with boldness to testify to the truth, they will be treated as the servants of God have been before them by the fallen churches; every church will cleave to its own way, and will unite in saying: "There is no need of these new things, the good old way is right;" while at the same time they are walking in as many different ways as there are sects, and only agree in persecuting and speaking all manner of evil against the fishers and hunters whom God shall send. But, thank heaven, there are individuals in every sect who are humbly seeking the truth, and who will know the voice of truth, and be gathered out, and planted in the New and Everlasting Covenant; and they will be adopted into the family of Israel, and will be gathered with them, and be partakers of the same covenant of promise. Yea, as Jeremiah says, in the sixteenth chapter of his Prophecies: "The Gentiles shall come unto thee from the ends of the earth, and shall say, surely our fathers have inherited lies, vanities, and things wherein there is no profit." But as the Jews overlooked Christ's first coming, by not understanding the Prophets, and fastening their whole expectations on His glorious coming in the last days, to restore the kingdom to Israel, and avenge them of their enemies, and, by this mistake, were broken and scattered; so the Gentiles will overlook the prophecies concerning His second coming, by confounding them with the last judgment, which is to take place more than a thousand years afterward. But this fatal mistake, instead of causing the Gentiles to be broken and scattered, will cause them to be ground to powder.

O my brethren, according to the flesh, my soul mourns over you, and had I a voice like a trumpet, I would cry, Awake, awake and arouse from your slumber, for the time is fulfilled, your destruction is at the door, "for I have heard from the Lord God of Hosts, a consumption, even determined upon the whole earth!" Prepare to meet your God I And again, Awake, O house of Israel, and lift up your heads, for your redemption draweth nigh: yea, depart ye, depart ye, go ye out from hence, gather home from your long dispersion, rebuild your cities; yea, go ye out from the nations, from one end of heaven to the other; but let not your flight be in haste, for the Lord shall go before you, and the God of Israel shall be your rearward! And finally, I would say to all, both Jew and Gentile, Repent ye, repent ye, for the great day of the Lord is at hand; for if I, who am a man, do lift up my voice, and call upon you to repent, and ye hate me, what will ye say when the day cometh, when the thunders shall utter their voices to the ends of the earth, speaking to the ears of all that live, saying: "Repent, and prepare for the great day of the Lord?" Yea, again, when the lightnings shall streak from the east unto the west, and shall utter forth their voices unto all that live, and make the ears of all that hear to tingle, saying these words: "Repent ye, for the great day of the Lord is come?" And again, the Lord shall utter His voice out of heaven, saying: "Hearken, O ye nations of the earth, and hear the words of that God who made you: O ye nations of the earth, how oft would I have gathered you together as a hen gathereth her chickens under her wings, but ye would not! How often have I called upon you by the mouth of my servants, and by the ministering of angels, and by mine own voice, and by the voice of thunderings, and by the voice of lightnings, and by the voice of tempests, and by the voice of earthquakes and great hailstorms, and by the voice of famine and pestilences of every kind, and by the great sound of a trumpet, and by the voice of judgments, and by the voice of mercy, all the day long, and by the voice of glory and honor, and the riches of eternal life, and would have saved you with an everlasting salvation, but you would not! Behold, the day has come, when the cup of the wrath of mine indignation is full."

Chapter Three - The Kingdom of God

"Seek first the Kingdom of God."

This was the command of the Savior, while on the earth, teaching the children of men.

Having taken a general view of the prophecies, past and future, we shall now proceed to fulfil this command, and search out the kingdom of God. But, before we advance, I would again caution the reader not to accompany me in this research, unless he is prepared to sacrifice everything, even to his good name, and life itself, if necessary, for the truth; for if he should once get a view of the kingdom of God, he will be so delighted that he never will rest satisfied short of becoming a subject of the same. And yet it will be so unlike every other system of religion now on earth, that he will be astonished that any person, with the Bible in his hand, should ever have mistaken any of the systems of men for the kingdom of God. There are certain powers, privileges, and blessings, pertaining to the kingdom of God, which are found in no other kingdom, nor enjoyed by any other people. By these it was over distinguished from all other kingdoms and systems, insomuch that the inquiring mind, seeking the kingdom of God, and being once acquainted with these peculiarities concerning it, need never mistake it, or be at a loss to know when he has found it. But, before we proceed any further in our research, let us agree upon the meaning of the term, the Kingdom of God, or the sense in which we will use it; for some apply this term to the kingdom of glory above, and some to the individual enjoyment of their own souls, while others apply it to His organized government on the earth. Now, when We speak of the kingdom of God, we wish it to be understood that we mean His organized government on the earth.

Now, reader, we launch forth into the wide field before us in search of a kingdom. But stop, let us consider—what is a kingdom? I reply, that four things are required in order to constitute any kingdom in heaven or on earth; namely, first, a king; secondly, commissioned officers duly qualified to execute his ordinances and laws; thirdly, a code of laws by which the subjects are governed; and fourthly, subjects who are governed. Where these exist in their proper order and regular authority, there is a kingdom, but where either of these ceases to exist, there is a disorganization of the kingdom; consequently an end of it, until reorganized after the same manner as before. It this respect the kingdom of God is like all other kingdoms; wherever we find officers duly commissioned and qualified by the Lord Jesus, together with His ordinances and laws existing in purity, unmixed with any precepts or commandments of men, there the kingdom of God exists, and there His power is manifest, and His blessings are enjoyed as in days of old.

We shall now take a view of the setting up of the kingdom of God in the days of the Apostles. The first intimation of its near approach was by an angel to Zachariah, promising him a son, who should go before the King to prepare his way. The next manifestation was to Mary, and finally to Joseph, by a holy angel, promising the birth of the Messiah: while at the same time, the Holy Ghost manifested unto Simeon, in the temple, that he should not die until he had seen the Savior. Thus, all these, together with the shepherds and the wise men from the east, began to rejoice with a joy unspeakable and full of glory, while the world around them knew not the occasion of their joy. After these things, all seemed to rest in silent expectation, until John had grown to manhood, when he came bounding from the wilderness of Judea, with a proclamation strange and new, crying: "Repent ye, for the kingdom of heaven is at hand," baptizing unto repentance, telling them plainly that their King was already standing among them, on the point of setting up His kingdom. And while he yet ministered, the Messiah came, and was baptized, and sealed with the Spirit of God, which rested on Him in the form of a dove; and soon after began the same proclamation as John, saying—"Repent ye, for the kingdom of heaven is at hand." Then, after choosing twelve disciples, He sent them forth into all the cities of Judea, with the same proclamation— "The kingdom of heaven is at hand;" and after them He sent seventy, and then another seventy, with the same news, so that all might be well warned and prepared for a kingdom which was soon to be organized amongst them.

But when these things had produced the desired effect, in causing a general expectation, more especially in the hearts of His disciples, who daily expected to triumph over their persecutors, by the coronation of this glorious personage, while they themselves were hoping for a reward for all their toil and sacrifices for His sake, by being exalted to dignity near His person, what must have been their disappointment, when they saw their King taken and crucified, having been mocked, derided, ridiculed, and finally overcome, and triumphed over, both by Jew and Gentile? They would gladly have died in battle to have placed Him upon the throne; but tamely to submit without a struggle, to give up all their expectations, and sink in despair from the highest pitch of enthusiasm to the lowest degradation, was more than they could well endure. They shrank back in sorrow, and returned every man to his own net, or to their several occupations, supposing all was over; probably with reflections like these: "Is this the result of all our labors? was it for this we forsook all worldly objects, our friends, our houses and lands, suffering persecution, hunger, fatigue and disgrace? And we trust it should have been He who would have delivered Israel; but alas, they have killed Him, and all is over. For three years we have awakened a general expectation through all Judea, by telling them that the kingdom of heaven was at hand, but now our King is dead, how shall we dare to look the people in the face?"

With these reflections, each pursuing his own course, all was again turned to silence, and the voice had ceased to be heard in Judea, crying: "Repent ye, for the kingdom of heaven is at hand." Jesus slept in the arms of death; a great stone with the seal of of state, secured the tomb where he lay, while the Roman guard stood in watchful silence, to see that all was kept secure; when suddenly, from the regions of glory, a mighty angel descended, at whoso presence the soldiers fell back as dead men, while he rolled the stone from the door of the sepulchre, and the Son of God awoke from His slumbers, burst the bonds of death, and soon after appearing to Mary, He sent her to the disciples with the joyful news of His resurrection, and appointed a place to meet them. When, after seeing Him, all their sorrow was turned into joy, and all their former hopes were suddenly revived, they had no longer to cry—"The kingdom of heaven is at hand," but were to tarry at Jerusalem until the kingdom was established; and they prepared to unlock the door of the kingdom, and to adopt strangers and foreigners into it as legal citizens, by administering certain laws and ordinances, which were invariably the laws of adoption, and without which no man could ever become a citizen.

Having ascended up on high, and having been crowned with all power in heaven and on earth, He again comes to His disciples, and gives them their authority, saying unto them: "Go ye into all the world, and preach the gospel to every creature. He that believeth, and is baptized, shall be saved; but he that believeth not shall be damned. And these signs shall follow them that believe: In my name shall they cast out devils; they shall speak with new tongues; they shall take up serpents; and if they drink any deadly thing it shall not hurt them; they shall lay hands on the sick, and they shall recover." Mark, xvi, 15-18. Now I wish the reader not to pass over this commission until he understands it, because when once understood, he never need mistake the kingdom of God, but will at once discover those peculiarities which were forever to distinguish it from all other kingdoms or religious systems on earth. Lest he should misunderstand, we will analyze it, and look at each part carefully in its own proper light; first, they were to preach the Gospel, or in other words, the glad tidings of a crucified and risen Redeemer, to all the world; secondly, he that believed, and was baptized, should be saved; thirdly, he that did not believe what they preached should be damned; and fourthly, these signs should follow them that believed: first, they were to cast out devils; second, to speak with new tongues; third, to take up serpents; fourth, if they drank any deadly thing, it should not hurt them; fifth, they were to lay hands on the sick, and they should recover.

Now, it is wilful blindness, or ignorance of the English language, that has ever caused any misunderstanding here. For some tell us that those signs were only to follow the Apostles; and others, that they were only to follow believers in that age. But Christ places the preaching, believing, salvation, and the signs that were to follow, all on an equal footing; where one was limited, the other must be; where one ceased, the other did. If the language limits these signs to the Apostles, it limits faith and salvation also to them. If no others were to have these signs follow them, then no others were to believe, and no others were to be saved. Again, if the language limits these signs to the first age or ages of Christianity, then it limits salvation to the first ages of Christianity, for one is precisely as much limited as the other; and where one is in force, the other is; and where one ends, the other must stop. And as well might we say, preaching of the Gospel is no longer needed; neither faith nor salvation; these were only given at first to establish the Gospel; as to say, the signs are no longer necessary, they were only given at first to establish the Gospel. But, says the astonished reader: "Have not these signs ceased from among men?" I reply, prove that they have ceased, and it will prove that the Gospel has ceased to be preached, that men have ceased to believe and be saved, and that the world is without the kingdom of God; or else it will prove that Jesus Christ was an impostor, and His promises of no effect.

Now, having analyzed and understood this commission, let us still pursue the subject of the organization of the kingdom of God in the days of the Apostles. The Savior, having given them their authority, commands them to tarry, and not undertake their mission, until they were endowed with power from on high. But why this delay? Because no man was ever qualified, or ever will be, to preach the Gospel, and teach all things whatsoever Jesus commanded him, without the Holy Ghost; and a very different Holy Ghost, too, from the one enjoyed by men who are not inspired, for the Holy Ghost of which Jesus spake would guide into all truth, bring all things to remembrance, whatsoever He had said unto them, and show them things to come—not to mention that it would enable them to speak in all the languages of the earth. Now, a man who preaches needs that Holy Ghost very much; first, to guide into all truth, that he may know what to teach; second, to strengthen his memory, lest he might neglect to teach some of the things which were commanded him; and, third, he needs to know things to come, that he may forewarn his hearers of approaching danger, and that would constitute him a prophet. From this, the reader may see how careful Jesus was that none should preach His Gospel without the Holy Ghost. He may also learn how different the Spirit of Truth is from the spirit now abroad in the earth, deceiving the world, under the name of the Holy Ghost. If the churches of the present day have the Holy Ghost, why are they so much at a loss to understand truth? Why do they walk in so many different ways and doctrines? Why do they need whole libraries of sermons, tracts, divinities, debates, arguments, and opinions, all written by the wisdom of men, without even professing to be inspired? Well doth the Lord complain, saying: "Their fear toward me is taught by the precepts of men." But to return; the Apostles tarried at Jerusalem until endowed with power, and then they commenced to proclaim the Gospel.

Here we have discovered several things towards a kingdom: first, we have found a King, crowned at the right hand of God, to whom is committed all power in heaven and on earth; second, commissioned officers, duly appointed to administer the affairs of government; third, the laws by which they were to be governed were ALL THINGS WHATSOEVER JESUS HAD COMMANDED HIS DISCIPLES TO TEACH THEM.

And now, if we can find how men became citizens of that kingdom, I mean as to the rules of adoption, then we have found the kingdom of God in that age, and shall be very much dissatisfied with every thing in our own age, professing to be the kingdom of God, which is not according to the pattern.

It happened that there were no natural born subjects of that kingdom, for both Jew and Gentile were included in sin and unbelief; and none could be citizens without the law of adoption. All that believed on the name of the King had power to be adopted, but there was but one invariable rule or plan by which they were adopted; and all that undertook to claim citizenship, in any other way whatever, were counted thieves and robbers, and could never obtain the seal of adoption. This rule was laid down in the Savior's teaching to Nicodemus, namely: "Except a man be born of water (that is, baptized in water), and of the Spirit (that is, baptized with the Spirit), he cannot enter into the kingdom of God."

Now, to Peter were given the keys of the kingdom; therefore it was his duty to open the kingdom to Jew and also to Gentile. We will therefore carefully examine the manner in which he did adopt the Jews into the kingdom on the day of Pentecost.

Now, when the multitude came running together on the day of Pentecost, the Apostle Peter, standing up with the eleven, lifted up his voice and reasoned with them from the Scriptures, testifying of Jesus Christ, and His resurrection and ascension on high—insomuch that many became convinced of the truth, and inquired what they should do. These were not Christians, but they were people who were that moment convinced that Jesus was the Christ; and because they were convinced of this fact, they inquired—"What shall we do?" Then Peter said unto them: "Repent and be baptized, every one of you, in the name of Jesus Christ, for the remission of sins, and you shall receive the gift of the Holy Ghost: for the promise is unto you, and your children, and to all that are afar of, even as many as the Lord our God shall call." My reader, do you understand this proclamation? If you do, you will see that this Gospel is not generally preached in modern times. Let us therefore analyze and examine it, sentence by sentence. You recollect they already believed, and the next thing was for them to repent; first, faith; second, repentance; third, baptism; fourth, remission of sins; and fifth, the Holy Ghost. This was the order of the Gospel. Faith gave the power to become sons, or citizens; repentance, and baptism in His name, was the obedience through which they were adopted; and the Holy Spirit of promise was the seal of their adoption, and this they were sure to receive if they would obey.

Now, reader, where do you hear such preaching in our day? Who teaches that those who believe and repent, should be baptized, and none others? Perhaps the reader may say the Baptists do; but do they call upon men to be baptized as soon as they believe and repent? And moreover, do they promise the remission of sins, with the gift of the Holy Ghost? Recollect, now, what effect the Holy Ghost has upon people who receive it. It will guide them into all truth, strengthen the memory, and show them things to come. And Joel has said, it would cause them to dream dreams, to see visions, and to prophesy. O! my reader, where do you find a Gospel like this preached among men? Would men go mourning for weeks upon weeks, without the forgiveness of sins, or the comfort of the Holy Spirit, if Peter stood among us to tell precisely how to get such blessings? Now, what would you think of a camp meeting, where three thousand men should come forward to be prayed for, and one of the ministers should (Peter like) command them every one to repent, and be baptized for the remission of sins, promising that all who obeyed should receive the remission of sins and the gift of the Holy Ghost, which should cause them to dream dreams and prophesy; and then should arise with his brethren of the same calling, and the same hour commence baptizing, and continue until they had baptized them all; and the Holy Ghost should fall upon them, and they begin to see visions, speak in other tongues, and prophecy? Would not the news go abroad, far and wide, that a new doctrine had made its appearance, quite different from any thing now practised among men? O yes, says the reader, this, to be sure, would be something new, and very strange to all of us. Well, strange as it may seem, it is the Gospel, as preached by Peter on the day of Pentecost; and Paul declares that he preached the same Gospel that Peter did; and he has also said: "Though we, or an angel from heaven, preach any other gospel, let him be accursed." Now, the reader need no longer be astonished to see that these signs do not follow them that believe some other gospel, or doctrine, different from that preached by the Apostles.

But now let us return to the kingdom of God organized in the days of the Apostles; you discover that three thousand persons were adopted into the kingdom the first day the door was opened. These, together with the numerous additions which were afterwards made, were the subjects of this kingdom; which, being fitly framed together, grew into a holy temple in the Lord. Thus, we have cleared away the rubbish of sectarian tradition and superstition, which arose in heaps around us; and having searched carefully, we have at length discovered the kingdom of God, as it existed at its first organization in the days of the Apostles; and we have seen that it differs widely from all modern systems of religion, both in its offices, ordinances, powers, and privileges, insomuch that no man need ever mistake the one for the other.

Having made this discovery, we shall proceed to examine the progress of the kingdom among Jew and Gentile; and what were its fruits, gifts, and blessings as enjoyed by its citizens.

Soon after the organization of the kingdom of God at Jerusalem, Philip came to Samaria, and there preached the Gospel: and when they believed Philip, they were baptized, both men and women, and had great joy. And afterwards, Peter and John came from Jerusalem, and prayed, and laid their hands on them, and they received the Holy Ghost. Mark here, they first believed, and then were baptized, having great joy, and yet had not received the

Holy Ghost. But that was afterwards given, by the laying on of hands and prayer, in the name of Jesus. O how different from the systems of men!

Witness Paul's conversion while on his journey to Damascus: the Lord Jesus appeared to him in the way; but instead of telling him his sins were forgiven, and pouring the Holy Ghost upon him, He sent him to Damascus, telling him that it should there be told him what he should do. And coming to Damascus, Ananias being sent, commanded him not to tarry, but to "arise and be baptized, and wash away his sins, calling on the name of the Lord;" then he arose and was baptized, and was even filled with the Holy Ghost, and straightway preached that Jesus was the Christ.

Again, witness Peter going to Cornelius, a Gentile of great piety, whose prayers were heard, and whose alms were remembered, and who had even attained to the ministering of an angel; yet with all his piety, and the Holy Ghost poured out upon him and his friends, before they were baptized, they must be baptized, or they could not be saved. Why? Because the Lord had commanded the Apostles to preach to every creature, and every creature who would not believe and be baptized, should be damned, without one exception. Witness the words of the angel to Cornelius: "He (Peter) shall tell thee words whereby thou and all thy house shall be saved." Now, query, could Cornelius have been saved without obeying the words of Peter? If so, the angel's errand was in vain.

Now, perhaps a minister, who should find a man as good as Cornelius was, would say to him: "Go on, brother, you can be saved, you have experienced religion, you may indeed be baptized to answer a good conscience, if you feel it your duty; or, if not, it is no matter, a new heart is all that is really necessary to salvation," etc.; as much as to say, that the commandments of Jesus are not absolutely necessary to salvation; a man may call him Lord, Lord, and be saved, just as well as by keeping His commandments. Oh vain and foolish doctrine! Oh ye children of men, how have you perverted the Gospel! In vain do ye call Him Lord, Lord, and do not obey His commandments.

Next, we call to mind the jailor and his household, who were baptized the same hour they believed, without waiting for the day; and Lydia and her household, who attended to the ordinance the first sermon they heard on the subject. Also Philip and the eunuch, who stopped the chariot at the first water they came to, in order to attend to the ordinance, although the eunuch had heard of Jesus, for the first time, only a few minutes before. Now, I gather from all those examples of ancient days, and from the precepts laid down in them, that baptism was the initiating ordinance, by which all those who believed and repented were received and adopted into the church or kingdom of God, so as to be entitled to the remission of sins, and the blessing of the Holy Ghost; indeed, it was the ordinance through which they became sons and daughters; and because they were sons, the Lord shed forth the Spirit of His Son into their hearts, crying, Abba, Father. It is true, the Lord poured out the Holy Ghost upon Cornelius and his friends, before they were baptized; but it seemed necessary, in order to convince the believing Jews that the Gentiles also had part in this salvation. And I believe this is the only instance, in the whole record, of the people receiving the Holy Ghost without first obeying the laws of adoption. But mark! Obeying the laws of adoption would not constitute a man an heir of the kingdom, a citizen entitled to the blessings and gifts of the Spirit, unless those laws and ordinances were administered by one who had proper authority, and was duly commissioned from the King; and a commission given to one individual could never authorize another to act in his stead. This is one of the most important points to be understood, as it brings to the test every minister in Christendom; and questions the organization of every church on earth, and all that have existed since direct inspiration ceased.

Now, in order to come at this subject in plainness, let us examine the constitution of earthly governments in regard to the authority and laws of adoption. We will say, for instance, the President of the United States writes a commission to A. B., duly authorizing him to act in some office in the government, and, during his administration, two gentlemen from Europe come to reside in this country, and, being strangers and foreigners wishing to become citizens, they go before A. B., and he administers the oath of allegiance in due form, and certifies the same, and this constitutes them legal citizens, entitled to all the privileges of those who are citizens or subjects by birth. After these things, A. B. is taken away by death, and C. D., in looking over his papers, happens to find the commission given to A. B., and, applying it to his own use, assumes the vacant office; meantime, two foreigners arrive, and apply for citizenship, and being informed by persons ignorant of the affairs of government, that C. D. could administer the laws of adoption, they submit to be administered unto by C. D., without once examining his authority; C. D. certifies of their citizenship, and they suppose they have been legally adopted, the same as the others, and are entitled to all the privileges of citizenship. But by and by, their citizenship is called in question, and they produce the certificate of C. D.; the President inquires— "Who is C. D.? I never gave him a commission to act in any office, I know him not, and you are strangers and foreigners to the commonwealth, until you go before the legally appointed successor of A. B., or some other of like authority, who has a commission from the President direct in his own name." In the meantime, C. D. is taken and punished according to law, for practising imposition, and usurping authority which was never conferred upon him.

And so it is with the kingdom of God. The Lord authorized the Apostles and others by direct revelation, and by the spirit of prophecy, to preach and baptize, and build up His church and kingdom; but after a while they died, and a long time passed away, and men, reading over their commission, where it says to the eleven Apostles—"Go ye into all the world and preach the Gospel to every creature," etc., have had the presumption to apply these sayings as their authority, and without any other commission, have gone forth professing to preach the Gospel, and baptize, and build up the church and kingdom of God; but those whom they baptize never receive the same blessings and gifts which characterized a saint or citizen of the kingdom in the days of the Apostles. Why? Because they are yet foreigners and strangers, for the commission given to the Apostles never commissioned any other man to act in their stead. This was a prerogative the Lord reserved unto himself. No man has a right to take this ministry upon himself, but he that is called by revelation, and duly qualified to act in his calling by the Holy Ghost.

But the reader inquires with astonishment, "What! are none of all the ministers of the present day called to the ministry, and legally commissioned?" Well, my reader, I will tell you how you may ascertain from their own mouths, and that will be far better than an answer from me; go to the clergy, and ask them if God has given them any direct revelation since the New Testament was finished; inquire of them whether the gift of prophecy ceased with the early age of the church; and, in short, ask them if revelations, prophets, the ministering of angels, etc., are needed or expected in these days, or whether they believe that these things are done away, no more to return to the earth; and their answer will be that the Bible contains sufficient, and that since the canon of Scripture was filled, revelation, the spirit of prophecy and the ministering of angels have ceased, because no longer needed. In short, they will denounce every man as an impostor who pretends to any such thing. And when you have obtained this answer, ask them how they themselves were called and commissioned to preach the Gospel, and they will be at a loss to answer you, and will finally tell you that the Bible commissioned them, saying—"Go ye into all the world," etc. Thus, you see, all who have no direct personal revelation from the King of heaven, either by angels, the voice of God, or the spirit of prophecy, are acting under authority which was given to others, who are dead, and their commission stolen, and their authority usurped; and the King will say—"Peter I know, and Paul I know, I commissioned them, but who are you? I know you not, I never spoke to you in my life; indeed you believed it was not necessary for me to speak in your day. Therefore you never sought in faith for any revelation, and I never gave you any; and even when I spake to others, you mocked them, and called them impostors, and persecuted them, because they testified of the things I had said unto them, therefore depart from me, ye cursed, into everlasting fire, prepared for the devil and his angels: for I was an hungered, and ye fed me not; I was naked, and ye clothed me not; I was a stranger, and ye took me not in; sick and in prison and ye visited me not." "Ah! Lord, when did we fail in any of these things?" "Inasmuch as you have not done it unto the least of these my brethren (taking them for impostors, because they testified of the things which I had revealed unto them), ye have not done it unto me." But to return: having examined the kingdom of God as to its offices and ordinances, and having discovered the only means of adoption into it, let us examine more fully what are the blessings, privileges, and enjoyments of its citizens. You have already seen that they were to cast out devils, speak with new tongues, heal the sick by the laying on of hands in the name of Jesus, as well as to see visions, dream dreams, prophesy, etc.

But let us look at the kingdom in its organized state, and see whether these promises were verified to Jew and Gentile, wherever the kingdom of God was found in all ages of the world.

Paul writing, first, "To the church of God at Corinth;" second, "To them that are sanctified in Christ Jesus;" third, "To them who are called to be saints;" and fourth, "To all that in every place call on the name of Jesus Christ our Lord," says to them all, in 1 Corinthians, xii, 1: "Now, concerning spiritual gifts, brethren, I would not have you ignorant." And then, continuing his instructions, a few verses further on, he says: "But the manifestation of the Spirit is given to every man to profit withal; for to one is given, by the Spirit, the word of wisdom; to another the word of knowledge by the same Spirit; to another faith by the same Spirit; to another, the gifts of healing by the same Spirit; to another, the working of miracles; to another, prophecy; to another, discerning of spirits; to another, divers kinds of tongues; to another, the interpretation of tongues; but all these worketh that one and the self-same Spirit, dividing to every man severally as He (Christ) will. For as the body is one, and hath many members, and all the members of that one body, being many, are one body; so also is Christ. For by one Spirit are we all baptized into one body, whether we be Jews or Gentiles, whether we be bond or free; and have been all made to drink into one Spirit. For the body is not one member, but many. If the foot shall say, because I am not the hand, I am not of the body; is it therefore not of the body? And if the ear shall say, because I am not the eye, I am not of the body; is it therefore not of the body? If the whole body were an eye, where were the hearing? If the whole were hearing, where were the smelling? But now hath Got set the members, everyone of them in the body, as it hath pleased Him. And if they were all one member, where were the body?" I reply, it would not exist. "But now are they many members, yet but one body. And the eye cannot say unto the hand, I have no need of thee; nor again, the head to the feet, I have no need of you. Nay, much more those members of the body which seem to be more feeble, are necessary; and those members of the body which we think to be less honorable, upon these we bestow more abundant honor: and our uncomely parts have more abundant comeliness. For our comely parts have no need: but God hath tempered the body together, having given more abundant honor to that part which lacked: that there should be no schism in the body; but that the members should have the same care for one another. And whether one member suffer, all the members suffer with it; or one member be honored, all the members rejoice with it. Now, ye are the body of Christ, and members in particular. And God hath set some in the church, first, apostles; secondarily, prophets; thirdly, teachers; after that, miracles, then gifts of healings, helps, governments, diversities of tongues. Are all apostles? are all prophets? are all teachers? are all workers of miracles? Have all the gifts of healing? do all speak with tongues? do all interpret? But covet earnestly the best gifts: and yet shew I unto you a more excellent way." From the thirteenth verse of the above chapter, we learn that the Apostle is still speaking to the whole church in all ages, whether Jew or Gentile, bond or free, even all who should ever compose the body of Christ, and showing that Christ's body consisted of many members, baptized by one spirit into one body, possessing all these different gifts, some one gift, and some another: and then expressly says, that one member possessing one gift, should not say to another member possessing another gift, we have no need of thee.

And having shown that it required apostles, prophets, evangelists, pastors, and teachers; together with the gifts of prophecy, miracles, healing, and all other gifts, to compose the church, or body of Christ, in any age, whether Jew or Gentile, bond or free; and having utterly forbidden any of the members ever to say, of any of these gifts: "We have no need of thee," He declares the body never could be perfected without all of them, and that if they were done away, there would be no body, that is, no church of Christ in existence. Having shown all these things clearly, he exhorts them to covet earnestly the best gifts. And in the thirteenth chapter, exhorts them to faith, hope, and charity, without which all these gifts would avail them nothing: and in the fourteenth chapter repeats the exhortation: "Follow after charity, and desire spiritual gifts, but rather that ye may prophesy." Again, in Ephesians, i, 17, Paul prays that the Lord would give unto the church the Spirit of WISDOM and of REVELATION, in the KNOWLEDGE of God. Again, in Ephesians, iv, he tells them there is one body and one Lord, one Spirit, one faith, and one baptism; and that Christ ascended up on high, led captivity captive, and gave gifts to men. And He gave some apostles; and some, prophets; and some, evangelists; and some, pastors and teachers. And if the reader inquire what these gifts or offices were for, let him read the twelfth verse: "For the perfecting of the saints, for the work of the ministry, for the edifying of the body of Christ." And if he inquire how long these were to continue, the thirteenth verse says: "Till we all come in the unity of the faith, and of the knowledge of the Son of God, unto a perfect man, unto the measure of the stature of the fulness of Christ." And if he still inquire what further object Christ had in giving these gifts, let him read the fourteenth verse: "That we henceforth be no more children, tossed to and fro, and carried about with every wind of doctrine, by the sleight of men, and cunning craftiness, whereby they lie in wait to deceive."

Now, without these gifts and offices, first, the saints cannot be perfected; second, the work of the ministry cannot proceed; third, the body of Christ cannot be edified; and fourth, there is nothing to prevent them from being carried about with every wind of doctrine. Now, I boldly declare that the cause of all the division, confusion, jars, discord, and animosities; and the fruitful source of so many faiths, lords, baptisms, and spirits; and of the understanding being darkened; and of men being alienated from the life of God, through the ignorance that is in them, because of the blindness of their hearts, is, because they have neither apostles, prophets, nor gifts, inspired from on high, to whom they give heed; for, if they had such gifts, and would give heed unto them, they would be built up in one body, in the pure doctrine of Christ, having one Lord, one faith, one baptism, and one hope of their calling; yea, they would be edified, built up unto Christ in all things, in whom the whole body, fitly joined together, would grow into an holy temple in the Lord.

But so long as the cunning craftiness of men can persuade them that they have no need of these things, so long they can toss them about with every wind of doctrine, just as they please.

Now, reader, I have done our examination of the kingdom of God, as it existed in the Apostles' days; and we cannot look at it in any other age, until renewed again in the last days, for it never did, nor never will exist, without apostles and prophets, and all the other gifts of the Spirit.

Were we to take a view of the churches, from the days that inspiration ceased until now, we should see nothing like the kingdom which we have been viewing with such admiration and delight. But instead of apostles and prophets, we should see false teachers, whom men had heaped to themselves; and instead of the gifts of the Spirit, we should see the wisdom of men; and instead of the Holy Ghost, many false spirits; instead of the ordinances of God, commandments of men; instead of knowledge, opinion; guess work, instead of revelation; division, instead of union; doubt, instead of faith; despair, instead of hope; hatred, instead of charity; a physician, instead of the laying on of hands for the healing of the sick; fables, instead of truth, evil for good, good for evil; darkness for light, light for darkness, and in a word, antiChrist instead of Christ; the powers of earth having made war with the saints, and overcome them, until the words of God should be fulfilled.

O my God, shut up the vision! for my heart sickens while I gaze; and let the day hasten on when the earth shall be cleansed by fire from such awful pollutions; but first, let Thy promise be fulfilled, which Thou didst make by the mouth of Thy servant John, that Thou wouldst call Thy people out of her, saying: "Come out of her, my people, that ye be not partakers of her sins, and that ye receive not of her plagues;" and then, O Lord, when Thou hast called Thy people out from the midst of her, by the fishers and hunters whom Thou hast promised to send in the last days to gather Israel; yea, when Thine everlasting covenant has been renewed, and Thy people established thereby; then let her plagues come in one day, death, mourning, and famine; let her be burned with fire; that the holy Apostles and Prophets, and all that fear Thy name, small and great, may rejoice, because Thou hast avenged the blood of Thy saints upon her. I ask these things in the name of Jesus Christ. Amen.

Chapter Four - The Book of Mormon—Origin of The American Indians, Etc.

Ye gloomy scenes, far hence, intrude no more!
Sublimer themes invite the muse to soar
In loftier strains, while scenes both strange and new
Burst on the sight, and open to the view.
Lo! from the opening heavens, in bright array
An angel comes—to earth he bends his way:
Reveals to man, in power, as at the first,
The fulness of the Gospel long since lost.
See earth, obedient, from its bosom yield
The sacred truth it faithfully concealed.
The wise, confounded, startle at the sight,
The proud and haughty tremble with affright.
The hireling priests against the truth engage,
While hell beneath stands trembling, filled with rage;
False are their hopes, and all their struggles vain;
Their craft must fall, and with it all their gain;
The deaf must hear, the meek their joy increase;
The poor be glad, and their oppression cease.

While darkness covered the earth, and gross darkness the people, every man walking in his own way, and looking for gain from his quarter, the Lord having for a long time held His peace, and the people having fondly flattered themselves that the voice of inspiration would never again sound in the ears of mortals, to disturb or molest them in their sinful career; while a few were looking for the consolation of Israel, and crying to God for the ushering in of that long-expected day, when an angel should fly through the midst of heaven, having the everlasting Gospel to preach unto them that dwell on the earth— suddenly, a voice is heard from the wilderness, a cry salutes the ears of mortals, a testimony is heard among them, piercing to the inmost recesses of their hearts, when all at once the heathen begin to rage, and the people to imagine a vain thing; the clergy lift a warning voice, crying impostor, false prophets, beware of delusion, etc.; while the professor of religion, the drunkard, the swearer, the learned, and the ignorant soon catch the sound and reiterate it again and again. Thus it re-echoes from one end of our country to the other, for a long time, and if any one should be so fortunate as to retain his sober senses, and should candidly inquire, "What is the matter?" the reply is: "We hardly know anything about it, but suffice it to say, some fellows have made their appearance, Paul like, who testify something about the ministering of angels, or some revelation or inspiration, just as though the religion of ancient days, and the faith once delivered to the saints, were returning to the earth in this enlightened age; so that not only this our craft is in danger, but our modern systems of religion, built upon the wisdom and learning of men, without direct inspiration, are like to be spoken against, and their great magnificence despised, though worshiped by all the world." And then all again cry with a loud voice, saying: "Great is the wisdom of man; great are the systems of modern divinity; great is the wisdom of uninspired priests, who come unto us with excellency of speech, and with man's wisdom, determined to know nothing among us save opinions and creeds of their own; and their speech, and their preaching, are with enticing words of man's wisdom, not in demonstration of the Spirit, and of power, for that is done away, that our faith should not stand in the power of God, but in the wisdom of man."

In the midst of the noise and clamor, and prejudice of an opposing world, it is difficult to get the people to understand the facts of the case, in relation to one of the most important subjects ever presented to the consideration of mankind.

The Book of Mormon has perhaps been less understood, and more misrepresented, by the world at large, than any other publication which has ever appeared.

America and England have, as it were, been flooded with publications against the said book; and many of them written by those who had never seen the book, or by those who had only read a page or two in it, or slightly looked it through with a biased mind, and a determination to find fault. By some of these it has been represented as a romance; by others, as a new Bible, calculated to displace the Bible, or do away with it. Some have pronounced it a "silly mess of stuff," not worth the perusal; and others, the most ingenious literary work ever put together. Some have found fault with it for being so much like the Bible, and agreeing with it; and others have condemned it for not being sufficiently like the Bible, and for disagreeing with it. Some have denounced it as notoriously corrupt, immoral, and blasphemous in its principles; and others have condemned it for being so exceedingly pure and moral in its principles, as to be just calculated to deceive. One clergyman, in particular, in a tract of sixty pages on this book, condemns it for being "a strange mixture of faith and works, of the mercy of God and the obedience of the creature." Some literary persons have pronounced it as altogether ancient in its style, language, and subjects, and as bearing great internal evidence of its own antiquity; while others have condemned it, as bearing every mark of being a modern production. Some have said that there were no definite predictions of the future contained in it, by the fulfilment or failure of which its prophetic merits might be tested; and others have quoted largely from its most plain and pointed predictions, which relate to circumstances about to be fulfilled, and have condemned it on account of its plainness.

In the midst of all these jarring statements, it now becomes our duty to show, as far as possible, what the Book of Mormon really is.

When the Lord confounded the languages at Babel, he led forth a colony from thence to the Western Continent, which is now called America. This colony, after crossing the ocean in eight vessels, and landing in that country, became, in process of time, a great nation—they inhabited America for some fifteen hundred years. They were at length destroyed for their wickedness, about six hundred years before Christ. A prophet by the name of Ether wrote their history, and an account of their destruction.

Ether lived to witness their entire destruction, and deposited his record where it was afterwards found by a colony of Israelites, who came from Jerusalem six hundred years before Christ, and re-peopled America. This last colony were the descendants of the tribe of Joseph; they grew and multiplied, and finally gave rise to two mighty nations. One of these nations was called Nephites—one Nephi being their founder; the other was called Lamanites, after a leader of the name Laman.

The Lamanites became a dark and benighted people, of whom the American Indians are still a remnant. The Nephites were an enlightened and civilized people, they were a people highly favored of the Lord, they had visions, angels, and the gift of prophecy among them from age to age; and finally, they were blessed with a personal appearance of Jesus Christ after his resurrection, from whose mouth they received the doctrine of the Gospel, and a knowledge of the future down through all succeeding ages. But after all the blessings and privileges conferred upon them, they fell into great wickedness in the third and fourth centuries of the Christian era, and finally were destroyed by the hands of the Lamanites. This destruction took place about four hundred years after Christ.

Mormon lived in that age of the world, and was a Nephite, and a Prophet of the Lord. He, by the commandment of the Lord, made an abridgment of the sacred records, which contained the history of his forefathers, and the Prophecies and Gospel which had been revealed among them; to which he added a sketch of the history of his own time, and the destruction of his nation. Previous to his death, the abridged records fell into the hands of his son Moroni, who continued them down to A. D. 420; at which time he deposited them carefully in the earth, on a hill which was then called Cumorah, but is situated in Ontario County, township of Manchester, and State of New York, North America. This he did in order to preserve them from the Lamanites, who overran the country, and sought to destroy them and all the records pertaining to the Nephites. This record lay concealed, or sealed up, from A. D. 420 to September 22, 1827, at which time it was found by Mr. Joseph Smith, jun., he being directed thither by an angel of the Lord.

The following account of the discovery and translation of this record is extracted from a tract by Elder Orson Pratt, published at Edinburgh, in 1840, entitled, "Remarkable Visions," etc., to which our readers are referred for further particulars:—

"'How far below the surface these records were placed by Moroni, I am unable to say; but from the fact that they had been some fourteen hundred years buried, and that, too, on the side of a hill so steep, one is ready to conclude that they were some feet below, as the earth would naturally wear, more or less, in that length of time; but they being placed toward the top of the hill, the ground would not remove as much as at two-thirds, perhaps. Another circumstance would prevent a wearing of the earth; in all probability, as soon as timber had time to grow, the hill was covered, after the Nephites were destroyed, and the roots of the same would hold the surface: however, on this point, I shall leave every man to draw his own conclusion, and form his own speculation.' But suffice it to say, 'a hole of sufficient depth was dug; at the bottom of this was laid a stone of suitable size, the upper surface being smooth; at each edge was placed a large quantity of cement, and into this cement, at the four edges of this stone, were placed erect four others; their bottom edges resting in the cement, at the outer edges of the first stone. The four last named, when placed erect, formed a box; the corners, or where the edges of the four came in contact, were also cemented so firmly, that the moisture from without was prevented from entering. It is to be observed, also, that the inner surface of the four erect or side stones was smooth. This box was sufficiently large to admit a breastplate, such as was used by the ancients to defend the chest, etc., from the arrows and weapons of their enemy. From the bottom of the box, or from the breastplate, arose three small pillars, composed of the same description of cement used on the edges; and upon these three pillars was placed the record. * * * This box containing the record was covered with another stone, the bottom surface being flat, and the upper crowning.' When it was first visited by Mr. Smith, on the morning of the twenty-second of September, 1823, 'a part of the crowning stone was visible above the surface, while the edges were concealed by the soil and grass. From which circumstance, it may be seen, that however deep this box might have been placed by Moroni at first, the time had been sufficient to wear the earth, so that it was easily discovered, when once directed, and yet not enough to make a perceivable difference to the passer by. * * * After arriving at the repository, a little exertion in removing the soil from the edges of the top of the box, and a light pry, brought to his natural vision its contents.'

"While viewing and contemplating this sacred treasure with wonder and astonishment, behold! the angel of the Lord, who had previously visited him, again stood in his presence, and his soul was again enlightened as it was the evening before, and he was filled with the Holy Spirit, and the heavens were opened, and the glory of the Lord shone round about and rested upon him. 'While he thus stood, gazing and admiring, the angel said, Look!' And as he thus spake, he beheld the Prince of Darkness, surrounded by his innumerable train of associates. All this passed before him, and the heavenly messenger said: 'All this is shown, the good and the evil, the holy and impure, the glory of God, and the power of darkness, that you may know hereafter, the two powers, and never be influenced or overcome by that wicked one. Behold, whatever entices and leads to good, and to do good, is of God, and whatever does not, is of that wicked one. It is he that fills the hearts of men with evil to walk in darkness, and blaspheme God; and you may learn from henceforth, that his ways are to destruction; but the way of holiness is peace and rest. You now see why you could not obtain this record, that the commandment was strict, and that if ever these sacred things are obtained, they must be by prayer and faithfulness in obeying the Lord. They are not deposited here for the sake of accumulating gain and wealth, for the glory of this world; they were sealed by the prayer of faith, and because of the knowledge which they contain, they are of no worth among the children of men, only for their knowledge. On them is contained the fulness of the Gospel of Jesus Christ, as it was given to His people on this land; and when it shall be brought forth by the power of God, it shall be carried to the Gentiles, of whom many will receive it, and after, will the seed of Israel be brought into the fold of their Redeemer by obeying it also. Those who kept the commandments of the Lord on this land, desired this at His hand, and through the prayer of faith obtained the promise, that if their descendants should transgress and fall away, a record might be kept, and in the last days, come to their children. These things are sacred, and must be kept so, for the promise of the Lord concerning them must be fulfilled. No man can obtain them if his heart is impure, because they contain that which is sacred. * * * By them will the Lord work a great and marvelous work; the wisdom of the wise shall become as naught, and the understanding of the prudent shall be hid, and because the power of God shall be displayed, those who profess to know the truth, but walk in deceit, shall tremble with anger; but with signs and with wonders, with gifts and with healings, with the manifestations of the power of God, and with the Holy Ghost, shall the hearts of the faithful be comforted. You have now beheld the power of God manifested, and the power of Satan; you see that there is nothing that is desirable in the works of darkness; that they cannot bring happiness; that those who are overcome therewith are miserable; while, on the other hand, the righteous are blessed with a place in the kingdom of God, where joy unspeakable surrounds them; there they rest beyond the power of the enemy of truth, where no evil can disturb them: the glory of God crowns them, and they continually feast upon His goodness, and enjoy His smiles. Behold, notwithstanding you have seen this great display of power, by which you may ever be able to detect the evil one, yet I give unto you another sign, and when it comes to pass, then know that the Lord is God, and that He will fulfil His purposes, and that the knowledge which this record contains, will go to every nation, and kindred, and tongue, and people under the whole heaven. This is the sign: when these things begin to be known, that is, when it is known that the Lord has shown you these things, the workers of iniquity will seek your overthrow; they will circulate falsehoods to destroy your reputation; and also will seek to take your life! but remember this, if you are faithful, and shall hereafter continue to keep the commandments of the Lord, you shall be preserved to bring these things forth; for in due time He will again give you a commandment to come and take them. When they are interpreted, the Lord will give the Holy Priesthood to some, and they shall begin to proclaim this Gospel and baptize by water, and after that, they shall have power to give the Holy Ghost by the laying on of their hands. Then will persecution rage more and more; for the iniquities of men shall be revealed, and those who are not built upon the Rock will seek to overthrow this Church; but it will increase the more opposed, and spread farther and farther, increasing in knowledge, till they shall be sanctified, and receive an inheritance where the glory of God will rest upon them; and when this takes place, and all things are prepared, the ten tribes of Israel will be revealed in the north country, whither they have been for a long season; and when this is fulfilled, will be brought to pass that saying of the Prophet, 'And the Redeemer shall come to Zion, and unto them that turn from transgression in Jacob, saith the Lord.' But, notwithstanding the workers of iniquity shall seek your destruction, the arm of the Lord will be extended, and you will be borne off conqueror, if you keep all His commandments. Your name shall be known among the nations, for the work which the Lord will perform by your hands shall cause the righteous to rejoice and the wicked to rage; with the one it shall be had in honor, and with the other in reproach; yet, with these it shall be a terror, because of the great and marvelous work which shall follow the coming forth of this fulness of the Gospel. Now, go thy way, remembering what the Lord has done for thee, and be diligent in keeping His commandments, and He will deliver thee from temptations, and all the arts and devices of the wicked one. Forget not to pray, that thy mind may become strong, that when he shall manifest unto thee, thou mayest have power to escape the evil, and obtain these precious things."

We here remark, that the above quotation is an extract from a letter written by Elder Oliver Cowdery, which was published in one of the numbers of the "Latter-day Saints' Messenger and Advocate."

Although many more instructions were given by the mouth of the angel to Mr. Smith, which we do not write in this book, yet the most important items are contained in the foregoing relation. During the period of the four following years, he frequently received instruction from the mouth of the heavenly messenger, and on the morning of the twenty-second of September, A. D. 1827, the angel of the Lord delivered the records into his hands.

These records were engraved on plates which had the appearance of gold. Each plate was not far from seven inches in width by eight inches in length, being not quite as thick as common tin. They were filled on both sides with engravings, in Egyptian characters, and bound together in a volume, as the leaves of a book, and fastened at one edge with three rings running through the whole. This volume was something near six inches in thickness, a part of which was sealed. The characters of letters upon the unsealed part were small, and beautifully engraved. The whole book exhibited many marks of antiquity in its construction, as well as much skill in the art of engraving. With the records was found a curious instrument, called by the ancients the Urim and Thummim, which consisted of two transparent stones, clear as crystal, set in the two rims of a bow. This was in use in ancient times by persons called Seers. It was an instrument by the use of which they received revelation of things distant, or of things past or future.

In the mean time the inhabitants of that vicinity, having been informed that Mr. Smith had seen heavenly visions, and that he had discovered sacred records, began to ridicule and mock at those things. And after having obtained those sacred things, while proceeding home through the wilderness and fields, he was waylaid by two ruffians, who had secreted themselves for the purpose of robbing him of the records. One of them struck him with a club before he perceived them; but being a strong man, and large in stature, with great exertion he cleared himself from them, and ran towards home, being closely pursued until he came near his father's house, when his pursuers, for fear of being detected, turned and fled the other way.

Soon the news of his discoveries spread abroad throughout all those parts. False reports, misrepresentations, and base slanders flew as if upon the wings of the wind in every direction. The house was frequently beset by mobs and evil designing persons. Several times he was shot at, and very narrowly escaped. Every device was used to get the plates away from him. And being continually in danger of his life, from a gang of abandoned wretches, he at length concluded to leave the place, and go to Pennsylvania; and accordingly packed up his goods, putting the plates into a barrel of beans, and proceeded upon his journey. He had not gone far, before he was overtaken by an officer with a search warrant, who flattered himself with the idea that he should surely obtain the plates; after searching very diligently, ho was sadly disappointed at not finding them. Mr. Smith then drove on; but before he got to his journey's end, he was again overtaken by an officer on the same business, and after ransacking the wagon very carefully, he went his way, as much chagrined as the first at not being able to discover the object of his research. Without any further molestation, he pursued his journey until he came into the northern part of Pennsylvania, near the Susquehanna River, in which part his father-in-law resided.

Having provided himself with a home, ho commenced translating the record, by the gift and power of God, through the means of the Urim and Thummim; and being a poor writer, he was under the necessity of employing a scribe, to write the translation as it tame from his mouth.

In the meantime, a few of the original characters were accurately transcribed and translated by Mr. Smith, which, with the translation, were taken by a gentleman named Martin Harris to the city of New York, where they were presented to a learned gentleman named Anthon, who professed to be extensively acquainted with many languages, both ancient and modern. He examined them, but was unable to decipher them correctly; but he presumed, that if the original records could be brought, he could assist in translating them.

But to return. Mr. Smith continued the work of translation, as his pecuniary circumstances would permit, until he had finished the unsealed part of the records. The part translated is entitled the "Book of Mormon," which contains nearly as much reading as the Old Testament.

"Well," says the objector, "if it were not for the marvellous, the book would be considered one of the greatest discoveries the world ever witnessed. If you had been ploughing, or digging a well or cellar and accidentally dug up a record containing some account of the ancient history of the American continent, and of its original inhabitants, together with the origin of the Indian tribes who now inhabit it; had this record had nothing to do with God, or angels, or inspiration, it would have been hailed by all the learned of America and Europe, as one of the greatest and most important discoveries of modern times, unfolding a mystery which had, until then, bid defiance to all the researches of the learned world. Every newspaper would have been filled with the glad tidings, while its contents would have poured upon the world a flood of light, on subjects before concealed in the labyrinth of uncertainty and doubt. But who can stoop, and so humble himself as to receive anything, in this enlightened age, renowned for its religion and learning, from the ministering of angels, and from inspiration? This is too much: away with such things, it comes in contact with the wisdom and popularity of the day." To this I reply, The Lord knew that before He revealed it; this was one principal object He had in view; it is just the manner of His dealing with the children of men; He always takes a different course from the one marked out for Him by the wisdom of the world, in order to "confound the wise, and bring to naught the understanding of the prudent;" He chooses men of low degree, even the simple and the unlearned, and those who are despised, to do His work and to bring about His purposes, that no flesh shall glory in His presence. O ye wise, and ye learned, who despise the wisdom that comes from above! Know ye not, that it was impossible for the world by wisdom to find out God? Know ye not that all your wisdom is foolishness with God? Know ye not that ye must become as a little child, and be willing to learn wisdom, from the least of His servants, or you will perish in your ignorance?

But what are the evidences which we gather from Scripture, concerning the coming forth of this glorious work? We shall attempt to prove: first, that America is a land promised to the seed of Joseph; second, that the Lord would reveal to them His truth as well as to the Jews; and third, that their record should come forth, and unite its testimony, with the record of the Jews, in time for the restoration of Israel, in the last days.

First, Genesis, xlviii, Jacob, while blessing the two sons of Joseph, says: "Let them grow into a multitude in the midst of the earth." In the same blessing, it is said of Ephraim, "His seed shall become a multitude of nations." Now put the sense of these sayings together, and it makes Ephraim a multitude of nations in the midst of the earth. In Genesis, xlix, it is prophesied concerning Joseph, while Jacob was blessing him, that he should be "a fruitful bough by a well, whose branches run over the wall: the archers have sorely grieved him, and shot at him, and hated him, but his bow abode in strength." Again, he further says: "The blessings of thy father have prevailed above the blessings of my progenitors, unto the utmost bound of the everlasting hills; they shall be on the head of Joseph, and on the crown of the head of him that was separate from his brethren." Now I ask, Who were Jacob's progenitors, and what was the blessing conferred upon him? Abraham and Isaac were his progenitors, and the land of Canaan was the blessing they conferred upon him, or that God promised them he should possess. Recollect that Jacob confers on Joseph a much greater land than that of Canaan; even greater than his fathers had conferred upon him, for Joseph's blessing was to extend to the uttermost bound of the everlasting hills. Now, reader, stand in Egypt, where Jacob then stood, and measure to the utmost bound of the everlasting hills, and you will land somewhere in the central part of America. Again, one of the Prophets says, in speaking of Ephraim: "When the Lord shall roar, the children of Ephraim shall tremble from the west." Now let us sum up these sayings, and what have we gained? First, that Ephraim was to grow into a multitude of nations in the midst of the earth; second, Joseph was to be greatly blessed in a large inheritance, as far off as America; third, this was to be on the west of Egypt or Jerusalem.

Now let the world search from pole to pole, and they will not find a multitude of nations in the midst of the earth, who can possibly have sprung from Ephraim, unless they find them in America; for the midst of all other parts of the earth is inhabited by mixed races, who have sprung from various sources; while here an almost boundless country was secluded from the rest of the world, and inhabited by a race of men, evidently of the same origin, although as evidently divided into many nations. Now, the Scriptures cannot be broken; therefore, these Scriptures must apply to America, for the plainest of reasons: they can apply to no other place.

Now, secondly, we are to prove that God revealed himself to the seed of Joseph or Ephraim—their location we have already proved—dwelling in America. For this, we quote Hosea, viii, 12; speaking of Ephraim, he says by the spirit of prophecy: "I have written to him the great things of my law, but they were counted as a strange thing." This is proof positive and needs no comment, that the great truths of Heaven were revealed unto Ephraim, and were counted as a strange thing.

Third: Were these writings to come forth just previously to the gathering of Israel? Answer: They were, according to Ezekiel, thirty-seventh chapter, where God commanded him to "Take one stick, and write upon it For Judah, and the children of Israel his companions; then take another stick, and write upon it For Joseph, the stick of Ephraim, and for all the house of Israel his companions; and join them one to another, into one stick, and they shall become one in thine hand. And when the children of thy people shall speak unto thee, saying, Wilt not thou show us what thou meanest by these? say unto them, Thus saith the Lord God, Behold, I will take the stick of Joseph, which is in the hand of Ephraim, and the tribes of Israel his fellows, and will put them with him, even with the stick of Judah, and make them one stick, and they shall be one in mine hand; and the sticks whereon thou writest shall be in thine hand before their eyes. And say unto them, Thus saith the Lord God, Behold, I will take the children of Israel from among the heathen, whither they be gone, and will gather them on every side, and bring them into their own land; and I will make them one nation in the land upon the mountains of Israel; and one king shall be king to them all: and they shall be no more two nations, neither shall they be divided into two kingdoms any more at all."

Now, nothing can be more plain than the above prophecy; there are presented two writings, the one to Ephraim, the other to Judah; that of Ephraim is to be brought forth by the Lord, and put with that of Judah, and they are to become one in their testimony, and grow together in this manner, in order to bring about the gathering of Israel. The eighty-fifth Psalm is very plain on the subject: speaking of the restoration of Israel to their own land, it says, "Mercy and Truth are met together; Righteousness and peace have kissed each other. Truth shall spring out of the earth: and Righteousness shall look down from heaven. Yea, the Lord shall give that which is good; and our land shall yield her increase. Righteousness shall go before Him, and shall set us in the way of His steps." Now the Savior, while praying for His disciples, said: "Sanctify them through Thy truth—Thy word is truth." From these passages we learn, that His word is to spring out of the earth, while Righteousness looks down from heaven. And the next thing that follows is, that Israel are set in the way of His steps, and partaking of the fruit of their own land. Jeremiah, xxxiii, 6, speaking of the final return from captivity of both Judah and Israel, says: "I will reveal unto them the abundance of peace and truth." And Isaiah, speaking of the everlasting covenant, which should gather them, makes this extraordinary and very remarkable expression: "Their seed shall be known amongst the Gentiles, and their offspring among the people." Now, reader, let me ask, can any one tell whether the Indians of America are of Israel, unless by revelation from God? Therefore this was a hidden mystery, which it was necessary to reveal in time for their gathering.

So much, then, we have produced from the Scriptures, in proof of a work, like the book of Mormon, making its appearance in these days; to say nothing of Isaiah, xxix. But says one, "What is the use of the Book of Mormon, even if it be true?" I answer: First, it brings to light an important history, before unknown to man. Second, it reveals the origin of the American Indians, which was before a mystery. Third, it contains important prophecies, yet to be fulfilled, which immediately concern the present generation. Fourth, it contains much plainness in regard to points of doctrine, insomuch that all may understand, and see eye to eye, if they take pains to read it.

"But what are its proofs, as to chosen witnesses who testify to its translation by inspiration?" For this testimony, I refer the reader to the testimony of the witnesses in the first page of the Book of Mormon; he will there find as positive testimony as has ever been found in the other Scriptures concerning any truth which God ever revealed. Men there testify, not only that they have seen and handled the plates, but that an angel of God came down from heaven, and presented the plates before them, while the glory of God shone round about them, and the voice of God spoke from heaven, and told them that these things were true, and had been translated by the gift and power of God, and commanded them to bear record of the same to all people.

Blessed be the Lord God of our fathers! He has visited His people, and the dayspring from on high has dawned upon our benighted world once more; for no sooner had the Book been translated, and men begun to bear record of the same, than the Angel of the Lord came down from heaven again, and commissioned men to preach the Gospel to every creature, and to baptize with water for the remission of sins. No sooner did the people begin to believe their testimony, and be baptized, than the Holy Ghost fell upon them, through the laying on of hands in the name of Jesus; and the heavens were opened: and while some had the ministering of angels, others began to speak in other tongues, and prophesy. From that time forth, many of them were healed by the laying on of hands in the name of Jesus; and thus mightily grew the word of God, and prevailed. And thus, thousands have been raised up to testify that they do know for themselves, and are not dependent on the testimony of any man, for the truth of these things, for these signs follow them that believe. And when a man believes the truth, through the testimony of God's witnesses, and then these signs follow, not only them, but him also; if he has the ministering of angels, if he has been healed, or heals others, by the laying on of hands in the name of Jesus, or if he speaks in other tongues, or prophesies, he knows it for himself; and thus is fulfilled the saying of Scripture, "If any man do my will, he shall know of the doctrine, whether it be of God." Thus faith comes by hearing, and knowledge by obeying; but hearing comes by preaching, and preaching comes by sending; as it is written—"How shall they preach, except they be sent?"

But there are many who say—"Show us a sign, and we will believe." Remember, faith comes not by signs, but signs come by faith. Gifts were not given to make men believe; but what saith the Scripture? "Gifts are for the edifying of the Church." If otherwise, why was it not written—"Faith comes by miracles," instead of "Faith comes by hearing?" I always take it for granted, that a man or woman who comes demanding a sign in order to make them believe, belongs to a wicked and adulterous generation, at least, to say no worse; for any person who will go to Jesus, with a pure heart, desiring and praying in faith, that he may know the truth concerning these things, the Lord will reveal it to him, and he shall know, and shall bear testimony, for by the Spirit of God they shall know truth from error: as it is written—"My sheep hear my voice." And he that will not come unto Jesus by faith, shall never know the truth, until, too late, he finds the harvest is over, and the summer is ended, and his soul not saved.

Thus the religion of Jesus, unlike all other religious systems, bears its own weight, and brings certainty and knowledge, leaving no room for imposition. And now I say unto all people, Come unto the Father in the name of Jesus; doubt not, but be believing, as in days of old, and ask in faith for whatsoever you stand in need of; ask not that you may consume it on your lusts, but ask with a firmness not to be shaken, that you will yield to no temptation, but that you will keep His commandments, as fast as He makes them manifest unto you; and if ye do this, and He reveals to you that He has sent us with a new and everlasting covenant, and commanded us to preach, and baptize, and build up His Church as in days of old, then come forward and obey the truth; but if you do not know, or are not satisfied that He has sent us, then do not embrace the doctrine we preach. Thus to your own master you shall stand or fall; and one day you shall know, yea, in that great day, when every knee shall bow, then shall you know that God has sent us with the truth, to prune His vineyard for the last time, with a mighty pruning.

We shall now introduce much circumstantial evidence, from American antiquities, and from the traditions of the natives, etc.

First, says Mr. Boudinot: "It is said among their principal or beloved men, that they have it handed down from their ancestors, that the book which the white people have, was once theirs: that while they had it they prospered exceedingly, etc. They also say, that their fathers were possessed of an extraordinary Divine Spirit, by which they foretold future events, and controlled the common course of nature; and this they transmitted to their offspring, on condition of their obeying the sacred laws; that they did, by these means, bring down showers of blessings upon their beloved people; but that this power, for a long time past, had entirely ceased." Colonel James Smith, in his journal, while a prisoner among the natives, says: "They have a tradition, that in the beginning of this continent, the angels or heavenly inhabitants, as they call them, frequently visited the people, and talked with their forefathers, and gave directions how to pray."

Mr. Boudinot, in his able work, remarks concerning their language: "Their language, in its roots, idiom, and particular construction, appears to have the whole genius of the Hebrew; and what is very remarkable, and well worthy of serious attention, has most of the peculiarities of that language." There is a tradition related by an aged Indian, of the Stockbridge tribe, that their fathers were once in possession of a "Sacred Book," which was handed down from generation to generation; and at last hid in the earth, since which time they had been under the feet of their enemies. But these oracles were to be restored to them again; and then they would triumph over their enemies, and regain their rights and privileges. Mr. Boudinot, after recording many traditions similar to the above, at length remarks: "Can any man read this short account of Indian traditions, drawn from tribes of various nations; from the west to the east, and from the south to the north, wholly separated from each other, written by different authors of the best character, both for knowledge and integrity, possessing the best means of information, at various and distant times, without any possible communication with each other; and yet suppose that all this is the effect of chance, accident, or design, from a love of the marvelous, or a premeditated intention of deceiving, and thereby ruining their well established reputation? Can any one carefully, and with deep reflection, consider and compare these traditions and nations with the position and circumstances of the long lost ten tribes of Israel, without at least drawing some presumptive inferences in favor of these wandering natives being descended from the ten tribes of Israel?"

"Joseph Merrick, Esq., a highly respectable character in Pitsfield, Mass., gave the following account: That in 1815, he was leveling some ground under and near an old wood-shed standing on a place of his, situated on Indian Hill. He ploughed and conveyed away old chips and earth to some depth. After the work was done, walking over the place, he discovered, near where the earth had been dug the deepest, a black strap, as it appeared, about six inches in length, and one and a half in breadth, and about the thickness of a leather trace to a harness. He perceived it had, at each end, a loop of some hard substance, probably for the purpose of carrying it. He conveyed it to his house, and threw it into an old tool box. He afterwards found it thrown out at the door, and again conveyed it to the box.

"After some time, he thought he would examine it; but in attempting to cut it, found it as hard as bone; he succeeded, however, in getting it open, and found it was formed of two pieces of thick rawhide, sewed and made watertight with the sinews of some animal, and gummed over; and in the fold was contained four folded pieces of parchment. They were of a dark yellow hue, and contained some kind of writing. The neighbors coming in to see the strange discovery, tore one of the pieces to atoms, in the true Hun and Vandal style. The other three pieces Mr. Merrick saved, and sent them to Cambridge, where they were examined, and discovered to have been written with a pen, in Hebrew, plain and legible. The writing on the three remaining pieces of parchment, was quotations from the Old Testament. See Deut., vi, from 4—9; also xi, 13—21; and Exodus, xiii, 11—16, to which the reader can refer, if he has the curiosity to read this most interesting discovery.

"On the banks of White River, in Arkansas Territory, have been found ruins erected no doubt by an enlightened population, of the most extraordinary character, on account of their dimensions, and the materials of which they were erected. One of these works is a wall of earth, which encloses an area of six hundred and forty acres, equal to a mile square, and having, in its centre, the foundation of a large circular building, or temple. Another, yet more strange, and more extensive, consists of the foundations of a great city, whose streets, crossing each other at right angles, are easily traced through the mighty forest. And besides these are found the foundations of houses, made of burnt bricks, like the bricks of the present time. These have been traced to the extent of a mile."

The foregoing is taken from Priest's American Antiquities, and from the same work we extract the following, page 246:

"Ruins of the City of Otolum, discovered in North America.—In a letter of C. S. Rafinesque, whom we have before quoted, to a correspondent in Europe, we find the following: 'Some years ago, the Society of Geography, in Paris, offered a large premium for a voyage to Guatemala, and for a new survey of the antiquities of Yucatan and Chiapa, chiefly those fifteen miles from Palenque.'"

"I have," says this author, "restored to them the true name of Otolum, which is yet the name of the stream running through the ruins. They were surveyed by Captain Del Rio, in 1787, an account of which was published in English, in 1822. This account describes partly the ruins of a stone city, of no less dimensions than seventy-five miles in circuit; length, thirty-two, and breadth twelve miles, full of palaces, monuments, statues, and inscriptions: one of the earliest seats of American civilization; about equal to Thebes of ancient Egypt."

It is stated in the Family Magazine, No. 34, p. 266, for 1833, as follows: "Public attention has been recently excited, respecting the ruins of an ancient city, found in Guatemala. It would seem that these ruins are now being explored, and much curious and valuable matter, in a literary and historical point of view, is anticipated. We deem the present a most auspicious moment, now that the public attention is turned to the subject, to spread its contents before our readers, as an introduction to future discoveries, during the researches now in progress."

The following are some of the particulars, as related by Captain Del Rio, who partially examined them, as above related, in 1787: "From Palenque, the last town northward in the province of Ciudad Real de Chiapa, taking a southwesterly direction, and ascending a ridge of high land, that divides the kingdom of Guatemala from Yucatan, at the distance of six miles, is the little river Micol, whose waters flow in a westerly direction, and unite with the great river Tulijah, which bends its course towards the province of Tobasco.

Having passed Micol, the ascent begins, and at half a league, or a mile and a half, the traveler crosses a little stream called Otolum; from this point heaps of stone ruins are discovered, which render the roads very difficult for another half league, when you gain the height whereon the stone houses are situated, being still fourteen in number in one place, some more dilapidated than others, yet still having many of their apartments perfectly discernible. These stand on a rectangular area, three hundred yards in breadth by four hundred and fifty in length, which is a fraction over fifty-six rods wide, and eighty-four rods long, being in the whole circuit, two hundred and eighty rods, which is three fourths of a mile, and a trifle over. This area presents a plain at the base of the highest mountain forming the ridge. In the centre of this plain is situated the largest of the structures which has been, as yet, discovered among these ruins. It stands on a mound, or pyramid, twenty yards high, which is sixty feet, or nearly four rods, in perpendicular altitude, which gives it a lofty and beautiful majesty, as if it were a temple suspended in the sky. This is surrounded by other edifices, namely, five to the northward, four to the southward, one to the southwest, and three to the eastward, fourteen in all.

"In all directions, the fragments of other fallen buildings are seen extending along the mountain, that stretches east and west either way from these buildings, as if it were the great temple of worship, or their government-house, around which they built their city, and where dwelt their kings and officers of state. At this place was found a subterranean stone aqueduct, of great solidity and durability, which in its course passes beneath the largest building."

Let it be understood, this city of Otolum, the ruins of which are so immense, is in North, not South America, in the same latitude with the island of Jamaica, which is about eighteen degrees north of the equator, being on the highest ground between the northern end of the Caribbean Sea and the Pacific Ocean, where the continent narrows towards the Isthmus of Darien, and is about eight hundred miles south of New Orleans.

The discovery of these ruins, and also of many others, equally wonderful, in the same country, is just commencing to arouse the attention of the schools of Europe, which hitherto have denied that America could boast of her antiquities. But these immense ruins are now being explored under the direction of scientific persons, a history of which, in detail, will, doubtless, be forthcoming in due time; two volumes of which, in manuscript, we are informed, have already been written, and cannot but be received with enthusiasm by Americans.

A gentleman who was living near the town of Cincinnati, in 1826, on the upper level, had occasion to sink a well for his accommodation; he persevered in digging to the depth of eighty feet, without finding water; but still persisting in the attempt, his workmen found themselves obstructed by a substance, which resisted their labor, though evidently not stone. They cleared the surface and sides from the earth bedded around it, when there appeared the stump of a tree, three feet in diameter, and two feet high, which had been cut down with an ax. The blows of the ax were yet visible. It was nearly of the color and apparent character of coal, but had not the friable and fusible quality of that substance. Ten feet below, the water sprang up, and the well is now in constant supply and high repute.

In Morse's Universal Geography, first volume, p. 142, the discovery of the stump is corroborated: "In digging a well in Cincinnati, the stump of a tree was found in a sound state, ninety feet below the surface; and in digging another well, at the same place, another stump was found, at ninety four feet below the surface, which had evident marks of the ax; and on its top there appeared as if some iron tool had been consumed by rust."

We might fill a volume with accounts of American antiquities, all going to show that this country has been inhabited by a people who possessed a knowledge of the arts and sciences, who built cities, cultivated the earth, and who were in possession of a written language. But the things which we have here introduced are abundantly sufficient for our purpose. If a few characters in Hebrew have been found in the earth in America, written on parchment, then it is just as easy to admit that a whole volume has been found in the earth in America, written on plates, in Egyptian characters. The astonishing facts of the stumps found eighty or ninety feet under ground at Cincinnati, and similar discoveries in many other parts of North and South America, such as buried cities, and other antiquities, all go to prove that there has been a mighty convulsion and revolution, not only of nations, but of nature; and such a convulsion as is nowhere else so reasonably accounted for, as in the following extraordinary and wonderful account of events, which transpired in this country, during the crucifixion of Messiah, which we extract from the Book of Mormon, Nephi, v, 2-11:

"And it came to pass, in the thirty and fourth year, in the first month, in the fourth day of the month, there arose a great storm, such an one as never had been known in all the land; and there was also a great and terrible tempest;

and there was terrible thunder, insomuch that it did shake the whole earth, as if it was about to divide asunder; and there were exceeding sharp lightnings, such as never had been known in all the land. And the city of Zarahemla did take fire; and the city of Moroni did sink into the depths of the sea, and the inhabitants thereof were drowned; and the earth was carried up upon the city of Moronihah, that, in the place of the city thereof, there became a great mountain; and there was a great and terrible destruction in the land southward. But, behold, there was a more great and terrible destruction in the land northward; for, behold, the whole face of the land was changed, because of the tempest, and the whirlwinds, and the thunderings, and the lightnings, and the exceeding great quaking of the whole earth; and the highways were broken up, and the level roads were spoiled, and many smooth places became rough, and many great and notable cities were sunk, and many were burned, and many were shook till the buildings thereof had fallen to the earth, and the inhabitants thereof were slain, and the places were left desolate; and there were some cities which remained, but the damage thereof was exceeding great, and there were many in them who were slain, and there were some who were carried away in the whirlwind, and whither they went, no man knoweth, save they know that they were carried away; and thus the face of the whole earth became deformed, because of the tempests, and the thunderings, and the lightnings, and the quaking of the earth. And, behold, the rocks were rent in twain; they were broken up upon the face of the whole earth, insomuch that they were found in broken fragments, and in seams, and in cracks, upon all the face of the land.

"And it came to pass, that when the thunderings, and the lightnings, and the storm, and the tempest, and the quakings of the earth did cease—for, behold, they did last for about the space of three hours: and it was said by some that the time was greater; nevertheless, all these great and terrible things were done in about the space of three hours; and then, behold, there was darkness upon the face of the land.

"And it came to pass that there was a thick darkness upon all the face of the land, insomuch that the inhabitants thereof, who had not fallen, could feel the vapor of darkness; and there could be no light because of the darkness, neither candles, neither torches; neither could there be fire kindled with their fine and exceeding dry wood, so that there could not be any light at all; and there was not any light seen, neither fire, nor glimmer, neither the sun, nor the moon, nor the stars, for so great were the mists of darkness which were upon the face of the land.

"And it came to pass, that it did last for the space of three days, that there was no light seen; and there was great mourning and howling, and weeping among all the people continually; yea, great were the groanings of the people, because of the darkness and great destruction which had come upon them. And in one place they were heard to cry, saying, O that we had repented before this great and terrible day, and then would our brethren have been spared, and they would not have been burned in that great city of Zarahemla! And in another place they were heard to cry and mourn, saying, O that we had repented before this great and terrible day, and had not killed and Stoned the prophets and cast them out; then would our mothers, and our fair daughters, and our children have been spared, and not have been buried up in that great city Moronihah; and thus were the howlings of the people great and terrible.

"And it came to pass, that there was a voice heard among all the inhabitants of the earth upon the face of this land, crying, Wo, wo, wo unto this people; wo unto the inhabitants of the whole earth, except they shall repent, for the devil laugheth, and his angels rejoice, because of the slain of the fair sons and daughters of my people; and it is because of their iniquity and abominations that they are fallen. Behold, that great city of Zarahemla have I burned with fire, and the inhabitants thereof. And behold, that great city Moroni have I caused to be sunk in the depth of the sea, and the inhabitants thereof to be drowned. And behold, that great city Moronihah have I covered with earth, and the inhabitants thereof, to hide their iniquities and their abominations from before my face, that the blood of the prophets and the saints shall not come any more unto me against them. And behold the city of Gilgal have I caused to be sunk, and the inhabitants thereof to be buried up in the depths of the earth: yea, and the city of Onihah and the inhabitants thereof, and the city of Mocum and the inhabitants thereof, and the city of Jerusalem and the inhabitants thereof, and waters have I caused to come up in the stead thereof, to hide their wickedness and abominations from before my face, that the blood of the prophets and the saints shall not come up any more unto me against them. And behold the city of Gadiandi, and the city of Gadiomnah, and the city of Jacob, and the city of Gimgimno, all these have I caused to be sunk, and made hills and valleys in the places thereof; and the inhabitants thereof have I buried up in the depths of the earth, to hide their wickedness and abominations from before my face, that the blood of the prophets and saints should not come up anymore unto me against them. And behold that great city of Jacobugath, which was inhabited by the people of the king of Jacob, have I caused to be burned with fire, because of their sins and their wickedness, which was above all the wickedness of the whole earth, because of their secret murders and combinations; for it was they that did destroy the peace of my people and the government of the land: therefore I did cause them to be burned, to destroy them from before my face, that the blood of the prophets and the saints should not come up unto me any more against them. And behold, the city of Laman, and the city of Josh, and the city of Gad, and tho city of Kishkumen, have I caused to be burned with fire, and the inhabitants thereof, because of their wickedness in casting out the prophets, and stoning those whom I did send to declare unto them concerning their wickedness and their abominations; and because they did cast them all out, that there were none righteous among them, I did send down fire and destroy them, that their wickedness and abominations might be hid from before my face, that the blood of the prophets and the saints whom I sent among them might not cry unto me from the ground against them; and many great destructions have I caused to come upon this land and upon this people, because of their wickedness and their abominations.

"O, all ye that are spared, because ye were more righteous than they, will ye not now return unto me, and repent of your sins, and be converted, that I may heal you? Yea, verily, I say unto you, if ye will come unto me, ye shall have eternal life. Behold, mine arm of mercy is extended towards you, and whomsoever will come, him will I receive; and blessed are those who come unto me. Behold, I am Jesus Christ, the son of God. I created the heavens and the earth, and all things that in them are. I was with the Father from the beginning. I am in the Father, and the Father in me; and in me hath the Father glorified his name. I came unto my own, and my own received me not. And the Scriptures concerning my coming are fulfilled. And as many as have received me, to them have I given to become the sons of God; and even so will I to as many as shall believe on my name; for, behold, by me redemption cometh, and in me is the law of Moses fulfilled. I am the light and life of the world. I am Alpha and Omega, the beginning and the end. And ye shall offer up unto me no more the shedding of blood: yea, your sacrifices and your burnt offerings shall be done away, for I will accept none of your sacrifices and your burnt offerings; and ye shall offer, for a sacrifice unto me, a broken heart and a contrite spirit. And whoso cometh unto me with a broken heart and a contrite spirit, him will I baptize with fire and with the Holy Ghost, even as the Lamanites, because of their faith in me, at the time of their conversion, were baptized with fire and with the Holy Ghost, and they knew it not. Behold, I have come unto the world to bring redemption unto the world, to save the world from sin: therefore, whoso repenteth and cometh unto me as a little child, him will I receive; for of such is the kingdom of God. Behold, for such I have laid down my life, and have taken it up again: therefore, repent and come unto me, ye ends of the earth, and be saved.

"And now, behold it came to pass, that all the people of the land did hear these sayings; and did witness of it. And after these sayings, there was silence in the land for the space of many hours: for so great was the astonishment of the people that they did cease lamenting and howling for the loss of their kindred which had been slain; therefore there was silence in all the land for the space of many hours.

"And it came to pass, that there came a voice again unto the people, and all the people did hear, and did witness of it, saying, O ye people of these great cities which have fallen, who are descendants of Jacob; yea, who are of the house of Israel, how oft have I gathered you as a hen gathereth her chickens under her wings, and have nourished you. And again, how oft would I have gathered you, as a hen gathereth her chickens under her wings; yea, O ye people of the house of Israel, who have fallen; yea, O ye people of the house of Israel; ye that dwell at Jerusalem, as ye that have fallen; yea, how oft would I have gathered you, as a hen gathereth her chickens, and ye would not. O, ye house of Israel, whom I have spared, how oft will I gather you, as a hen gathereth her chickens under her wings, if ye will repent and return unto me with full purpose of heart. But if not, O house of Israel, the places of your dwellings shall become desolate, until the time of the fulfilling of the covenant to your fathers.

"And now it came to pass, that after the people had heard these words, behold, they began to weep and howl again, because of the loss of their kindred and friends. And it came to pass that thus did three days pass away. And it was in the morning, and the darkness dispersed from off the face of the land, and the earth did cease to tremble, and the rocks did cease to rend, and the dreadful groanings did cease, and all the tumultuous noises did pass away, and the earth did cleave together again, that it stood; and the mourning, and the weeping, and the wailing of the people who were spared alive, did cease, and their mourning was turned into joy, and their lamentations into the praise and thanksgiving unto the Lord Jesus Christ, their Redeemer. And thus far were the Scriptures fulfilled, which had been spoken by the prophets."

Here, then, is an account which shows, clearly and definitely, how and when the American antiquities became buried; how the stumps of trees were placed eighty or ninety feet under ground; how cities were sunk, and overwhelmed; how mountains fell and valleys rose; how the rocks were rent, and how the whole face of the continent became altered and deformed. We now close this subject by saying to all the people, if you wish information on the antiquities of America; if you wish historical, prophetical, or doctrinal information of the highest importance, read carefully the Book of Mormon.

Chapter Five - The Resurrection of The Saints, and the Restoration of All Things Spoken by The Prophets.

This is one of the most important subjects upon which the human mind can contemplate; and one perhaps as little understood, in the present age, as any other now lying over the face of prophecy. But, however neglected at the present time, it was once the groundwork of the faith, hope, and joy of the Saints. It was a correct understanding of this subject, and firm belief in it, that influenced all their movements. Their minds once fastening upon it, they could not be shaken from their purposes; their faith was firm, their joy constant, and their hope like an anchor to the soul, both sure and steadfast, reaching to that within the veil. It was this that enabled them to rejoice in the midst of tribulation, persecution, sword, and flame; and in view of this, they took joyfully the spoiling of their goods, and gladly wandered as strangers and pilgrims on the earth. For they sought a country, a city, and an inheritance that none but a saint ever thought of, understood, or even hoped for.

Now, we can never understand precisely what is meant by restoration, unless we understand what is lost or taken away; for instance, when we offer to restore anything to a man, it is as much as to say he once possessed it, but had lost it, and we propose to replace, or put him in possession of, that which he once had; therefore, when a Prophet speaks of the restoration of all things, he means that all things have undergone a change, and are to be again restored to their primitive order, even as they first existed.

First, then, it becomes necessary to take a view of creation, as it rolled in purity from the hand of its Creator; and if we can discover the true state in which it then existed, and understand the changes that have taken place since, then we shall be able to understand what is to be restored; and thus, our minds being prepared, we shall be looking for the very things which will come, and shall be in no danger of lifting our puny arm in ignorance, to oppose the things of God. First, then, we will take a view of the earth, as to its surface, local situation, and productions.

When God had created the heavens and the earth, and separated the light from the darkness, His next great command was to the waters, Genesis, i, 9: "And God said, Let the waters under the heaven, be gathered together into one place, and let the dry land appear: and it was so." From this we learn a marvelous fact, which very few have ever realized or believed in this benighted age; we learn that the waters, which are now divided into oceans, seas, and lakes, were then all gathered together, into one vast ocean; and, consequently, that the land, which is now torn asunder, and divided into continents and islands, almost innumerable, was then one vast continent or body, not separated as it now is.

Second, we hear the Lord God pronounce the earth, as well as everything else, very good. From this we learn that there were neither deserts, barren places, stagnant swamps, rough, broken, rugged hills; nor vast mountains covered with eternal snow; and no part of it was located in the frigid zone, so as to render its climate dreary and unproductive, subject to eternal frost, or everlasting chains of ice—

Where no sweet flowers the dreary landscape cheer,
Nor plenteous harvests crown the passing year.

But the whole earth was probably one vast plain, or interspersed with gently rising hills, and sloping vales, well calculated for cultivation; while its climate was delightfully varied, with the moderate changes of heat and cold, of wet and dry, which only tended to crown the varied year with the greater variety of productions, all for the good of man, animal, fowl, or creeping thing; while from the flowery plain or spicy grove, sweet odors were wafted on every breeze; and all the vast creation of animated being breathed naught but health, and peace, and joy.

Next, we learn from Genesis, i, 29, 30: "And God said, Behold, I have given you every herb bearing seed, which is upon the face of all the earth, and every tree, in which is the fruit of a tree, yielding seed; to you it shall be for meat. And to every beast of the earth, and to every fowl of the air, and to everything that creepeth upon the earth, wherein there is life, I have given every green herb for meat: and it was so." From these verses we learn, that the earth yielded neither nauseous weeds nor poisonous plants, nor useless thorns and thistles; indeed every thing that grew was just calculated for the food of man, beast, fowl, and creeping thing; and their food was all vegetable. Flesh and blood were never sacrificed to glut their souls, or gratify their appetites; the beasts of the earth were all in perfect harmony with each other; the lion ate straw like the ox, the wolf dwelt with the lamb, the leopard lay down with the kid, the cow and bear fed together, in the same pasture, while their young ones reposed, in perfect security, under the shade of the same trees; all was peace and harmony, and nothing to hurt nor disturb, in all the holy mountain.

And to crown the whole, we behold man created in the image of God, and exalted in dignity and power, having dominion over all the vast creation of animated beings, which swarmed through the earth, while, at the same time, he inhabits a beautiful and well watered garden, in the midst of which stood the tree of life, to which he had free access; while he stood in the presence of his Maker, conversed with Him face to face, and gazed upon His glory, without a dimming veil between. O reader, contemplate, for a moment, the beautiful creation, clothed with peace and plenty; the earth teeming with harmless animals, rejoicing over all the plain; the air swarming with delightful birds, whose never-ceasing notes filled the air with varied melody; and all in subjection to their rightful sovereign, who rejoiced over them; while in a delightful garden—the capitol of creation, man was seated on the throne of this vast empire, swaying his sceptre over all the earth with undisputed right; while legions of angels encamped round about him, and joined their glad voices in grateful songs of praise, and shouts of joy; neither a sigh nor groan was heard throughout the vast expanse; neither were there sorrow, tears, pain, weeping, sickness, nor death; neither contentions, wars, nor bloodshed; but peace crowned the seasons as they rolled, and life, joy, and love reigned over all God's works. But, O, how changed the scene!

It now becomes my painful duty to trace some of the important changes which have taken place, and the causes which have conspired to reduce the earth and its inhabitants to their present state.

First, man fell from his standing before God, by giving heed to temptation; and this fall affected the whole creation, as well as man, and caused various changes to take place; he was banished from the presence of his Creator, and a veil was drawn between them, and man was driven from the garden of Eden, to till the earth, which was then cursed for his sake, and should begin to bring forth thorns and thistles; and with the sweat of his face he should earn his bread, and in sorrow eat of it, all the days of his life, and finally return to dust. But as to Eve, her curse was a great multiplicity of sorrow and conception; and between her seed and the seed of the serpent there was to be a constant enmity; it should bruise the serpent's head, and the serpent should bruise his heel.

Now, reader, contemplate the change. This scene, which was so beautiful a little before, had now become the abode of sorrow and toil, of death and mourning: the earth groaning with its production of accursed thorns and thistles; man and beast at enmity; the serpent slyly creeping away, fearing lest his head should get the deadly bruise; and man startling amid the thorny path, in fear, lest the serpent's fangs should pierce his heel; while the lamb yields his blood upon the smoking altar. Soon man begins to persecute, hate, and murder his fellow, until at length the earth is filled with violence, all flesh becomes corrupt, the powers of darkness prevail, and it repented Noah that God had made man, and it grieved him at his heart, because the Lord should come out in vengeance, and cleanse the earth by water.

How far the flood may have contributed to produce the various changes, as to the division of the earth into broken fragments, islands and continents, mountains and valleys, we have not been informed; the change must have been considerable. But after the flood, in the days of Peleg, the earth was divided. See Gen., x, 25. A short history, to be sure, of so great an event; but still it will account for the mighty revolution which rolled the sea from its own place in the north, and brought it to interpose between different portions of the earth, which were thus parted asunder, and moved into something near their present form; this, together with the earthquakes, revolutions, and commotions which have since taken place, have all contributed to reduce the face of the earth to its present state; while the great curses which have fallen upon different portions, because of the wickedness of men, will account for the stagnant swamps, the sunken lakes, the dead seas, the great deserts; witness, for instance, the denunciations of the Prophets upon Babylon, how it was to become perpetual desolations, a den of wild beasts, a dwelling of unclean and hateful birds, a place for owls; and should never be inhabited, but should lie desolate from generation to generation. Witness also the plains of Sodom, filled with towns, cities, and flourishing gardens, well watered; but O, how changed! A vast sea of stagnant water alone marks the place. Witness the land of Palestine; in the days of Solomon, it was capable of sustaining millions of people, besides yielding a surplus of wheat, and other productions, which were exchanged with the neighboring nations; whereas, now it is desolate, and hardly capable of sustaining a few miserable inhabitants. And when I cast mine eyes over our own land, and see the numerous swamps, lakes, and ponds of stagnant waters, together with the vast mountains, and innumerable rough places, rocks having been rent, and torn asunder, from centre to circumference, I exclaim, Whence all this?

When I read the Book of Mormon, it informs me, that while Christ was crucified among the Jews, this whole American continent was shaken to its foundation, that many cities were sunk, and waters came up in their places; that the rocks were all rent in twain; that mountains were thrown up to an exceeding height; and that other mountains became valleys; the level roads spoiled, and the whole face of the land changed. I then exclaim, These things are no longer a mystery; I have now learned to account for the many wonders, which I everywhere behold, throughout our whole country. When I am passing a ledge of rocks, and see they have all been rent and torn asunder, while some huge fragments are found deeply imbedded in the earth, some rods from whence they were torn, I exclaim, with astonishment, These were the groans! the convulsive throes of agonizing nature! while the Son of God suffered upon the cross!

But men have degenerated, and greatly changed, as well as the earth. The sins, the abominations, and the many evil habits of the latter ages, have added to the miseries, toils, and sufferings of human life. The idleness, extravagance, pride, covetousness, drunkenness, and other abominations, which are characteristics of the latter times, have all combined to sink mankind to the lowest state of wretchedness and degradation; while priestcraft and false doctrines have greatly tended to lull mankind to sleep, and cause them to rest infinitely short of the powers and attainments which the ancients enjoyed, and which are alone calculated to exalt the intellectual powers of the human mind, to establish noble and generous sentiments, to enlarge the heart, and to expand the soul to the utmost extent of its capacity. Witness the ancients conversing with the Great Jehovah, learning lessons from the angels, and receiving instruction by the Holy Ghost, in dreams by night, and visions by day, until at length the veil is taken off, and they are permitted to gaze, with wonder and admiration, upon all things past and future; yea, even to soar aloft amid unnumbered worlds, while the vast expanse of eternity stands open before them, and they contemplate the mighty works of the Great I AM, until they know as they are known, and see as they are seen.

Compare this intelligence with the low smatterings of education and worldly wisdom which seem to satisfy the narrow mind of man in our generation; yea, behold the narrow-minded, calculating, trading, overreaching, penurious sycophant of the nineteenth century, who dreams of nothing here, but how to increase his goods, or take advantage of his neighbor; and whose only religious exercise or duties consist of going to meeting, paying the priest his hire, or praying to his God, without expecting to be heard or answered, supposing that God has been deaf and dumb for many centuries, or altogether stupid and indifferent like himself. And having seen the two contrasted, you will be able to form some idea of the vast elevation from which man has fallen; you will also learn how infinitely beneath his former glory and dignity he is now living, and your heart will mourn, and be exceedingly sorrowful, when you contemplate him in his low estate—and then think he is your brother; and you will be ready to exclaim, with wonder and astonishment: "O man! how art thou fallen! Once thou wast the favorite of heaven; thy Maker delighted to converse with thee, and angels, and the spirits of just men made perfect, were thy companions; but now thou art degraded, and brought down to a level with the beasts; yea, far beneath them, for they look with horror and affright at your vain amusements, your sports, and your drunkenness, and thus often set an example worthy of your imitation. Well did the Apostle Peter say of you, that you know nothing, only what you know naturally as brute beasts, made to be taken and destroyed. And thus you perish, from generation to generation, while all creation groans under its pollution; and sorrow and death, mourning and weeping, fill up the measure of the days of man!" But, O my soul, dwell no longer on this awful scene! let it suffice to have discovered, in some degree, what is lost. Let us turn our attention to what the Prophets have said should be restored.

The Apostle Peter, while preaching to the Jews, says: "And He shall send Jesus Christ, which before was preached unto you, whom the heavens must receive, until the times of the restitution (restoration) of all things which God hath spoken, by the mouth of all His holy prophets since the world began." It appears from the above, that all the holy Prophets from Adam to Christ, and those that followed after, had their eyes upon a certain time, when all things should be restored to their primitive beauty and excellence. We also learn, that the time of restitution was to be at or near the time of Christ's second coming; for the heavens are to receive Him, until the times of restitution, and the Father shall send Him again to the earth.

We will now proceed to notice Isaiah, xl, 1-5. "Comfort ye, comfort ye my people, saith your God. Speak ye comfortably to Jerusalem, and cry unto her, that her warfare is accomplished, that her iniquity is pardoned; for she hath received of the Lord's hand, double for all her sins. The voice of him that crieth in the wilderness, Prepare ye the way of the Lord, make straight in the desert a highway for our God. Every valley shall be exalted, and every mountain and hill shall be made low; and the crooked shall be made straight, and the rough places plain; and tho glory of the Lord shall be revealed, and all flesh shall see it together; for the mouth of the Lord hath spoken it."

From these verses we learn, first, that the voice of one shall be heard in the wilderness, to prepare the way of the Lord, just at tho time when Jerusalem has been trodden down of the Gentiles long enough to have received, at the Lord's hand, double for all her sins, yea, when the warfare of Jerusalem is accomplished, and her iniquities pardoned. Then shall this proclamation be made as it was before by John, yea, a second proclamation, to prepare the way of the Lord, for His second coming; and about that time every valley shall exalted, and every mountain and hill shall be made low, and the crooked shall be made straight, and the rough places plain, and then the glory of the Lord shall be revealed, and all flesh shall see it together, for the mouth of the Lord hath spoken it.

Thus you see, every mountain being made low, and every valley exalted, and the rough places being made plain, and the crooked places straight—that these mighty revolutions will begin to restore the face of the earth to its former beauty. But all this done, we have not yet gone through our restoration; there are many more great things to be done in order to restore all things.

Our next, is Isaiah, twenty-fifth chapter, where we again read of the Lord's second coming, and of the mighty works which attend it. The barren desert should abound with pools and springs of living water, and should produce grass, with flowers blooming and blossoming as the rose, and that, too, about the time of the coming of their God, with vengeance and recompense, which must allude to His second coming; and Israel is to come at the same time to Zion, with songs of everlasting joy, and sorrow and sighing shall flee away. Here, then, we have the curse taken off the deserts, and they becomes fruitful, well-watered country.

We will now inquire whether the islands return again to the continents, from whence they were separated. For this subject we refer you to Revelations, vi, 14. "And every mountain and island were moved out of their places." From this we learn that they moved somewhere; and as it is the time of restoring what has been lost, they accordingly return and join themselves to the land whence they came.

Our next is Isaiah, xiii, 13, 14, where "The earth shall remove out of her place, And shall be as the chased roe, which no man taketh up." Also Isaiah, lxii, 4: "Thou shalt no more be termed Forsaken; neither shall thy land any more be termed Desolate; but thou shalt be called Hephzibah, and thy land Beulah; for the Lord delighteth in thee, and thy land shall be married."

In the first instance, we have the earth on a move like a chased roe; and in the second place, we have it married. And from the whole, and various Scriptures, we learn, that the continents and islands shall be united in one, as they were on the morn of creation, and the sea shall retire and assemble in its own place, where it was before; and all these scenes shall take place during the mighty convulsion of nature, about the time of the coming of the Lord.

Behold! the mount of Olives rent in twain:
While on its top He sets His feet again,
The islands, at His word, obedient, flee;
While to the north He rolls the mighty sea;
Restores the earth in one, as at the first,
With all its blessings, and removes the curse.

Having restored the earth to the same glorious state in which it first existed—leveling the mountains, exalting the valleys, smoothing the rough places, making the deserts fruitful, and bringing all the continents and islands together, causing the curse to be taken off, that noxious weeds, and thorns, and thistles shall no longer be produced; the next thing is to regulate and restore the brute creation to their former state of peace and glory, causing all enmity to cease from off the earth. But this will never be done until there is a general destruction poured out upon man, which will entirely cleanse the earth, and sweep all wickedness from its face. This will be done by the rod of His mouth, and by the breath of His lips; or, in other words, by fire as universal as the flood. Isaiah xi, 4, 6-9: "But with righteousness shall He judge the poor, and reprove with equity for the meek of the earth; and He shall smite the earth with the rod of His mouth, and with the breath of His lips shall He slay the wicked. The wolf also shall dwell with the lamb, and the leopard shall lie down with the kid; and the calf and the young lion, and the falling together; and a little child shall lead them. And the cow and the bear shall feed; their young ones shall lie down together; and the lion shall eat straw like the ox. And the suckling child shall play on the hole of the asp, and the weaned child shall put his hand on the cockatrice's den. They shall not hurt nor destroy in all my holy mountain; for the earth shall be full of the knowledge of the Lord, as the waters cover the sea."

Thus, having cleansed the earth, and glorified it with the knowledge of God, as the waters cover the sea, and having poured out His Spirit upon all flesh, both man and beast becoming perfectly harmless, as they were in the beginning, and feeding on vegetable food only, while nothing is left to hurt or destroy in all the vast creation, the Prophets then proceed to give us many glorious descriptions of the enjoyments of its inhabitants. "They shall build houses and inhabit them; and they shall plant vineyards and eat the fruit of them; they shall not build and another inhabit; they shall not plant and another eat; for as the days of a tree are the days of my people, and mine elect shall long enjoy the work of their hands. They shall not labor in vain, nor bring forth for trouble; for they are the seed of the blest of the Lord, and their offspring with them; and it shall come to pass, that before they call I will answer, and while they are yet speaking I will hear." In this happy state of existence it seems that all people will live to the full age of a tree, and this, too, without pain or sorrow, and whatsoever they ask will be immediately answered, and even all their wants will be anticipated. Of course, then, none of them will sleep in the dust, for they will prefer to be translated, that is, changed in the twinkling of an eye, from mortal to immortal; after which they will continue to reign with Jesus on the earth.

Thus we have traced the Prophets through the varying scenes which conspire to restore the earth, and its inhabitants, to that state of perfection in which they first existed, and in which they will exist during the great Sabbath of creation. Having seen all things restored among the living, we will now inquire after those who sleep in the dust; but, in order to understand precisely the nature of their restoration, we must ascertain the particulars concerning the resurrection of Jesus, for He was an exact pattern after which all His Saints will be raised. We recollect, first, that he was clothed upon with flesh, and blood, and bones, like another man, and every way subject to hunger, thirst, pain, weariness, sickness, and death, like any other person—with this difference, that He was capable of enduring more than any other human body. Second, this same body was hung upon the cross, torn with nails, which were driven through His hands and feet, and His side pierced with a spear, from which there came out blood and water. Third, this same body, being perfectly lifeless, like any other corpse, was taken, without a bone being broken, and carefully wrapped in linen and laid in the tomb, where it continued until the third day; when, early in the morning, the women came to the sepulchre, and His disciples also, and found the linen clothes lying useless, and the napkin which was about His head carefully folded and laid by itself, but the body which had lain there was gone.

From all these circumstances, we discover that the same flesh and bones which were laid in the tomb were actually re-animated, and did arise and lay aside the linen which was no longer needed. And Jesus Christ came forth triumphant from the mansions of the dead, possessing the same body which had been born of a woman, and which was crucified; but no blood flowed in His veins, for blood was the natural life, in which were the principles of mortality, and a man restored to flesh and blood would be mortal, and, consequently, again subject unto death, which was not the case with our Savior, although He had flesh and bones after He arose, for when He appeared to His disciples, and they were afraid, supposing it was only a spirit, in order to show them their mistake, He said: "Handle me and see, for a spirit hath not flesh and bones as ye see me have." And calling for something to eat, He was provided with a piece of broiled fish and honeycomb, and He did eat. And even afterwards, Thomas was invited to put his finger into the prints of the nails in His hands and feet, and to thrust his hand into His side, from which it was evident that He not only possessed the same body, but the same wounds also continued to show themselves for a witness, and will continue until He comes again, when the Jews will look upon Him whom they have pierced, and inquire, "What are these wounds in thy hands and in thy feet?"

O ye hard hearted, ye ungodly children of men! your eyes will very soon behold Him who was crucified for your sins; then shall ye see that the resurrection of the dead is a reality, something tangible, and that eternity is not a land of shades, nor a world of phantoms, as some suppose.

Among other things which Jesus did after the resurrection, we find Him in the humble attitude of broiling fish, and calling His disciples to come and dine. O what simplicity, what love, what condescension! Wonder, O heavens! Be astonished, O earth! Behold the Redeemer clothed upon with immortality, and yet seated by a fire of coals, in the open air, with His brethren, humbly partaking of a meal of fish, actually prepared by His own hands! O ye great and noble of the earth, who roll in luxury and refinement! O ye priests, who are loaded with the honors, titles, dignities, riches, and splendor of the world, here is a lesson for you, which will make you blush: boast no more of being followers of the meek and lowly Jesus!

But to return to the subject of the resurrection. Having proved to a demonstration, that our Savior rose from the dead, with the same body which was crucified—possessing flesh and bones, that He ate and drank with His disciples, it puts the matter forever at rest respecting the resurrection of the Saints. But if more proof were wanting, we have it in the prophecy of Job, quoted in a former part of this work, where he declares that his Redeemer will stand, in the latter-day, upon the earth, and he should see Him in the flesh, though worms should destroy the body which he then had. The fact is, the Saints will again receive their bodies, every joint being in its proper and perfect frame, and clothed upon with flesh, sinews, and skin, like as we now are; the whole being immortal, no more to see corruption, and clothed with a white robe of fine linen, suitable for immortality to wear. Well did the Apostle say, In heaven we have a more enduring substance (not shadow).

But in order to illustrate this subject still farther, we will carefully examine Ezekiel xxxvii, which we have touched upon before. In this vision, the Prophet is carried away in the Spirit, and a valley of dry bones is presented before him, and they are very numerous and very dry; and while he stands musing and contemplating the awful scene, a very wonderful question is proposed to him: "Son of man, can these dry bones live?" and he answered: "O Lord God, thou knowest." And the Lord said: "Son of man, prophesy upon these bones, and say, O ye dry bones, hear the word of the Lord." So he prophesied as he was commanded, and, as he prophesied, there was a noise, and behold, a shaking, and the bones came together, bone to his bone, and the sinews and the flesh came upon them, and the skin covered them. And again he prophesied to the winds, saying: "Come from the four winds, O breath, and breathe upon these slain, that they may live;" and the breath entered into them, and they lived and stood upon their feet, an exceeding great army. We have heard many comments upon this vision; some compare it to sinners being converted, and some to the body of Christ, the Church, when dead as to the spiritual gifts; but the Church becoming dead, can no longer be said to be the body of Christ, as when she abides in the true vine, she lives and bears fruit, and is not dead, and when she does not abide in Him, she is cut off as a branch withered, and burned, instead of rising again. But did you ever hear the Lord's own explanation of this vision, in the same chapter? It so far surpasses all other comments, I am inclined to believe it; I will therefore write it in preference to any other, and run the risk of becoming unpopular by so doing. The Lord says: "Son of man, these bones are the whole house of Israel; behold, they say, Our bones are dried, and our hope is lost: we are cut off for our parts. Therefore, prophesy and say unto them, Thus saith the Lord God, Behold, O my people, I will open your graves, and cause you to come up out of your graves, and bring you into the land of Israel: and ye shall know that I am the Lord, when I have opened your graves, O my people, and brought you up out of your graves, and shall put my Spirit in you, and ye shall live; and I shall place you in your own land. Then shall ye know that I the Lord have spoken it, and performed it, saith the Lord." Thus you have the whole vision unfolded plainly, if the Lord's authority can once be allowed, which is seldom the case in this age of wisdom and learning. The fact is, all the seed of Israel are to be raised from the dead, and are to be brought into the land of Israel, which was given to them for an everlasting inheritance. And in order to do this, their old dry bones are to be brought together, bone to its bone, and every part of their bodies is to be reinstated; and it will make a great noise, and a wonderful shaking when they come together; and surely when they stand upon their feet they will make an exceeding great army.

This just explains the promise, so oft repeated in Scripture: "My servant David shall be their prince for ever;" indeed this same chapter makes the promise to them, that His servant David shall be raised up, and shall be a prince among them, while the Lord shall be their King; while both they that are alive, and they that are dead, shall be restored, and become one nation, in the land, upon the mountains of Israel; while David comes forth and reigns as a prince and shepherd over them for ever; and the Lord Jesus reigns as King of kings, and Lord of lords, in Mount Zion, and in Jerusalem, and before His ancients gloriously.

O glorious day! O blessed hope!
My soul leaps forward at the thought;
When in that happy, happy land,
We'll take the ancients by the hand;
In love and union hail our friends;
And Death and Sorrow have an end.

I now no longer marvel, when I call to mind that Abraham counted himself a stranger and a pilgrim, seeking a better country, and a city whose builder and maker is God. It seems after this restoration there will be but one more change necessary, in order to fit the earth for man's eternal inheritance; and that change is to take place at the last day, after man has enjoyed it in peace a thousand years. We have now discovered the great secret, which none but the Saints have understood (but was well understood by them in all ages of the world), which is this, that man is to dwell in the flesh, upon the earth, with the Messiah, with the whole house of Israel, and with all the Saints of the Most High, not only one thousand years, but for ever and ever. There our father Adam, whose hair is white like the pure wool, will sit enthroned in dignity, as the Ancient of Days, the great Patriarch, the mighty Prince; while thousands of thousands stand before him, and ten thousand times ten thousand minister to him; there he will hail all his children, who died in the faith of the Messiah; while Abel, Enoch, Noah, Abraham, Job, and Daniel, with all the Prophets and Apostles, and all the Saints of God of all ages, hail each other in the flesh. Jesus, the great Messiah, will stand in the midst, and, to crown the whole, will gird himself, and administer bread and wine to the whole multitude, and He himself will partake of the same with them on the earth, all being clothed in fine linen, clean and white. This is the marriage supper of the Lamb, Blessed are they who partake thereof.

Having traced the great restoration of the earth and its inhabitants, until we find them in the full enjoyment of the promises made to their fathers; and having learned that a future state is not a state of shadows and fables, but something tangible, even a more enduring substance, we shall now take a view of the division of their land, and the laying out of their city, oven the holy city, where the tabernacle of God and His sanctuary shall be forevermore, for of course this was the city sought for by Abraham and others, who found it not.

This view is given in the last chapter of Ezekiel, where he divides the land, by lot, to the whole twelve tribes; and lays off the city, and sanctuary in the midst, with its twelve gates, three on each side, the whole lying four square. But in the forty-seventh chapter, we have a description of a beautiful river, which will issue forth from the eastern front of the temple, from under the sanctuary, and run eastward into the Dead Sea, healing the waters, and causing a very great, multitude of fishes; so that from Engedi, and Eneglaim, the fishers spread forth their nets; while the miry places shall not be healed, but shall be given to salt. And on either side shall grow all trees for meat, whose leaf shall not fade, nor shall the fruit thereof be consumed; it shall bring forth new fruit according to its months, because of the waters issuing from the sanctuary; and their fruits shall be for meat, and their leaves for medicine.

But to set forth more fully the building of the city, and the materials of which it will be built, we quote Isaiah, liv, 11, to the end of the chapter: "O thou afflicted, tossed with tempest, and not comforted, behold, I will lay thy stones with fair colors, and lay thy foundations with sapphires. And I will make thy windows of agates, and thy gates of carbuncles, and all thy borders of pleasant stones. And all thy children shall be taught of the Lord; and great shall be the peace of thy children. In righteousness shalt thou be established; thou shalt be far from oppression; for thou shalt not fear: and from terror; for it shall not come near thee. Behold, they shall surely gather together, but not by me: whosoever shall gather together, against thee shall fall for thy sake. Behold I have created the smith that bloweth the coals in the fire, and that bringeth forth an instrument for his work; and I have created the waster to destroy. No weapon that is formed against thee shall prosper; and every tongue that shall rise against thee in judgment thou shalt condemn. This is the heritage of the servants of the Lord, and their righteousness is of me, saith the Lord."

From these verses we learn something of the beauty of their city, and of the materials of which it is composed. Their stones of fair colors, their foundations of sapphires, their windows of agates, their gates of carbuncles, and all their borders of pleasant stones, are well calculated to beautify the place of His sanctuary, and to make the place of His feet glorious, as well as to give a lustre and magnificence to the whole city, of which the Gentiles, with all their boasted wealth and grandeur, can form but a faint idea; and then to mark, in the same description, the knowledge, as well as the peace and security, of all the inhabitants; while they who gather together against them to battle are sure to fall for their sake: surely this is the heritage of the servants of the Lord, surely this is a delightful city, and well worth a pilgrimage like Abraham's.

But in order to form a still more striking idea of the prosperity, wealth, beauty and magnificence of the cities of Zion and Jerusalem, we will quote Isaiah lx: "Arise, shine; for thy light is come, and the glory of the Lord is risen upon thee. For, behold, the darkness shall cover the earth, and gross darkness the people: but the Lord shall arise upon thee, and His glory shall be seen upon thee. And the Gentiles shall come to thy light, and kings to the brightness of thy rising. Lift up thine eyes, round about, and see; all they gather themselves together, they come to thee: thy sons shall come from far, and thy daughters shall be nursed at thy side. Thou thou shalt see, and flow together, and thine heart shall fear, and be enlarged; because the abundance of the sea shall be converted unto thee, the forces of the Gentiles shall come unto thee. The multitude of camels shall cover thee, the dromedaries of Midian and Epha; all they from Sheba shall come: they shall bring gold and incense; and they shall show forth the praises of the Lord. All the flocks of

Kedar shall be gathered together unto thee, the rams of Nebaioth shall minister unto thee: they shall come up with acceptance on mine altar, and I will glorify the house of my glory. Who are these that fly as a cloud, and as the doves to their windows? Surely the isles shall wait for me, and the ships of Tarshish first, to bring thy sons from far, their silver and their gold with them, unto the name of the Lord thy God, and to the Holy One of Israel, because He hath glorified thee. And the sons of strangers shall build up thy walls, and their kings shall minister unto thee: for in my wrath I smote thee, but in my favor have I had mercy on thee. Therefore thy gates shall be open continually; they shall not be shut day nor night; that men may bring unto thee the forces of the Gentiles, and that their kings may be brought. For the nation and kingdom that will not serve thee shall perish: yea, those nations shall be utterly wasted. The glory of Lebanon shall come unto thee, the fir-tree, the pine-tree, and the box together, to beautify the place of my sanctuary; and I will make the place of my feet glorious. The sons also of them that afflicted thee shall come bending unto thee; and all they that despised thee shall bow themselves down at the soles of thy feet; and they shall call thee, The city of the Lord, the Zion of the Holy One of Israel.

"Whereas thou hast been forsaken and hated, so that no man went through thee, I will make thee an eternal excellency, a joy of many generations. Thou shalt also suck the milk of the Gentiles, and shalt suck the breast of kings: and thou shalt know that I the Lord am thy Savior and thy Redeemer, the Mighty One of Jacob. For brass I will bring gold, and for iron I will bring silver, and for wood brass, and for stones iron: I will also make thy officers peace, and thine exactors righteousness. Violence shall no more be heard in thy land, wasting nor destruction within thy borders; but thou shalt call thy walls Salvation, and thy gates Praise. The sun shall be no more thy light by day; neither for brightness shall the moon give light unto thee: but the Lord shall be unto thee an everlasting light, and thy God thy glory. Thy sun shall no more go down; neither shall thy moon withdraw itself: for the Lord shall be thine everlasting light, and the days of thy mourning shall be ended. Thy people also shall be all righteous: they shall inherit the land for ever, the branch of my planting, the work of my hands, that I may be glorified. A little one shall become a thousand, and a small one a strong nation: I the Lord will hasten it in his time."

In this chapter we learn—First, that there is a city to be built in the last days, unto which, not only Israel, but all the nations of the Gentiles, are to flow; and the nation and kingdom that will not serve the city shall perish and be utterly wasted. Second, we learn that the name of that city is Zion, the city of the Lord. Third, we learn that it is called the place of His sanctuary, and the place of His feet. Fourth, that the best of timber, consisting of fir, pine, and boxwood, is to be brought in great plenty, to beautify the place of His sanctuary, and make the place of His feet glorious. Fifth, the precious metals are to abound in such plenty, that gold is to be in the room of brass, silver in the room of iron, brass in the room of wood, and iron in the room of stones. Their officers are to be peace officers, and their exactors righteous exactors; violence is no more to be heard in the land; wasting nor destruction within their borders. Their walls are to be Salvation, and their gates Praise: while the glory of God, in the midst of the city, outshines the sun. The days of their mourning are ended; their people are ail righteous, and are to inherit the land forever, being the branch of the Lord's planting, that He may be glorified. A little one shall become a strong nation, and the Lord will hasten it in His time.

The Psalmist David has told us, concerning the time of the building of this city, in his one hundred and second Psalm, from the thirteenth to the twenty-second verse: "Thou shalt arise and have mercy upon Zion; for the time to favor her, yea, the set time, is come. For Thy servants take pleasure in her stones, and favor the dust thereof. So the heathen shall fear the name of the Lord, and all the kings of the earth Thy glory. When the Lord shall build up Zion, He shall appear in His glory. He will regard the prayer of the destitute, and not despise their prayer. This shall be written for the generation to come: and the people which shall be created shall praise the Lord. For He hath looked down from the height of His sanctuary; from Heaven did the Lord behold the earth; to hear the groaning of the prisoner; to loose those that are appointed to death; to declare the name of the Lord in Zion, and His praise in Jerusalem; when the people are gathered together, and the kingdoms, to serve the Lord."

From this scripture we learn—First, that there is a set time to build up Zion, or the city of which Isaiah speaks, namely, just before the second coming of Christ; and that when this city is built, the Lord will appear in His glory, and not before. So from this we affirm, that if such a city is never built, then the Lord will never come. Second, we learn that the people and kingdoms are to be gathered together, to serve the Lord, both in Zion and Jerusalem; and third, that this Psalm was written expressly for the generation to come, and the people which shall be created shall praise the Lord, when they read it and see it fulfilled.

I will now call the attention of the reader to the first paragraph of the sixth chapter of the Record of Ether, contained in the Book of Mormon: "For he truly told them of all things from the beginning of man; and how that after the waters had receded from off the face of this land (America), it became a choice land above all other lands, a chosen land of the Lord, wherefore, the Lord would have that all men should serve Him who dwell upon the face thereof; and that it was the place of the New Jerusalem, which should come down out of heaven, and the holy sanctuary of the Lord. Behold, Ether saw the days of Christ, and he spake concerning a New Jerusalem upon this land: and he spake also concerning the house of Israel, and the Jerusalem from whence Lehi should come; after it should be destroyed, it should be built up again a holy city unto the Lord; wherefore, it could not be a New Jerusalem, for it had been in a time of old; but it should be built up again, and become a holy city of the Lord, and it should be built up unto the house of Israel; and that a New Jerusalem should be built up upon this land, unto the remnant of the seed of Joseph, for which things there has been a type; for as Joseph brought his father down into the land of Egypt, even so he died there; wherefore, the Lord brought a remnant of the seed of Joseph out of the land of Jerusalem, that He might be merciful unto the seed of Joseph, that they should perish not, even as He was merciful unto the father of Joseph, that he should perish not; wherefore, the remnant of the house of Joseph shall be built up on this land, and it shall be a land of their inheritance; and they shall build up a holy city unto the Lord, like unto the Jerusalem of old, and they shall no more be confounded, until the end come, when the earth shall pass away. And there shall be a new heaven and a new earth, and they shall be like unto the old, save the old have passed away, and all things have become new. And then cometh the New Jerusalem: and blessed are they who dwell therein, for it is they whose garments are white through the blood of the Lamb; and they are they who are numbered among the remnant of the seed of Joseph who were of the house of Israel. And then also cometh the Jerusalem of old, and the inhabitants thereof; blessed are they for they have been washed in the blood of the Lamb; and they are they who were scattered and gathered in from the four quarters of the earth, and from the north countries, and are partakers of the fulfilling of the covenant which God made with their father Abraham. And when these things come, bringeth to pass the Scripture which saith, "There are they who were first, who shall be last: and there are they who were last, who shall be first."

From this prophecy we learn—First, that America is a chosen land of the Lord, above every other land. Second, that it is the place of the New Jerusalem, which shall come down from God, out of heaven, upon the earth, when it is renewed. Third, that a New Jerusalem is to be built in America, to the remnant of Joseph, after a similar pattern, or like unto the old Jerusalem in the land of Canaan; and that the old Jerusalem shall be rebuilt at the same time, and, this being done, both cities will continue in prosperity on the earth, until the great and last change, when the heavens and the earth are to be renewed. Fourth, we learn that when this change takes place, the two cities, together with the inhabitants thereof, are to be caught up into heaven, and being changed and made new, the one comes down upon the American land, and the other to its own place as formerly: and, fifth, we learn that the inhabitants of these two cities are the same that gathered together and first builded them. The remnant of Joseph, and those gathered with them, inherit the New Jerusalem. And the tribes of Israel, gathered from the north countries, and from the four quarters of the earth, inhabit the other; and thus all things being made new, we find those who were once strangers and pilgrims on THE EARTH, in possession of that better country, and that city, for which they sought.

We will now turn to John's Revelation, and examine the city after it is made new, and see if it is anything like the pattern which it exhibited previous to its final change, Rev. xxi: "And I saw a new heaven and a new earth: for the first heaven and the first earth were passed away; and there was no more sea. And I, John, saw the holy city, New Jerusalem, coming down from God out of heaven, prepared as a bride adorned for her husband. And I heard a great voice out of heaven, saying, Behold, the tabernacle of God is with men, and He will dwell with them, and they shall be His people, and God himself shall be with them, and be their God. And God shall wipe away all tears from their eyes; and there shall be no more death, neither sorrow, nor crying, neither shall there be any more pain: for the former things are passed away. And He that sat upon the throne said, Behold, I make all things new. And He said unto me, Write, for these words are true and faithful. And He said unto me, It is done. I am Alpha and Omega, the beginning and the end. I will give unto him that is athirst, of the fountain of the water of life freely. He that overcometh shall inherit all things; and I will be his God, and he shall be my son. But the fearful, and unbelieving, and the abominable, and murderers, and whoremongers, and sorcerers, and idolaters, and all liars, shall have their part in the lake which burneth with fire and brimstone: which is the second death.

"And there came unto me one of the seven angels which had the seven vials full of the seven last plagues, and talked with me, saying, Come hither, I will show thee the bride, the Lamb's wife. And he carried me away in the spirit to a great and high mountain, and showed me that great city, the holy Jerusalem, descending out of heaven from God, having the glory of God: and her light was like unto a stone most precious, even like a jasper stone, clear as crystal; and had a wall great and high, and had twelve gates, and at the gates, twelve angels, and names written thereon, which are the names of the twelve tribes of the children of Israel. On the east, three gates; on the north, three gates; on the south, three gates; on the west, three gates. And the wall of the city had twelve foundations, and in them the names of the twelve Apostles of the Lamb. And he that talked with me had a golden reed to measure the city, and the gates thereof, and the wall thereof. And the city lieth four square, and the length is as large as the breadth. And he measured the city with the reed, twelve thousand furlongs: the length and the breadth and the height of it are equal. And he measured the wall thereof, an hundred and forty and four cubits, according to the measure of a man, that is, of the angel. And the building of the wall of it was of jasper: and the city was of pure gold, like unto clear glass. And the foundations of the wall of the city were garnished with all manner of precious stones. The first foundation was jasper; the second, sapphire; the third, a chalcedony; the fourth, an emerald; the fifth, sardonyx; the sixth, sardius; the seventh, chrysolyte; the eighth, beryl; the ninth, a topaz; the tenth, a chrysoprasus; the eleventh, a jacinth; the twelfth, an amethyst. And the twelve gates were twelve pearls; every several gate was of one pearl: and the street of the city was pure gold, as it were transparent glass. And I saw no temple therein: for the Lord God Almighty and the Lamb are the temple of it. And the city had no need of the sun, neither of the moon, to shine in it; for the glory of God did lighten it, and the Lamb is the light thereof. And the nations of them which are saved shall walk in the light of it; and the kings of the earth do bring their glory and honor into it. And the gates of it shall not be shut at all by day; for there shall be no night there. And they shall bring the glory and honor of the nations into it. And there shall in no wise enter into it anything that defileth, neither whatsoever worketh abomination, or maketh a lie; but they which are written in the Lamb's book of life." Also, twenty-second chapter, he says: "And He showed me a pure river of water of life, clear as crystal, proceeding out of the throne of God and of the Lamb. In the midst of the street of it, and on either side of the river, was there the tree of life, which bare twelve manner of fruits, and yielded her fruit every month: and the leaves of the tree were for the healing of the nations. And there shall be no more curse: but the throne of God and of the Lamb shall be in it; and His servants shall serve Him. And they shall see His face; and His name shall be in their foreheads. And there shall be no night there; and they need no candle, neither light of the sun; for the Lord God giveth them light: and they shall reign forever and ever. And He said unto me, These sayings are faithful and true: and the Lord God of the holy prophets sent His angel to show unto His servants the things which must shortly be done. Behold, I come quickly: blessed is he that keepeth the sayings of the prophecy of this book."

From this beautiful description, we learn—First, that the new earth is not to be separated by any sea, consequently, what is now called the Eastern and Western Continents will then be one land. Secondly, we learn that the Lord will make not only the heavens and earth, but all things new (including of course, the cities of Jerusalem and Zion, where His tabernacle will have been for more than a thousand years). Thirdly, we learn that the city will lie four square, and have twelve gates, with the names of the twelve tribes of Israel, inserted, one on each gate; three gates on the north, three on the south, three on the east, and three on the west; precisely after the same manner in which it will exist temporally during the thousand years, as described by Ezekiel. Fourthly, we learn that it will be composed of precious stones, and gold, as the temporal city also will be, as described by Isaiah. Fifthly, a pure river of the water of life, clear as crystal, will flow through this renewed city, proceeding from the throne of God, just as living waters will flow from the sanctuary in the temporal city, as described by Ezekiel. Sixthly, the tree of life will stand on either side of the river, even the tree which will have once borne twelve manner of fruits, and have yielded its fruit every month, its leaves having been for the healing of the nations. But now, when John sees it, the nations have no need of healing, for there is no more death, neither pain, nor sorrow, for the former things have passed away, and all things are become new, consequently, he speaks in the past tense, and says they were for the healing of the nations; of course, referring to the times when they existed temporally, according to Ezekiel, before their final change.

Now, of the things which we have spoken this is the sum: Ezekiel and the other Prophets have presented us with the view of the cities of Zion and Jerusalem, as they will exist during the one thousand years of rest called the

Millennium; and John has given us a view of the same cities, after their final change, when they come down from God out of heaven, and rest upon the new earth. But Ether has given us a sketch of them as they are to exist, both in their temporal and in their eternal state: and he has told us plainly concerning their location, first and last, namely, the New Jerusalem, in America, inhabited by the remnant of Joseph, and those gathered with them, who have washed their robes, and made them white, in the blood of the Lamb: and the other Jerusalem, in its former place, inhabited by the house of Israel gathered from the north countries, and from all countries where they were scattered, having washed their robes, and made them white, in the blood of the Lamb. And here is the end of the matter.

I would only add, that the government of the United States has been engaged, for upwards of nine years, in gathering the remnant of Joseph to the very place where they will finally build a New Jerusalem, a city of Zion, with the assistance of the Gentiles, who will gather them from all the face of the land: and this gathering is clearly predicted in the Book of Mormon, and other revelations, and the place before appointed, and the time set for its fulfilment. And except the Gentiles repent of all their abominations, and embrace the same covenant, they will soon be utterly destroyed from off the face of this land; as it is written by Isaiah: "The nation and kingdom that will not serve thee shall perish. Yea, those nations shall be utterly wasted." And as it is written by the Prophet Nephi in the Book of Mormon (n. e.), 3 Nephi, xxi:

"And, verily, I say unto you, I give unto you a sign, that ye may know the time when these things shall be about to take place, that I shall gather in from their long dispersion, my people, O house of Israel, and shall establish again among them my Zion.

"And behold, this is the thing which I will give unto you for a sign, for verily I say unto you, that when these things which I declare unto you, and which I shall declare unto you hereafter of myself, and by the power of the Holy Ghost, which shall be given unto you of the Father, shall be made known unto the Gentiles, that they may know concerning this people who are a remnant of the house of Jacob, and concerning this my people who shall be scattered by them.

"Verily, verily, I say unto you, when these things shall be made known unto them of the Father, and shall come forth of the Father, from them unto you;

"For it is wisdom in the Father that they should be established in this land, and be set up as a free people by the power of the Father, that these things might come forth from them unto a remnant of your seed, that the covenant of the Father may be fulfilled which He hath covenanted with His people, O house of Israel;

"Therefore, when these works, and the works which shall be wrought among you hereafter, shall come forth from the Gentiles, unto your seed, which shall dwindle in unbelief because of iniquity;

"For thus it behoveth the Father that it should come forth from the Gentiles, that He may shew forth His power unto the Gentiles, for this cause, that the Gentiles, if they will not harden their hearts, that they may repent and come unto me, and be baptized in my name, and know of the true points of my doctrine, that they may be numbered among my people, O house of Israel;

"And when these things come to pass, that thy seed shall begin to know these things, it shall be a sign unto them, that they may know that the work of the Father hath already commenced unto the fulfilling of the covenant which He hath made unto the people who are of the house of Israel.

"And when that day shall come, it shall come to pass that kings shall shut their mouths; for that which had not been told them shall they see; and that which they had not heard shall they consider.

"For in that day, for my sake shall the Father work a work, which shall be a great and marvellous work among them; and there shall be among them who will not believe it, although a man shall declare it unto them.

"But behold, the life of my servant shall be in my hand; therefore they shall not hurt him, although he shall be marred because of them. Yet I will heal him, for I will shew unto them that my wisdom is greater than the cunning of the devil.

"Therefore it shall come to pass, that whosoever will not believe in my words, who am Jesus Christ, whom the Father shall cause him to bring forth unto the Gentiles, and shall give unto him power that he shall bring them forth unto the Gentiles (it shall be done even as Moses said), they shall be cut off from among my people who are of the covenant.

"And my people who are a remnant of Jacob, shall be among the Gentiles, yea, in the midst of them as a lion among the beasts of the forest, as a young lion among the flocks of sheep, who, if he go through both treadeth down and teareth in pieces, and none can deliver.

"Their hand shall be lifted up upon their adversaries, and all their enemies shall be cut off.

"Yea, wo be unto the Gentiles, except they repent, for it shall come to pass in that day, saith the Father, that I will cut off thy horses out of the midst of thee, and I will destroy thy chariots,

"And I will cut off the cities of thy land, and throw down all thy strongholds;

"And I will cut off witchcrafts out of thy hand, and thou shalt have no more soothsayers;

"Thy graven images I will also cut off, and thy standing images out of the midst of thee, and thou shalt no more worship the works of thy hands;

"And I will pluck up thy groves out of the midst of thee; so will I destroy thy cities.

"And it shall come to pass that all lyings, and deceivings, and envyings, and strifes, and priestcrafts, and whoredoms, shall be done away.

"For it shall come to pass, saith the Father, that at that day whosoever will not repent and come unto my beloved Son, them will I cut off from among my people, O house of Israel;

"And I will execute vengeance and fury upon them, even as upon the heathen, such as they have not heard.

"But if they will repent, and hearken unto my words, and harden not their hearts, I will establish my Church among them, and they shall come in unto the covenant, and be numbered among this the remnant of Jacob, unto whom I have given this land for their inheritance,

"And they shall assist my people, the remnant of Jacob, and also, as many of the house of Israel as shall come, that they may build a city, which shall be called the New Jerusalem;

"And then shall they assist my people that they may be gathered in, who are scattered upon all the face of the land, in unto the New Jerusalem,

"And then shall the power of heaven come down among them; and I also will be in the midst;

"And then shall the work of the Father commence at that day, even when this Gospel shall be preached among the remnant of this people. Verily I say unto you, at that day shall the work of the Father commence among all the dispersed of my people; yea, even the tribes which have been lost, which the Father hath led away out of Jerusalem.

"Yea, the work shall commence among all the dispersed of my people, with the Father, to prepare the way whereby they may come unto me, that they may call on the Father in my name;

"Yea, and then shall the work commence, with the Father, among all nations, in preparing the way whereby His people may be gathered home to the land of their inheritance

"And they shall go out from all nations; and they shall not go out in haste, nor go by flight, for I will go before them, saith the Father, and I will be their rearward."

O ye remnant of Joseph, your secret is revealed, ye who are despised, smitten, scattered, and driven by the Gentiles from place to place, until you are left few in number! "O thou afflicted, tossed with tempest and not comforted," lift up your heads and rejoice, for your redemption draweth nigh: yea, we have found your record, the oracles of God once committed to your forefathers, which have been hidden from you for a long time, because of unbelief. Behold! they are about to be restored to you again; then shall you rejoice; for you shall know that it is a blessing from the hand of God; and the scales of darkness shall begin to fall from your eyes; and the Gentiles shall not again have power over you; but you shall be gathered by them, and be built up, and again become a delightsome people; and the time has come; yea, the work has already commenced; for we have seen you gathered together, from all parts of the land, unto the place which God has appointed for the Gentiles to gather you; therefore lay down your weapons of war, cease to oppose the Gentiles in the gathering of your various tribes, for the hand of your great God is in all this, and it was all foretold by your forefathers, ten thousand moons ago. Therefore suffer them peaceably to fulfil this last act of kindness, as a kind reward for the injuries you have received from them.

It is with mingled feelings of joy and sorrow that I reflect upon these things. Sorrow, when I think how you have been smitten; joy, when I reflect upon the happy change that now awaits you; and sorrow again, when I turn my thoughts to the awful destruction that awaits the Gentiles, except they repent. But the eternal purposes of Jehovah must roll on, until all His promises are fulfilled, and none can hinder; therefore, O God, Thy will be done! But while I still linger upon this subject, with feelings that are easier felt than described, methinks I can almost hear the Indian's mournful chant resounding through his native woods. It whispers thus:

Great Spirit of our fathers, lend an ear;
Pity the red man, to his cries give ear;
Long hast Thou scourged him with Thy chastening sore;
When will Thy vengeance cease, Thy wrath be o'er?

105

When will the white man's dire ambition cease,
And let our scattered remnants dwell in peace?
Or shall we, driven to the western shore,
Become extinct, and fall to rise no more?
Forbid, great Spirit! make Thy mercy known;
Reveal Thy truth; Thy wandering captives own;
Make bare Thine arm of power, for our release,
And o'er the earth extend the reign of peace.

Chapter Six - The Dealings of God with All Nations, in Regard to Revelation

"And hath made of one blood all nations of men for to dwell on all the face of the earth, and hath determined the times before appointed, and the bounds of their habitation; that they should seek the Lord, if haply they might feel after Him, and find Him, though He he not far from every one of us; for in Him we live, and move, and have our being."—Acts, xvii, 26-28.

In this text we learn—First, that all nations are made of one blood. Secondly, they are designed to dwell on all the face of the earth (America not excepted). Thirdly, that the Lord has determined the bounds of their habitation, that is, He has divided the earth among His children, giving each nation that portion which seemed Him good—for instance the land of Canaan, to Israel; Mount Seir, to Esau; Arabia, to Ishmael; America, to the remnant of Joseph, etc., as a father parcels off a large tract of land to his several children. And fourthly, He has granted unto all the nations of the earth the privilege of feeling after Him and finding Him; since He is not so very far from every one of them, whether they be in Asia, Africa, Europe, America, or even upon the islands of the sea. Now, if any nation, in any age of the world, or in any part of the earth, should happen to live up to their privilege, what would they obtain? I answer, revelation, for the best of reasons, because no people ever found God in any other way, nor ever will. Therefore, if they found God, they found Him by revelation, direct from Himself, He revealing His will to them; and if they did not find Him in this way, they never knew Him. And if they did obtain revelation, it was their privilege to write it, and make a record of the same, and teach it to their children; and this record would be sacred, because it would contain the word of God; and thus it would be a HOLY BIBLE, no matter whether it was written by the Jews, the Ten Tribes, the Nephites, or the Gentiles. I would just as soon have the Gospel written by Nephi, Mormon, Moroni or Alma, as the Gospel written by Matthew, Mark, Luke, or John. Again, I would just as soon believe a revelation given in America, as believe a revelation given in Asia; for if ever a nation failed to get a revelation, it was because they did not attain unto that which was their privilege But why, then, was any nation over left in darkness, from age to age, without the light of revelation to guide them? I answer, because their forefathers, in some age of the world, rejected revelation, cast out and killed the Prophets, and turned a deaf ear to the things of God, until God took away that which they enjoyed, and committed it to some other people, and left them from generation to generation to grow up in ignorance, until He should see fit again to send His light and truth to that nation; but those who reject no light are under no condemnation, and the mercy of God hath claim upon them, through the blood of Christ which atoneth for the sins of the world. The heathen who never had the light of revelation will be saved by the blood of Christ; while their forefathers who rejected the light are condemned, for this is their condemnation, that when light came they rejected it.

Now on this subject, let us examine the history of various ages. In the morn of creation, men had light by direct revelation, for Adam, Cain and Abel talked with the Lord. In the next age, men had light by revelation, for Enoch walked with the Lord, and not only saw the first coming of Christ, but His second coming also, and he exclaimed: "Behold, the Lord cometh with ten thousand of His saints, to take vengeance on the ungodly," etc., as it is written in Jude. From which it appears that Enoch knew and prophesied concerning the Messiah, with all the plainness of an Apostle. Again, in Noah's day there was positive revelation. And all these were Gentiles, or, rather, the word Israel had not yet been named upon Jacob by the angel. Now, if it was the privilege of so many Gentiles to get the word of the Lord, and to have the knowledge of the true God by revelation, it was the privilege of all the rest; and if any ran into darkness and worshiped idols, until God gave them over to work all uncleanness with greediness, and finally took the oracles of God from them, and confined them more particularly to Abraham, it was because they had for a long time rejected them, and rendered themselves unworthy of them; so that from the days of Israel the oracles of God seemed to pertain more particularly to the chosen seed, chosen for that very purpose, namely, that to them might be committed the oracles of God, the Priesthood, the service of God, and the promises which had been in existence from the beginning, among the Gentiles, who had long rendered themselves unworthy of such blessings.

But in process of time Israel rendered themselves unworthy of a continuance of such blessings, by stoning and killing the Prophets, and rejecting the Messiah, and all those that God sent unto them, until at length the Lord took the kingdom from them as a nation, and gave it again to the Gentiles; in the meantime winking at all the ignorance through which the Gentiles had passed, from the time the kingdom had been taken from them until restored again. But as soon as the kingdom of God was restored again to the Gentiles, He commanded them all everywhere to repent, and then if they did not do it they were under condemnation, but not before. But no sooner was the kingdom taken from the Jews, than the fruits of it disappeared from among them, and they were dispersed into all the nations of the earth where they have never again heard the voice of inspiration commanding them to repent. And if any Gentile has commanded them to repent and be baptized (in the name of the Lord), without being inspired and commanded to do it, it was an imposition practised upon them. Not that repentance was any harm, but the imposition consisted in professing to be sent with a message when they were not, for when God commands men to repent, He sends somebody with the command, in order that they may teach it to those for whom He designs it; and when He does not command them to do a thing, He does not require it at their hand. Any man who says that the Jews, as a nation, have been commanded to repent and be baptized, for the last seventeen hundred years, says that which he cannot prove, unless he can prove that there has been a new revelation within that time, commissioning some man to go to them with such an errand; neither will any generation of Jews, which have existed since inspiration ceased, be condemned for rejecting any message from God, for He has sent no message to them, consequently they have rejected none; but their forefathers, who did reject the things of God, are under condemnation.

Again, when men were sent with the Gospel to the Gentiles, they were commanded to repent; and this command was in force, whenever men came preaching, who were sent by proper authority, and inspired by the Holy Ghost; but when they had killed the Apostles and inspired men, and abused their privileges, until God took them away, and left them without inspiration, then the sin was answered upon that generation; and those who have since come upon the stage of action have never been commanded to repent and be baptized (except by some new revelation), and any man who says that God

108

has commanded a Gentile to repent and obey the Gospel since the days that inspiration ceased, or since the days that Apostles and Prophets ceased from among men, says that which he will not be able to prove, unless he proves that some revelation has been given since that time, again commissioning men to go to the Gentiles with such an errand.

The fact is, God requires nothing more of a generation than to do those things which He commands them, and a generation to whom He reveals nothing, or to whom He does not send men with a message from Him, have no message to obey, and none to reject, and consequently nothing is binding on them, except the moral principles of right and wrong, which are equally binding on all ages of the world, according to the knowledge people have of moral rectitude.

But in these last days God has again spoken from the heavens, and commissioned men to go, first to the Gentiles, commanding them everywhere to repent and obey the Gospel; and then He has commanded them to go to the Jews also, and command them to repent, and obey the Gospel; thus restoring again that which has been so long lost from the earth. And wherever their voices shall be heard issuing this proclamation, in the name of Jesus, according as He has commanded them, then and there the people are under obligation to repent and be baptized. And he that repents and is baptized shall be saved; and he that does not believe their testimony, and repent and be baptized, shall be damned, for this plain reason, because God has sent them, by revelation, with this very errand, to this very generation, and they who reject the least of God's ambassadors reject Him that sent him, and therefore they are under condemnation from that time forth. But the message which God has sent these men with, is binding only on the generation to whom it is sent, and is not binding at all upon those who are dead and gone before it came; neither will it be binding on any generation which shall come after, unless God should raise up men and send unto them with the same Gospel, and then that generation to whom He sends them, will be saved or damned, according as they receive or reject their testimony.

People frequently ask this question—"If God has sent men with certain truths which are binding on the people, and without which they cannot be saved, what will become of the good people who have died before the message came?" I answer, if they obey the message which God sent to their own generation, they will be saved; but if not, they will be damned: but if God sent no message to that generation, then they rejected none, and, consequently, are under no condemnation; and they will rise up in judgment against this generation, and condemn it; for if they had received the same blessings which are now offered to us, they would no doubt have received them gladly. The principle of condemnation, in all ages of the world, is no other than rejecting the very message which God sends to them while they pretend to cleave closely to that which He has sent in former ages.

Woe unto you, Scribes and Pharisees, hypocrites! ye garnish the sepulchres of the Prophets, and say: "If we had lived in the days of our fathers, we would not have stoned and killed the Prophets as they did." But ye yourselves are witnesses, that you allow the deeds of your fathers; for they killed the Prophets, and you build their sepulchres. This was the testimony of the Savior to the Jews, who were pretending to stand stiffly for their former Prophets, and at the same time rejecting Jesus and His Apostles. And so it is now in the nineteenth century. You Christians (so called) garnish the tombs of the Messiah and His former Apostles, and even build fine chapels to their memory, entitling them Saint Peter's Church, Saint Paul's Church, Saint John's Church, etc.; and you say: "If we had lived in the days of the Apostles, we would not have stoned and killed them." But ye yourselves are witnesses, that ye allow the deeds of your fathers: for they killed the Apostles, and you build chapels in honor of them; while at the same time, if a Prophet or an Apostle comes among you, you will forthwith shut your houses against him, as soon as he testifies of what God has sent him to testify, for you say there are to be no more Prophets or Apostles on the earth, and you forthwith pronounce him a false Prophet; and if a mob rise and kill him, or burn his house, or destroy his goods, you will either rejoice, or sit in silence and give countenance to the deed, and perhaps cry, "False Prophet!" while your press and pulpits teem with all manner of lies concerning him. Woe unto you, priests, Pharisees, hypocrites! but fill ye up the measure of your fathers, for as they did, so do ye. Vengeance belongs to God. He will speedily avenge His elect, who cry unto Him day and night.

But to return to the subject of Revelation. "There is nothing secret that shall not be revealed: neither hid that shall not be known;" this was a maxim of the Savior. And again: "The knowledge of the Lord is to cover the earth, as the waters do the sea." Now, I ask how this great overturn is to be brought about? And I know no better way to answer this question, than to quote the prophecy of Nephi, Book of Mormon (n.e.), 2 Nephi, xxix, 11-14: "For I command all men, both in the east, and in the west, and in the north, and in the south, and in the islands of the sea, that they shall write the words which I speak unto them: for out of the books which shall be written, I will judge the world, every man according to their works, according to that which is written.

"For behold, I shall speak unto the Jews, and they shall write it; and I shall also speak unto the Nephites, and they shall write it; and I shall also speak unto the other tribes of the house of Israel which I have led away, and they shall write it; and I shall also speak unto all the nations of the earth, and they shall write it.

"And it shall come to pass that the Jews shall have the words of the Nephites, and the Nephites shall have the words of the Jews; and the Nephites and the Jews shall have the words of the lost tribes of Israel; and the lost tribes of Israel shall have the words of the Nephites and the Jews.

"And it shall come to pass, that my people which are of the house of Israel, shall be gathered home unto the lands of their possessions; and my word also shall be gathered in one. And I will show unto them that fight against my word, and against my people who are of the house of Israel, that I am God, and that I covenanted with Abraham, that I would remember his seed for ever."

[Transcriber's note: the material in the following chapter was originally printed in two side by side columns. Side by side pairs of paragraphs are separated from following pairs by three asterisks.]

Chapter Seven - A Contrast Between the Doctrine of Christ and the Doctrines of Nineteenth Century

"Whosoever transgresseth, and abideth not in the doctrine of Christ, hath not God. He that abideth in the doctrine of Christ, he hath both the Father and the Son."—2 JOHN, 2.

DOCTRINE OF CHRIST.
DOCTRINES OF MEN.
* * *

And these signs shall follow them that believe.

And these signs shall not follow them that believe, for they are done away and no longer needed.

* * *

In my name shall they cast out devils.

111

In His name they shall not cast out devils.

* * *

They shall speak with new tongues.

The gift of tongues is no longer needed.

* * *

They shall take up serpents, and if they drink any deadly thing it shall not hurt them; they shall lay hands on the sick, and they shall recover.

If they take up serpents, they will bite them; if they drink any deadly thing it will kill them. They shall not lay hands on the sick, and if they do they shall not recover; for such things are done away.

* * *

He that believeth on me, the works that I do shall he do also; and greater works than these shall he do; because I go to the Father.

He that believeth on Christ shall not do any of the miracles and mighty works that He did, for such things have ceased.

* * *

There is nothing secret that shall not be revealed, neither hid that shall not be known.

There is to be no more revelation, for all things necessary are already revealed.

* * *

And He shall send His angels, and they shall gather His elect from the four winds, etc.

And there is to be no more ministering of angels, for such things are done away.

* * *

And I saw an angel flying in the midst of heaven, having the everlasting Gospel to preach to them that dwell on the earth, etc.

Angels do not appear in this enlightened age, because they are no longer needed.

* * *

And when He, the Spirit of Truth, is come, He will guide you into all truth; again, "He shall show you things to come."

And inspiration is no longer needed in this age of learning and refinement. Again, it shall not show you things to come: for then you would be a Prophet, and there are to be no Prophets in these days.

* * *

If ye abide in me, and my words abide in you, you shall ask what you will, in my name, and I will give it you.

It is not so in these days, we must not expect to heal the sick and work miracles, consequently we must not expect to receive what we ask for.

* * *

Father, neither pray I for these alone, but for all them that shall believe on me through their words, that they may all be one, even as we are one.

And we are all good Christians, and we all believe on Him through the Apostles' words, although divided into several hundred sects.

* * *

One Lord, one faith, and one baptism.

Many Lords, many faiths, and three or four kinds of baptism.

* * *

And by one Spirit are ye all baptized into one body.

And by many spirits are we all torn asunder into different bodies.

* * *

And God gave some Apostles; and some, Prophets; and some, Evangelists; and some, Pastors and Teachers; for the perfecting of the Saints, for the work of the ministry, for the edifying of the body of Christ.

And there are to be no more Apostles, and no more Prophets. But the work of the ministry, the perfecting of the Saints, and the edifying of the different bodies of Christ, can all be done very well without these gifts of God, only give us money enough to educate and employ the wisdom of men.

* * *

These gifts and offices were to continue until we all come into the unity of the faith, and of the knowledge of the Son of God, unto a perfect man, unto the measure of the stature of the fulness of Christ.

Apostles, miracles and gifts were to continue during the first age of Christianity, and then were to cease, because no longer needed, having accomplished their purpose.

* * *

These gifts and offices were given that we henceforth be no more children, tossed to and fro, and carried about with every wind of doctrine, by the sleight of men, and cunning craftiness, whereby they lie in wait to deceive.

Tracts, creeds, sermons and commentaries of uninspired men, together with a hireling priesthood, are now necessary in order to keep men from being carried about with every wind of doctrine, etc.

* * *

For no man taketh this honor unto himself, but he that is called of God, as was Aaron.

For no man taketh this honor unto himself, but one who has been educated for the purpose, and commissioned by men.

* * *

But how shall they preach, except they be sent (of God)?

But how shall they preach except they be well educated for the purpose, and sent (by the board of officers)?

* * *

Is any sick among you? let him call for the Elders of the Church; and let them pray over him, anointing him with oil in the name of the Lord: and the prayer of faith shall save the sick, and the Lord shall raise him up; and if he have committed sins they shall be forgiven him.

If any are sick among you, do not send for the Elders of the Church; or, if the Elders come, do not let them lay hands on them, neither let them anoint them in the name of the Lord, for this is all "Mormon" delusion, but send for a good physician, and perhaps they may get well.

* * *

Repent and be baptized every one of you in the name of Jesus Christ, for the remission of sins, and ye shall receive the gift of the Holy Ghost; for the promise is unto you, and to your children, and to all that are afar off, even as many as the Lord our God shall call.

Repent and come to the anxious seat (penitent form), every one of you, and cry, "Lord, Lord," and may be you will get forgiveness of sins; and you may be baptized or not; but if you do, you will not get the Holy Ghost as they did anciently, for such things are done away.

* * *

It shall come to pass in the last days, saith God, that I will pour out my Spirit upon all flesh: and your sons and your daughters shall prophesy, and your young men shall see visions, and your old men shall dream dreams; etc.

And in these last days the Lord will not pour out His Spirit so as to cause our sons and daughters to prophesy, our old men to dream dreams, and our young men to see visions; for such things are no longer needed, and it is all a delusion, and none but the ignorant believe such things.

* * *

Covet earnestly the best gifts, but rather that ye prophesy.

Do not covet any of the supernatural gifts, but especially beware of prophesying, for such things are done away.

* * *

Covet to prophesy, and forbid not to speak with tongues.

Do not prophesy, and it is all a delusion to speak in tongues.

* * *

But in vain do they worship me, teaching for doctrines the commandments of men.

It matters not what kind of doctrine, or what system, a man embraces, if he is only sincere and worships Jesus Christ.

* * *

I thank thee, O Father, Lord of heaven and earth, because thou hast hid these things from the wise and prudent, and hast revealed them unto babes; even so, Father, for so it seemed good in thy sight.

We thank God that He has revealed nothing to any person, wise or simple, for many hundred years, but that our wise and learned men have been able to know God without a revelation, and that we shall never be favored with any more.

* * *

No man knoweth the Son but the Father, neither knoweth any man the Father save the Son, and he to whomsoever the Son will reveal Him.

We all know God in this enlightened age, and yet neither the Father nor the Son has revealed any thing to any of us, for we do not believe revelations are necessary now.

* * *

And this is life eternal, that they might know Thee the only true God, and Jesus Christ, whom Thou hast sent.

And we cannot know for ourselves, by any positive manifestation, in these days, but must depend on the wisdom and learning of men.

* * *

I thank my God always on your behalf, for the grace of God which is given you by Jesus Christ, that in everything ye are enriched by Him in all utterance, and in all knowledge, even as the testimony of Christ (the spirit of prophecy) was confirmed in you, so that ye come behind in no good gift, waiting for the coming of our Lord Jesus Christ.

We thank the Lord always, in behalf of the Church in these days, that she has no supernatural gifts given unto her, and that she is not enriched by Christ, neither in the gift of utterance, nor in the gift of knowledge; neither has she the testimony of Jesus (the spirit of prophecy) confirmed in her, and she comes behind in all the gifts; nor is she waiting for, or expecting, the coming of the Lord; for He has come once, and never will come again till the great and last day, the end of the earth.

* * *

The foolishness of God is wiser than men; and the weakness of God is stronger than men. For you see your calling, brethren, how that not many wise men after the flesh, not many mighty, not many noble, are called: but God hath chosen the foolish things of the world to confound the wise; and God hath chosen the weak things of the world to confound the things which are mighty, and base things of the world, and things which are despised, hath God chosen; yea, and things which are not, to bring to nought things that are; that no flesh should glory in His presence.

The wisdom of men, and the learning of men, are better than the inspiration of the Almighty, for that is not needed any longer; for you see your calling, brethren, how that the wise and learned, and noble, and mighty are called in these days; for we have chosen such to confound the foolish, the unlearned, and the ignorant; yea, to confound the base things of the world which are despised, that flesh might glory in His presence.

* * *

And I, brethren, when I came to you, came not with excellency of speech or of wisdom, declaring unto you the testimony of God; for I determined not to know anything among you, save Jesus Christ and Him crucified. And I was with you in weakness, and in fear, and in much trembling. And my speech and my preaching was not with enticing words of man's wisdom, but in demonstration of the Spirit and of power; that your faith should not stand in the wisdom of men, but in the power of God.

And we, brethren, when we came unto you, came with excellency of speech, and with the wisdom and learning of man; and our speech and our preaching were with enticing words of man's wisdom, not in demonstration of the Spirit and power, for that is done away; that your faith should not stand in the power of God, but in the wisdom of man.

* * *

But we speak the wisdom of God in a mystery, even the hidden wisdom, which God ordained before the world unto our glory; which none of the princes of this world knew: for had they known it, they would not have crucified the Lord of glory.

But we speak the wisdom of man in a mystery, even the hidden wisdom which none but the learned knew; for had others known it, they would never have been under the necessity of employing us to tell it to them.

116

* * *

But God hath revealed them unto us, by His Spirit; for the Spirit searcheth all things, yea, the deep things of God.

But God hath revealed nothing unto us by His Spirit; for the wisdom and learning of man search all things; yea, all the deep things which are necessary for us to know.

* * *

For what man knoweth the things of a man, save the spirit of man which is in him? Even so the things of God knoweth no man, but the Spirit of God.

For what man knoweth the things of man, save the spirit of man, which is in him? even so the things of God knoweth no man by the Spirit of God in these days, for it is done away, or it reveals nothing.

* * *

Now we have received not the spirit of the world, but the Spirit which is of God: that we might know the things that are freely given to us of God.

Now we have not received the Spirit of God, but the spirit of the world, that we might not know for a certainty, but that we might guess at, or give our opinion of, the things of God.

* * *

Which things also we speak, not in the words which man's wisdom teacheth, but which the Holy Ghost teacheth: comparing spiritual things with spiritual.

Which things also we speak, not in the words which the Holy Ghost teacheth, but which man's wisdom teacheth; for the inspiration of the Holy Ghost is done away.

* * *

But the natural man receiveth not the things of the Spirit of God: for they are foolishness unto him; neither can he know them, because they are spiritually discerned.

But the learned man may receive and understand the things of God by his own wisdom, without the inspiration of the Spirit; for who will be so foolish as to believe in visions and revelations in this religious age?

* * *

Let no man deceive himself. If any man among you seemeth to be wise in this world, let him become a fool, that he may be wise.

Let no man deceive himself. If any man among you seemeth to be wise in the things of God, let him get the wisdom of men, that he may be wise.

* * *

117

For the wisdom of this world is foolishness with God: for it is written, He taketh the wise in their own craftiness. And again, The Lord knoweth the thoughts of the wise, that they are vain. Therefore, let no man glory in men.

For the wisdom of God is foolishness with the world, for it is written, Let us educate young men for the ministry; and again, Let no man preach who has not been educated for the purpose; and especially, receive no man who professes to be inspired.

* * *

Now concerning spiritual gifts, brethren, I would not have you ignorant.

Now, concerning spiritual gifts, brethren, we would have you entirely ignorant, for they are not needed at all in this generation.

* * *

But the manifestation of the Spirit is given to every man to profit withal.

But the manifestation of the Spirit is given to no man to profit at all.

* * *

For to one is given by the Spirit the word of wisdom; to another, the word of knowledge by the same Spirit.

But to one is given, by the learning of men, the word of wisdom; and to another, the word of knowledge by human learning.

* * *

To another, faith by the same Spirit; to another, the gifts of healing by the same Spirit.

And to another, faith, by the same Spirit; but to none the gift of healing by the same Spirit.

* * *

To another, the working of miracles; to another, prophecy; to another, discerning of spirits; to another, divers kinds of tongues; to another, the interpretation of tongues.

And to none the working of miracles, and to none to prophesy; and to none discerning of spirits; and to none to speak with divers kinds of tongues, and to none to interpret tongues.

* * *

For as the body is one, and hath many members, and all the members of that one body, being many, are one body, so also is Christ.

For as the body is composed of many sects and parties who are opposed to each other, and have no gifts, and being many sects, are but one body, so also is Antichrist.

* * *

For by one Spirit are we all baptized into one body, whether we be Jews or Gentiles, whether we be bond or free; and have been all made to drink into one Spirit.

For by many spirits are we all baptized into many bodies, whether we be Catholics or Protestants, Presbyterians or Methodists, but have all drunk into one spirit, even the spirit of the world.

* * *

For the body is not one member, but many.

For the body is not one sect, but many.

* * *

But now hath God set the members every one of them in the body, as it hath pleased Him.

But now hath the God (of this world) set the sects and parties in the body (of Antichrist) as it hath pleased him.

* * *

And if they were all one member, where were the body?

And if they were all one sect, where were the body?

* * *

But now are they many members, but one body.

But now are they many sects, yet but one body (even Babylon).

* * *

Now ye are the body of Christ, and members in particular.

Now ye are the body of Antichrist, and members in particular.

* * *

And God hath set some in the Church: first, Apostles; secondly, Prophets; thirdly, Teachers; after that, miracles; then, gifts of healings, helps, governments, diversities of tongues.

And man hath set some in the church, first, a hireling priest; secondly, a board of officers; thirdly, tracts; then commentaries, creeds, and diversities of opinions; hence, societies and wondrous helps.

* * *

Blessed are ye, when men shall revile you, and persecute you, and shall say all manner of evil against you falsely, for my sake: rejoice, and be exceeding glad; for great is your reward in heaven; for so persecuted they the Prophets which were before you.

Woe unto you, when men revile you, and persecute you, and say all manner of evil against you falsely for Christ's sake. Lament ye, and be exceedingly sorrowful in that hour, for little is your reward among men, for so persecute they the Latter-day Saints.

* * *

Give to him that asketh thee; and from him that would borrow of thee turn thou not away.

Give to him that asketh of thee, if he be able to make thee a similar present; and from him that would borrow of thee turn not thou away, if he be able to pay thee again with good interest.

* * *

Be ye therefore perfect even as your Father who is in heaven is perfect.

Do not think to be perfect, for it is impossible to live without sin.

* * *

Take heed that you do not your alms before men, to be seen of them; otherwise ye have no reward of your Father who is in heaven.

Take heed that you do your alms before men, to be seen of them; otherwise, you have no reward nor praise from the children of men.

* * *

Therefore, when thou doest thine alms, do not sound a trumpet before thee, as the hypocrites do in the synagogues and in the streets, that they may have glory of men. Verily I say unto you, They have their reward.

Therefore when thou doest thine alms, publish it in the Missionary Herald, or some other paper, that you may get praise of the world. Verily I say unto you, You shall have your reward.

* * *

And when thou prayest, thou shalt not be as the hypocrites are; for they love to pray standing in the synagogues and in the corners of the streets, that they may be seen of men.

And when thou prayest, be like the hypocrites in days of old; go before the public and cry mightily, not expecting to be heard and answered, for that would be miraculous, and miracles have ceased.

* * *

Moreover, when ye fast, be not, as the hypocrites, of a sad countenance: for they disfigure their faces, that they may appear unto men to fast. Verily I say unto you, They have their reward.

Moreover, when ye fast, be like the hypocrites, of a sad countenance, that ye may appear unto men to fast; so that you may get your reward.

* * *

Lay not up for yourselves treasures upon earth, where moth and rust doth corrupt, and where thieves break through and steal: but lay up for yourselves treasures in heaven, where neither moth nor rust doth corrupt, and where thieves do not break through nor steal; for where your treasure is, there will your heart be also.

Lay up for yourselves abundance of treasures on the earth, where moth and rust doth corrupt, and where thieves break through and steal; for if your heart is only in heaven, it is no matter how rich you are in this world; for now it is come to pass that ye can serve God and mammon.

    * * *

Therefore all things whatsoever ye would that men should do to you, do ye even so to them: for this is the law and the Prophets.

Therefore all things whatsoever men do to you, do ye even so to them; for this is the law and the practice.

    * * *

Enter ye in at the straight gate; for wide is the gate, and broad is the way, that leadeth to destruction, and many there be which go in thereat.

Enter ye in at the wide gate, where the multitude go: for it cannot be that all our great and learned men are wrong, and nobody right but a few obscure individuals.

    * * *

Because straight is the gate, and narrow is the way, that leadeth unto life, and few there be that find it.

For the narrow way is not altogether too straight, but only a very few travel in it.

    * * *

Beware of false prophets, which come to you in sheep's clothing, but inwardly they are ravening wolves. Ye shall know them by their fruits. Do men gather grapes of thorns, or figs of thistles?

Beware of Prophets who come to you with the Word of God; you may know at once they are false, without hearing them or examining their fruits; popular opinion is against them; whereas, if they were men of God, the people would speak well of them.

    * * *

Wherefore, by their fruits ye shall know them. Not every one that saith unto me, Lord, Lord, shall enter into the kingdom of heaven; but he that doeth the will of my Father who is in heaven.

If we are only sure that we have experienced religion, and we pray often, we shall be saved, whether we do the Lord's will or not; for it mattereth not what system we embrace, whether it be right or wrong, if we are only sincere.

* * *

And it came to pass, when Jesus had ended these sayings, the people were astonished at His doctrine: for He taught them as one having authority, and not as the scribes.

And it came to pass, when men had ended these sayings, the people were pleased with their doctrines, for they taught them not as men having authority, but as the scribes.

Key to the Science of Theology

Fly—fly—these thoughts on the lightning car,
With the speed of light to the realms afar!
Mount—mount the car with the horse of fire;
Outstrip the wind, he will never tire,
Let the wild bird scream as he lags behind,
And the hurricane a champion find.
Search the darkest spot where mortals dwell:
With a voice of thunder the tidings tell,
Proclaim the dawn of a brighter day,
When the King of kings shall his sceptre sway.
Bid pain, and anguish, and sorrow cease,
And open the way for the Prince of Peace.
He will conquer death, bid mourning flee,
And give to the nations a Jubilee.

Preface

The present is an age of progress, of change, of rapid advance, and of wonderful revolutions.

The very foundations of society—social, political, commercial, moral and religious, seem to be shaken as with a mighty earthquake, from centre to circumference. All things tremble; creation groans; the world is in travail, and pains to be delivered.

A new era has dawned upon our planet, and is advancing with accelerated force—with giant strides.

The rail-roads and the steam-boats, with their progressive improvements in speed, safety and convenience, are extending and multiplying the means of travel, of trade, of association, and intercommunication between countries whose inhabitants have been comparatively unknown to, or estranged from, each other.

But, as if even these means were too slow for the God-like aspirations, the mighty throes of human thought, and its struggles for light and expansion, man seizes the lightning, tames and subdues it, and makes it the bearer of his thoughts and despatches. While these things are in progress by one portion of mankind, another learns to seize and control a sunbeam, in a manner subservient to the progress of the fine arts: and by which means a man performs in a minute, the work which a short time since would have employed the most active years of a lifetime.

While every science, every art is being developed; while the mind is awakened to new thought; while the windows of heaven are opened, as it were, and the profound depths of human intellect are stirred—moved from the foundation on all other subjects, religious knowledge seems at a stand still.

The creeds of the Fathers seem to have been cast in the mould of other ages, to be adapted to a more narrow sphere of intellectual development, and to be composed of material too much resembling cast iron; or, at least, not sufficiently elastic to expand with the expansion of mind, to grow with the growth, and advance with the progressive principles of the age.

For these reasons, perhaps more than any other, the master spirits of the age are breaking loose from the old moorings, and withdrawing from estab-

124

lished and venerated systems, by which means society is distracted, divided, broken up, thrown, as it were, into a chaos of confused, disorganized individualization, without a standard or rallying point, without a nucleus by which to concentrate or re-organise this chaotic mass, these atoms of thought.

One thing is certain—according to ancient prophecy, and agreeable to the general expectation of this and other ages, the day approaches which will flood the earth with the pure principles of religious knowledge; a day when none will have to teach his neighbour, saying, Know ye the Lord; for all persons shall know Him, from the least to the greatest.

It should be a matter of serious thought and investigation—without respect to party, sect, or creed, whether there should not, in the very nature of present circumstances, and future Millennial hopes, be an entire remodelling, or re-organization of religious society, upon the broad basis of revealed knowledge, tangible fact, and philosophical, scientific and spiritual Truth—a universal "standard," of immutable Truth, instead of numberless systems founded on uncertainty, opinion, mere human impression, or conjecture.

Can anything short of such a standard unite society, enlighten the world, establish real peace, brotherhood and fellowship, and put a final end to all religious ignorance, superstition, jargon, or discord? Is not a difference of opinion, or a disagreement on any given subject, a proof positive of existing ignorance, or want of light or information, on the part of the parties disagreeing? If so, the present age is certainly in the dark, or, in a great measure, ignorant on religious subjects. A knowledge of the Truth can alone bring the desired union, and bid discord cease. If the Scriptures be true, it is not religious opinion which will cover the earth, and universally pervade every bosom, but it is, a KNOWLEDGE, "The knowledge of God." "God is Truth." To know Him, is to know the Truth.

The present Volume aims to embody, in a concise and somewhat original manner and style, a general view of the Science of Theology, as gathered from revelation, history, prophecy, reason and analogy.

If the Work proves an introductory key to some of the first principles of the divine science of which it treats; if it serves to open the eyes of any of his fellowmen, on the facts of the past, the present, and the future; if it leads to investigation and inquiry, and calls public attention to the greater and more particular truths which have been, or are about to be, revealed as a standard by which to unite the people of all nations and of all religions upon the rock, the sure foundation of divine, eternal, uncreated, infinite and exhaustless Truth, it will have accomplished the end aimed at by...

Chapter One - Theology—Its Definition—
Historical Illustrations

Eternal Science! who would fathom thee
Must launch his bark upon a shoreless sea.
Thy knowledge yet shall overwhelm the earth,
Thy truth to immortality to give birth;
Thy dawn shall kindle to eternal day,
And man, immortal, still shall own thy sway.

First. THEOLOGY is the science of communication, or of correspondence, between God, angels, spirits, and men, by means of visions, dreams, interpretations, conversations, inspirations, or the spirit of prophecy and revelation.

Second. It is the science by which worlds are organized, sustained, and directed, and the elements controlled.

Third. It is the science of knowledge, and the key and power thereof, by which the heavens are opened, and lawful access is obtained to the treasures of wisdom and intelligence—inexhaustible, infinite, embracing the past, the present, and the future.

Fourth. It is the science of life—endless and eternal, by which the living are changed or translated, and the dead raised.

Fifth. It is the science of faith, reformation, and remission of sins, whereby a fallen race of mortals may be justified, cleansed, and restored to the communion and fellowship of that Holy Spirit which is the light of the world, and of every intelligence therein.

Sixth. It is the science of spiritual gifts, by which the blind see, the deaf hear, the lame walk, the sick are healed, and demons are expelled from the human system.

Seventh. It is the science of all other sciences and useful arts, being in fact the very fountain from which they emanate. It includes philosophy, astronomy, history, mathematics, geography, languages, the science of letters; and blends the knowledge of all matters of fact, in every branch of art, or of research. It includes, also, all the scientific discoveries and inventions—agriculture, the mechanical arts, architecture, shipbuilding, the properties and applications of the mariner's compass, navigation, and music. All that is useful, great, and good; all that is calculated to sustain, comfort, instruct, edify, purify, refine, or exalt intelligences; originated by this science, and this science alone, all other sciences being but branches growing out of this— root.

Some of the facts stated in the foregoing, are beautifully illustrated in Theological history, of which the following is an imperfect summary—

God spake, and the worlds were framed by His word.

He spake, darkness dispersed, and light prevailed.

He commanded, and the elements—water and earth, separated, and assumed their proper bounds.

He commanded, and the earth brought forth vegetable and animal life in countless variety.

He commanded, and man, male and female, took upon them a tabernacle of flesh, and prepared to multiply and perpetuate their species in the new creation.

"The Lord God planted a garden," and thus introduced agriculture.

"He made coats of skins," hence the tailor's art.

The Lord God commanded and gave pattern for Noah's Ark, thus introducing the art of shipbuilding.

He revealed the patterns for the Tabernacle in the wilderness, with all its arrangements and furniture; and afterwards developed the entire plan and all the designs of that most stupendous of all works of art—the great Temple of Solomon, with all its furniture; thus developing and improving the art of architecture.

The Lord God wrote with His own finger on the "tables of stone," on Mount Sinai; thus showing that the science of letters was cultivated and used by the highest Intelligence of the eternal heavens.

The Lord God has revealed by Ezekiel the Prophet, a plan for the survey and division of Palestine to the Twelve Tribes of Israel, on their return to the land of their fathers; also for laying out the new city of Jerusalem, with its squares, blocks, public grounds, and suburbs, and its temple.

Thus Theology includes the surveyor's art, and the planning of cities, as well as temples, and shows that these arts are cultivated in heaven, and that the very highest Intelligence of the Heaven of heavens, stoops, or condescends, to grace these arts by His own particular attention and example.

In the Revelation of John the Apostle, on the Isle of Patmos, we have a specimen, a masterpiece, a climax of all that is great and grand in design, and splendid and glorious in execution, in cities, thrones, palaces, streets, pavements, outgrounds, gates, walks, squares, fountains, rivulets, gardens, fruits, groves, specimens of dress, poetry, song, music, marriage, bridal dress, feasting, books, literature, public worship, prophesying, prayer, and praise, as existing in and around the palaces of the New Jerusalem, the capital of heaven, the seat of government of the Eternal King.

The very gates of the city are numbered and named, together with the particular names of the precious stones forming the foundations thereof; the gold which composed the pavement of the streets—all are portrayed in the description.

And what is still more marvellous, all this surpassing grandeur of design, and stupendous wisdom and display in execution, were explored, comprehended, and described by a poor, illiterate fisherman, by the aid of the science and arts of Theology.

Having reviewed some of the works of the great Head—the President or First Teacher in the school of Theology, we will still continue the historic illustrations of this wonderful science, as developed and exemplified by the most eminent students and professors of the same.

By this science Adam obtained from his Father, the promise of the eternal dominion over the planet on which he was placed.

By this science Enoch overcame death, and ascended to a higher sphere of immortality and eternal life, without even being separated from his fleshly tabernacle.

By this science Noah foretold the flood, prepared to meet the event, and, with his family, survived the same, and became the greatest landed proprietor since Adam.

By the perversion and unlawful use of this science king Nimrod built the stupendous Tower of Babel, but was frustrated, and his works were destroyed before their completion.

By this science various tongues and languages were instituted, and colonies—the germs of nations, planted beyond the seas and in all the earth.

By this science Abraham escaped the idolatry and priestcraft of the Egyptians, and of the world around him; obtained a good land secured to him and his seed by an immutable oath, covenant, and an everlasting, unchangeable title.

By this science he conversed with angels, and was favoured with a personal interview with the Great Head and Founder of the science, who became his guest, and, after eating and drinking with him, blessed him and his wife, promised them an heir in their old age, and finally, on parting, told him His design on Sodom and its neighbourhood.

By this science Lot escaped the flames of Sodom, the knowledge being communicated by two angels.

By this science Isaac and Jacob also obtained promises, and conversed with angels.

By it Joseph was exalted from a dungeon to a palace, for the salvation, from famine, of a nation and of his father's house.

By this science Moses performed his wonders in Egypt, in the Red Sea, and in the wilderness.

By the perversion and unlawful use of this science the magicians of Egypt withstood Moses for a time, and performed their enchantments.

By this science Joshua controlled the motions of the earth, and lengthened out the day by a simple command.

By this science the walls of Jericho were levelled with the earth, and the city was taken.

By this science the Jordan river was divided, while a nation crossed dry shod, to take possession of the promised land.

By this science Elijah controlled the heavens, that it rained not for three years and six months in Palestine. And by it he called forth and restored rain.

By it he overthrew the priests of Baal, and the kingdom of Ahab; put an end to the royal family of this idolatrous king; and placed Jehu on the throne.

By it he rose, like Enoch, to a higher sphere, without returning to dust.

By this science Samuel prophesied, raised up a mighty king and nation, and afterwards dethroned Saul, and exalted an obscure shepherd boy to the throne of Israel.

By this science Isaiah, Jeremiah, Ezekiel, Daniel, and others, foretold the fate of Babylon, Egypt, Tyre, Jerusalem, and other cities and nations; and the exact career and final doom of Nebuchadnezzar, Belteshazzar, Cyrus, and other great and important personages, who were destined in turn to influence and decide the fate of nations.

By this science the furnace of fire was overcome, and the months of lions were closed, that no harm should befall the holy men of God.

By this science Zachariah, Elizabeth, John the Baptist, Simeon, Anna, Joseph, Mary, the wise men from the east, and the shepherds of Judea, enjoyed visions, communion with angels, and the spirit of prophecy, so as to understand and welcome with joy the events of the birth and approaching ministry of Jesus Christ, when, as yet, all those not versed in this science, were in darkness on the subject, and as liable to reject the Saviour as to receive him.

Dreams and visions, enjoyed by means of this science, led and protected the Son of God in all his career of mortal life.

Finally—By this same power a mighty angel descended, shook the earth, frightened the Roman guards, rolled away the great stone, broke the seal of the tomb, and called to life the sleeping body of Jesus Christ.

By this power the risen Jesus, eating, drinking, and conversing with his disciples, after his resurrection, commissioned and instructed them in the same science, ordained them to act in the same, and to impart its power to others, in all the world, with signs following them that believed.

By this science he ascended to the Father, and lives for ever in the flesh, to shed forth the gifts and powers of the same science, according to his own will, and the will of his Father, to reign henceforth until he descends to the earth, conquers death in a last great conflict, and puts all enemies under his feet.

By this same power his Apostles, being clothed with the full powers of the same on the day of Pentecost, ministered the powers and knowledge of this science to others, both Jew and Gentile, insomuch that the sick were healed, the blind saw, the dumb spake, the deaf heard, the lame walked, devils were cast out, and the dead were raised, while everywhere, dreams, visions, the ministering of angels, and the gift of prophecy were enjoyed.

Chapter Two - Decline and Loss of This Science Among the Jews

O horrid! awful! melancholy sight!
A nation, wont to soar 'mid realms of light,
Degraded, fallen, sunk in dark despair,
The hiss, the scorn, the bye-word everywhere;
No eye to pity, and no arm to save,
Till wearied nature finds an exile's grave.

It now becomes our painful task to trace the decline of the science of Theology and its powers among the nations, and to review the awful consequences of such decline.

We will commence with the Jewish nation.

The science of Theology, as we have just reviewed, was enjoyed, and its powers were wonderfully developed, under the several dispensations called Patriarchal, Mosaic, and Jewish.

There had, however, been a great decline, a retrogression of the powers and knowledge of the same, previous to their restoration by John the Baptist and Jesus Christ.

This was owing to the general prevalence of sectarian principles, divisions, precepts, commandments, and doctrines of men, by which the Law and the Prophets were made void, and a veil was thrown over them, or over the hearts of men, by which means they were misunderstood, or rather, not understood at all.

It therefore became the duty of Jesus Christ and his Apostles and Elders, as well as of his forerunner, to reprove those sects, denounce their doctrines and traditions, and restore that which was lost in this great science.

This restoration was at first confined strictly to the nation of the Jews. But seeing they turned from it, and judged themselves unworthy of eternal life, preferring their own powerless forms and doctrines, to the science of revelation, miracles, visions, and prophecy, which had ever illuminated the pathway of their more ancient fathers, the Apostles turned from them, by the commandment of the Lord, and translated this science, with its keys and legitimate powers, to the Gentiles.

The nation had rejected and slain the Messiah, stoned the Prophets, and imprisoned and even murdered many of the Apostles and Elders; and Jesus had already, in tears of anguish, announced their doom—

"O Jerusalem, Jerusalem, thou that killest the Prophets, and stonest them which are sent unto thee, how often would I have gathered thy children together, even as a hen gathereth her chickens under her wings, and ye would not! Behold, your house is left unto you desolate. For I say unto you, ye shall not see me henceforth till ye shall say, Blessed is He that cometh in the name of the Lord."

Again, on another occasion, the Messiah uttered his voice, saying—"There shall be great distress in the land, and wrath upon this people. And they shall fall by the edge of the sword, and shall be led away captive into all nations: and Jerusalem shall be trodden down of the Gentiles, until the times of the Gentiles be fulfilled."

Again he spake, concerning the Temple, saying—"There shall net be left here one stone upon another, that shall not be thrown down."

All these things, foretold by the science of Theology, were fulfilled in that generation. And Jerusalem has been destroyed, trodden down by the Gentiles, and the Jews have remained in captivity among the nations until now.

Our readers will readily discern the entire loss of the science and powers of Theology among this nation; the time, circumstances, and reasons of its decline; and the time or circumstances which will restore it unto them.

They lost it when, by the hand of the Apostles, it was taken from them and given to the Gentiles.

The result was, the destruction of their city and temple, and of their national existence.

Their temple, priesthood, and offerings were no longer attended by divine power. Its outward forms were, therefore, of no possible use.

From that very time to the present—One thousand eight hundred and fifty-one of the Christian era, the voice of a Prophet has not been heard among the Jews.

Angels have not ministered unto them.

There has been no vision from the Lord.

No dream or interpretation.

No answer by Urim or Thummim.

No Prophet.

No voice.

No sound.

No reproof.

No comforting whisper.

All is silence—stillness—solemn blackness of despair.

All is as the similitude and shadow of death.

Oh the weariness, the painful suspense, the watchings, the wanderings, the anxieties, the pains and sorrows of eighteen centuries! Oh the mist of ages which has shrouded a nation as it were in the gloom of an endless night!

When—O when, will their day dawn, and the day star of their ancient science appear above the horizon, disperse the cloud, and usher in the morning of a brighter day?

When the times of the Gentiles are fulfilled.

When they shall welcome a messenger in the name of the Lord.

Chapter Three - Progress, Decline, and Final Loss of the Science of Theology Among the Gentiles—Foreshadowings of Its Restoration for the Ushering in of The Millennium

Oh Mystic Babel, long has been thy reign!
What direful evils follow in thy train!
The veil is rent—thy mystery revealed,
Angels cry wo! and God thy doom has sealed.
The nations, from thy long and dreary night,
Are waking now to everlasting light.

Returning to the Gentile Church, we find the science of Theology, with all its miraculous powers of visions, dreams, angels, revelations, prophecy, healings, &c., everywhere enjoyed. It had abated none of its powers, in its transition from Jew to Gentile. The wild branches, being engrafted into the good old stock, immediately partook of the root and fatness of the tame olive tree, and thus was produced the natural fruit.

But Paul, the great Apostle of the Gentiles, in his writings to the Romans, cautioned them to beware lest they should fall away after the same example as the Jews had done before them.

Said he—"If God spared not the natural branches, take heed lest he also spare not thee."

John the Apostle also predicted the rise and universal sway of a certain mystical power, a Babel of spiritual or religious confusion, in short—"Mystery, Babylon the great, the mother of harlots and abominations of the earth."

This power should bear rule among all nations. The kings and rulers of the earth should be drunken with the wine of her fornication. The merchants of the earth should become rich through the abundance of her delicacies.

This power should, according to the Prophet Daniel and the Apostle John, "wear out the Saints of the Most High;" "change times and laws;" "be drunken with the blood of the Saints, and with the blood of the martyrs of Jesus;" "destroy the mighty and the holy people;" "make war with the Saints, and overcome them" until a set time.

All these predictions, and many others, foretell the doom of the Gentile Church—its destruction from the earth, and the consequent decline and cessation of the science of Theology, and of its powers and blessings in the Gentile world.

Connected with these predictions, we have the most positive prophetic declarations of Holy Writ concerning the overthrow and entire destruction of this same mystical power, which had made war with the Saints.

Its judgments are set forth as far more terrible than those which befell Jerusalem. Plague, pestilence, sword, earthquake, and the flame of devouring fire will cause her to cease to be.

Then will usher in the kingdom of our God, and the power of His Christ. Then will the Saints of the Most High take the kingdom, and the greatness of the kingdom under the whole heaven.

Thus are to be revived the ancient powers and blessings, the knowledge and wisdom, of the science of Theology.

In the fulfilment of the foregoing predictions, the science of Theology declined, and passed away from among the Gentiles, just in proportion as the Church, or the Saints of the Most High, were warred against and overcome.

For years, centuries, ages, there has been no voice from heaven among the Gentiles, any more than among the Jews. They have fallen "after the same example of unbelief," notwithstanding the caution of their great Apostle.

No Gentile Prophet has arisen and uttered his voice.

No kind angel has ministered to them.

No vision from the Lord.

No answer.

No inspired dream.

No voice.

No sound from the heavens.

No revelation has burst upon the silence of midnight darkness which has brooded over the nations.

Or, if such voice, such vision, such Prophet has occasionally burst forth with the testimony of Jesus, the spirit of prophecy, his testimony has been unheeded by the mass of the people called Christians, his voice silenced in death, or himself and his followers have been banished from society, to wander in the mountains, forests, caves, or deserts of the earth; or, on the other hand, compelled to drag out an existence in the solitude of the dungeon.

Ages, centuries have passed, and Oh! what suffering! what torture! what rivers of tears! what oceans of blood! what groanings! what strong crying and tears on the earth! what prayers in heaven!

"How long, O Lord, holy and true, dost thou not judge and avenge our blood, on them that dwell on the earth?"

The fire consumed.

The sword devoured.

Hell's artillery bellowed.

Devils hugely grinned.

Widows and orphans mourned.

Heaven wept.

Saints prayed.

Justice stood aghast.

Mercy, retiring, dropped a tear of blood.

Angels, starting, half-drew their glittering swords.

And the Gods, in solemn council, decreed a just vengeance.

Protest upon protest! reforms and re-reforms; revolutions, struggles, exertions of every kind, of mere human invention, have been tried, and tried in vain. The science of Theology, with all its keys and powers, once lost, could never, consistent with the ancient Prophetic testimony, be restored to either Jew or Gentile, until the full time should arrive—"The times of restitution of all things, which God hath spoken by the mouth of all his holy prophets, since the world began."

The time for a mighty angel to fly in the midst of heaven, having the everlasting Gospel to preach to them who dwell on the earth; to every nation, kindred, tongue, and people. (See John's revelation.)

The time of judgment for "Mystery Babylon."

The times of "the fulness of the Gentiles."

The times for the grafting in again of the Jews, and all the natural branches of Israel.

Then, and not till then, could the science, the keys, the powers of Theology, be restored to man.

No individual or combined human action could obtain or restore again these keys—this science.

A mighty angel held the keys of this science for the last days. A mighty angel was to restore the keys of the ancient Priesthood, Apostleship, power and blessings. A voice from heaven was to reveal the time, and send forth the cry—"Come out of her my people, that ye be not partakers of her sins, and that ye receive not of her plagues. For her sins have reached unto heaven, and God hath remembered her iniquities."

All the darkness of the middle ages; all the priestcraft or kingcraft of every age, since the slaughter of the Apostles; all the oppressions, persecutions, or abuses of power; all the extravagancies and idleness on the one hand, and all the sufferings and miseries of the toiling millions for want of the comforts of life, on the other; all the ignorance, superstitions, errors, divisions and contentions which have transpired in the name of "Christianity" down to the present time; have been the results of the decline, and loss of the keys and powers, of the science of Theology, or for want of attention to them when existing on the earth.

Nor will the "Christian" world ever attain to any considerable degree of knowledge, power, or union in religious progress, until they discover their loss of this science, become sensible of the need of its restoration, and humble themselves as in the dust, and welcome a messenger who comes in the name of the Lord, with a commission from heaven, and with keys committed by the Angels of God—a new Apostolic commission, a restoration of the Kingdom and Church, and power and gifts of God; a new dispensation, universally proclaimed in all the world, with power and signs following; and the whole consummated by the glorious restoration of Israel and Judah to their own land and nationality, and to the true fold of God; together with the second advent of Messiah and all his Saints with him, to overthrow "Mystery Babylon," and reign on the earth.

Such are the events, such is the remedy for the past and present evils.

Chapter Four - Rise, Progress, Decline, and Loss of the Science of Theology

...on the Western Hemisphere, As Brought to Light by The Late Discovery of Ancient American Records.

The spirit world is moved, the silence broken,
The ancient Seers from out the ground have spoken.
The appointed years on time's fleet wings have fled.
And voices whisper from the ancient dead.
Volumes of truth the sacred archives yield.
The past, the glorious future, stand revealed.

We are now, of necessity, carried back in our research to the cradle of nations, the Tower of Babel, in order to trace the history of this wonderful science, from the first emigration of a colony to the western hemisphere, till its final decline and overthrow, for the knowledge of which we are indebted to many ancient records, written by the fathers, or ancient students and professors of this science, on the western hemisphere.

Among these we will make honourable mention of the Prophets Jared, Ether, Lehi, Nephi, Mosiah, Alma, Abinadi, Mormon, and Moroni, who wrote and prophesied in the western hemisphere, during the several ages intervening between the time of the dispersion at Babel, and the fifth century of the Christian era.

By the science of Theology Jared and his brother led a colony from the great tower to the sea coast, conversing with the Lord, and walking by the light of His revelations on the way.

By this science they were instructed in the building of eight barges similar to the ark of Noah.

By this science their leader saw God, face to face, and talked with Him in plain humility, as one man talks with another, thus obtaining a knowledge of His future coming and Kingdom, and of the great events of all ages and generations.

By this science they were preserved on the great waters three hundred and forty-four days, and were then landed, with their eight barges, in the western hemisphere, together with their women, children, cattle, and seeds of every kind.

By this science they became a great nation, peopling the entire continent, and enjoying all the blessings of civilization and heavenly light.

By the abuse and neglect of it they were at length exterminated, in the days of their Prophet Ether, who lived about six hundred years before Christ came in the flesh.

By this science the Prophets Lehi and Nephi came out with a colony from Jerusalem, in the days of Jeremiah the Prophet, and after wandering for eight years in the wilderness of Arabia, came to the sea coast, built a vessel, obtained from the Lord a compass to guide them on the way, and finally landed in safety on the coast of what is now called Chili, in South America.

By this science they also became a great nation, enjoyed many visions, had the ministering of angels, and of many Prophets, by which means they knew of the coming, birth, ministry, death, resurrection, and ascension of Jesus Christ.

By this science they also enjoyed a personal visit of the risen Redeemer, who descended from heaven in their presence, taught them his Gospel, chose and ordained twelve of their number as Apostles, and prophesied many things.

By this science these twelve and others established the Gospel, Church, and ordinances of God throughout the entire western hemisphere.

By this science their sick were healed, demons were expelled, the lame walked, the blind saw, the dumb spake, the deaf heard, and their dead were raised.

By this science three of those Apostles, having a change wrought upon them, tarried in the flesh upon the earth, ministered the Gospel and its blessings nearly four hundred years, and then withdrew from the people because of their iniquity, took away the keys of Apostleship and of the Gospel, and its powers, sealed up the records, and caused the work of healing, and of gifts and miracles, to cease from among the people, because of iniquity, bloodshed, and persecution.

By this science they yet live in the flesh upon the earth, holding keys of Apostleship and power upon the western hemisphere, being now about one thousand eight hundred years old.

By this science (being held in reserve above the powers of mystery Babylon,) they will soon go forth, prophesying, preaching the Gospel, and doing mighty signs and wonders in the midst of all nations, in order to complete and mature the Gentile fulness, and restore the tribes of Israel. Nor is this all—John, the beloved disciple among the Jews, is yet alive in the flesh, and is held in reserve, to "prophesy again before many peoples, and nations, and tongues, and kings" as it is written.

But to return to our history of the western hemisphere. After the science of Theology had ceased to be cultivated and enjoyed among this branch of Israel, terrible wars and bloodshed ensued. Governments and civilization were broken up, cities and countries were overthrown, all records and vestiges of truth were diligently sought and destroyed, as far as obtained.

And, finally, the whole face of the country was soaked, as it were, in blood, and strewed with the dead and dying.

The wild beasts of the forest and fowls of heaven devoured their flesh, and their bones were left to moulder unburied.

In other instances bodies were heaped up, and covered with mounds of earth.

All government became extinct, and the countries overrun by tribes and bands of robbers at war with each other.

In this situation the records of Moroni leave them, in the fifth century of the Christian era, and much in the same situation, with some exceptions, the Europeans found them after the lapse of another thousand years.

Oh! who can contemplate the disgusting deformity, the dark features, the filthy habits, the idleness, the cruelty, the nakedness, the poverty, the misery, the sufferings, the ignorance of the descendants of this once favoured branch of the royal blood of Abraham and Joseph, and not weep for very anguish, while his bosom yearns, and the fountains—the depths of his inmost soul, are stirred and moved within him!

Reader, all these things have come upon them, on account of the abuses, the consequent decline, and final loss of the keys and powers, of the science of Theology.

But comfort your heart, their redemption is at the door.

Chapter Five - Keys of the Mysteries of the God-head

Eternal Father, Being without end!
Thy glorious fulness who can comprehend!
Thine own infinitude alone is fraught
With attributes to swell a human thought,
To grasp thy knowledge, or thy nature scan.
As Father of the endless race of man.

"This is life eternal: to know the only true and living God, and Jesus Christ whom he hath sent."

Since the decline of the science of Theology, a mystery, dark and deep, has shrouded the human mind, in regard to the person and nature of the Eternal Father, and of Jesus Christ, His son.

Councils of the fathers, and wise men of Christendom, have assembled again and again, in order to solve the mystery of Godliness, and fix some standard or creed upon which all parties might rest and be agreed.

This, however, was not in their power. It is impossible for the world by its wisdom to find out God. "Neither knoweth any man the Father save the son, and he to whomsoever the son will reveal him."

The key to the science of Theology, is the key of divine revelation. Without this key, no man, no assemblage of men, ever did, or ever will know the Eternal Father, or Jesus Christ.

When the key of revelation was lost to man, the knowledge of God was lost. And as life eternal depended on the knowledge of God, of course the key of eternal life was also lost.

Oh the mysteries, the absurdities, the contentions, the quarrels, the bloodshed, the infidelity, the senseless and conflicting theories, which have grown and multiplied among sectaries on this subject!

Among these theories, we will notice one, which is, perhaps, more extensively received by different sects than any other. The language runs thus—"There is one only living and true God, without body, parts, or passions; consisting of three persons—the Father, Son, and Holy Ghost."

It is painful to the human mind to be compelled to admit, that such wonderful inconsistencies of language or ideas, have ever found place in any human creed. Yet, so it is.

It is but another way of saying, that there is a God who does not exist, a God who is composed of nonentity, who is the negative of all existence, who occupies no space, who exists in no time, who is composed of no substance, known or unknown, and who has no powers or properties in common with any thing or being known to exist, or which can possibly be conceived of, as existing either in the heavens or on the earth.

Such a God could never be seen, heard, or felt, by any being in the universe.

There never has been a visible idol worshipped among men, which was so powerless as this "God without body, parts, or passions."

The god of Egypt, the crocodile, could destroy.

The images of different nations could be felt and seen.

The Peruvian god, the Sun, could diffuse its genial warmth, light, and influence.

But not so with the God without "body, parts, or passions."

That which has no parts, has no whole.

Beings which have no passions, have no soul.

Before we can introduce the keys and powers of practical Theology to the understanding of men in this age, we must, of necessity, place within their comprehension some correct ideas of the true God.

It is written that, "without faith it is impossible to please Him." Those who do not please Him, can never partake of the powers and gifts of the science of Theology, because the keys and powers of this science emanate from Him as a free gift, but they are never given to those with whom He is not well pleased. The individual who would partake of this power, must therefore have faith in Him. But how can he believe in a being of whom he has no correct idea?

So vague, so foreign from the simple, plain truth, are the ideas of the present age, so beclouded is the modern mind with mysticism, spiritual nonentity, or immateriality in nearly all of its ideas of the person or persons of the Deity, that we are constrained to use the language of an ancient Apostle, as addressed to the learned of Athens—"Whom therefore ye ignorantly worship. Him declare I unto you."

Although there are facts in our own existence, which are beyond our present comprehension or capacity, which is true, in a higher sense, in relation to the Godhead, still the limited knowledge we are able to comprehend in relation to ourselves, may at least be rational, and be as clearly conveyed and understood as any other subject. So with our knowledge of Deity. Although there are facts beyond our reach in relation to His existence, attributes, and power, yet that which we may know and comprehend or express of Him, should be divested of all mystery, and should be as clearly conceived, expressed, and conveyed as any other item of truth or of science.

Jesus Christ, a little babe like all the rest of us have been, grew to be a man, was filled with a divine substance or fluid, called the Holy Spirit, by which he comprehended and spake the truth in power and authority; and by which he controlled the elements, and imparted health and life to those who were prepared to partake of the same.

This man died, being put to death by wicked men.

He arose from the dead the third day, and appeared to his disciples.

These disciples, on seeing him, supposed him to be a spirit only.

They may have possessed some of the vague ideas of men in more modern times, in regard to an immaterial existence beyond the grave: an existence unconnected with any real or tangible matter, or substance.

But their risen Lord adopted the most simple means of dispersing their mysticism, their spiritual vagaries or immateriality. He called upon them to handle him and see, "For" said he, "a spirit hath not flesh and bones, as ye see me have."

They accordingly handled him, examined the prints of the nails in his hands and feet, and the mark of the spear in his side. But, as if this was not enough in order to familiarize them still more with the facts of a material or tangible immortality, he ate and drank with them—partaking of a broiled fish and an honey-comb.

In short, he was with them for forty days, in which he walked, talked, ate, drank, taught, prophesied, commanded, commissioned, reasoned with and blessed them, thus familiarizing to them that immortality and eternal life which he wished them to teach in all the world.

He then ascended up in their presence, toward that planet where dwelt his Father and their Father, his God and their God.

While he was yet in sight in the open firmament, and they stood gazing upward, behold! two men stood by them in white raiment, and said—

"Ye men of Galilee why stand ye gazing up into heaven? This same Jesus which is taken up from you into heaven shall so come in like manner as ye have seen him go into heaven."

Here, then, we have a sample of an immortal God—a God who is often declared in the Scriptures to be like his father, "being the brightness of his glory, and the express image of his person," and possessing the same attributes as his Father, in all their fulness; a God not only possessing body and parts, but flesh and bones, and sinews, and all the attributes, organs, senses, and affections of a perfect man.

He differs in nothing from his Father, except in age and authority, the Father having the seniority, and, consequently, the right, according to the Patriarchal laws of eternal Priesthood, to preside over him, and over all his dominions, for ever and ever.

While on the one hand, this God claims affinity and equality, as it were, with his Father, he claims, on the other hand, affinity and equality with his brethren, on the earth, with this difference, however, that his person is a specimen of Divine, eternal Humanity, immortalized, and with attributes perfected; while his brethren who dwell in mortal flesh, although children of the same royal Parent in the heavens, are not yet immortalized, as it regards their fleshly tabernacles, and are not perfected in their attributes; and although joint heirs, are younger, he being the first born among many brethren in the spiritual world. They are therefore subject to him.

But every man who is eventually made perfect—raised from the dead, and filled, or quickened, with a fulness of celestial glory, will become like them in every respect, physically, and in intellect, attributes or powers.

The very germs of these Godlike attributes, being engendered in man, the offspring of Deity, only need cultivating, improving, developing, and advancing by means of a series of progressive changes, in order to arrive at the fountain "Head," the standard, the climax of Divine Humanity.

The difference between Jesus Christ and his Father is this—one is subordinate to the other, does nothing of himself, independently of the Father, but does all things in the name and by the authority of the Father, being of the same mind in all things. The difference between Jesus Christ and another immortal and celestial man is this—the man is subordinate to Jesus Christ, does nothing in and of himself, but does all things in the name of Christ, and by his authority, being of the same mind, and ascribing all the glory to him and his Father.

On account of the double relationship of Jesus Christ—with God the Father on one hand, and with man on the other, many have adopted the creed, that "Two whole and perfect natures" were blended in the person of Jesus Christ; that he was every way a God, and every way a man; as if God and man were two distinct species. This error came by reason of not knowing ourselves. For just in proportion as we comprehend ourselves in our true light, and our relationships and affinities with the past, present and future, with time and eternity, with Gods, angels, spirits and men, who have gone before us, and who will come after us, so, in proportion, we may be able to benefit by the keys of the mysteries of the Godhead, or, in other words, to know and comprehend Jesus Christ and his Father.

Gods, angels and men, are all of one species, one race, one great family widely diffused among the planetary systems, as colonies, kingdoms, nations, &c.

The great distinguishing difference between one portion of this race and another, consists in the varied grades of intelligence and purity, and also in the variety of spheres occupied by each, in the series of progressive being.

An immortal man, possessing a perfect organization of spirit, flesh, and bones, and perfected in his attributes, in all the fulness of celestial glory, is called a God.

An immortal man, in progress of perfection, or quickened with a lesser degree of glory, is called an angel.

An immortal spirit of man, not united with a fleshly tabernacle, is called a spirit.

An immortal man, clothed with a mortal tabernacle, is called a man.

It may then consistently enough be said, that there are, in a subordinate sense, a plurality of Gods, or rather of the sons of God; although there is one Supreme Head, who is over all, and through all, and in all His sons, by the power of His Spirit.

Jesus Christ and his Father are two persons, in the same sense as John and Peter are two persons. Each of them has an organized, individual tabernacle, embodied in material form, and composed of material substance, in the like-ness of man, and possessing every
organ, limb, and physical part that man possesses.

There is no more mystery connected with their oneness, than there is in the oneness of Enoch and Elijah, or of Paul and Silas.

Their oneness consists of a oneness of spirit, intelligence, attributes, knowledge, or power.

If Enoch, Elijah, Abraham, Peter, Paul, and millions of others ever attain to the immortal life, and their fleshly tabernacles be quickened by a fulness of celestial life and light, intelligence and power, then it can be said of them, they are one, as the Father and Son are one.

It could then be said of each of them, in him dwells all the fulness of the powers and attributes of the Eternal God, or, in other words, he possesses endless life, together with all intelligence, knowledge, light, and power. He therefore has the same mind as all the others—is in communication and in perfect union with each and all of them.

All these are Gods, or sons of God—they are the Kings, Princes, Priests, and Nobles of Eternity. But over them all there is a Presidency or Grand Head, who is the Father of all. And next unto him is Jesus Christ, the eldest born, and first heir of all the realms of light.

Every person knows, by reflection, that intelligence may be imparted without diminishing the store possessed by the giver. Therefore it follows, that millions of individual beings may each receive all the attributes of eternal life, and light, and power.

Again it follows, that in the use of this power, by consent and authority of the head, any one of these Gods may create, organize, people, govern, control, exalt, glorify and enjoy worlds on worlds, and the inhabitants thereof; or, in other words, each of them can find room in the infinitude of space, and unoccupied chaotic elements in the boundless storehouse of eternal riches, with which to erect for himself thrones, principalities, and powers, over which to reign in still increasing might, majesty and dominion, for ever and ever.

All these are kingdoms which, together with their Kings, are in subordination to the great Head and Father of all, and to Jesus Christ the first born, and first heir, among the sons of God.

All these kingdoms, with all their intelligences, are so many acquisitions to His dominion who is Lord of lords, and King of kings, and of whom it is written, by the Prophet Isaiah, "Of the increase of his kingdom there shall be no end."

All these are so many colonies of our race, multiplied, extended, transplanted, and existing for ever and ever, as occupants of the numberless planetary systems which do now exist, or which will roll into order, and be peopled by the operations of the Holy Spirit, in obedience to the mandates of the sons of God.

These kingdoms present every variety and degree in the progress of the great science of life, from the lowest degradation amid the realms of death, or the rudimental stages of elementary existence, upward through all the ascending scale, or all the degrees of progress in the science of eternal life and light, until some of them in turn arise to thrones of eternal power.

Each of these Gods, including Jesus Christ and his Father, being in possession of not merely an organized spirit, but a glorious immortal body of flesh and bones, is subject to the laws which govern, of necessity, even the most refined order of physical existence.

All physical element, however embodied, quickened, or refined, is subject to the general laws necessary to all existence.

Some of these laws are as follows—

First. Each atom, or embodiment of atoms, necessarily occupies a certain amount of space.

Second. No atom, or embodiment of atoms, can occupy the identical space occupied by other atoms or bodies.

Third. Each individual organized intelligence must possess the power of self motion to a greater or less degree.

Fourth. All voluntary motion implies an inherent will, to originate and direct such motion.

Fifth. Motion, of necessity, implies that a certain amount of time is necessary, in passing from one portion of space to another.

These laws are absolute and unchangeable in their nature, and apply to all intelligent agencies which do or can exist.

They, therefore, apply with equal force to the great, supreme, eternal Father of the heavens and of the earth, and to His meanest subjects.

It is, therefore, an absolute impossibility for God the Father, or Jesus Christ, to be everywhere personally present.

The omnipresence of God must therefore be understood in some other way than of His bodily or personal presence.

This leads to the investigation of that substance called the Holy Spirit.

As the mind passes the boundaries of the visible world, and enters upon the confines of the more refined and subtle elements, it finds itself associated with certain substances in themselves invisible to our gross organs, but clearly manifested to our intellect by their tangible operations and effects.

The very air we breathe, although invisible to our sight, is clearly manifested to our sense of feeling. Its component parts may be analyzed. Nay more, the human system itself is an apparatus which performs a chemical process upon that element. It is received into the system by the act of respiration, and there immediately undergoes the separation of its component parts.

The one part, retained and incorporated in the animal system, diffuses life and animation, by supplying the necessary animal heat, &c., while the other part, not adapted to the system, is discharged from the lungs to mingle with its native element.

There are several of these subtle, invisible substances but little understood as yet by man, and their existence is only demonstrated by their effects. Some of them are recognized under the several terms, electricity, galvanism, magnetism, animal magnetism, spiritual magnetism, essence, spirit, &c.

The purest, most refined and subtle of all these substances, and the one least understood, or even recognized, by the less informed among mankind, is that substance called the Holy Spirit.

This substance, like all others, is one of the elements of material or physical existence, and therefore subject to the necessary laws which govern all matter, as before enumerated.

Like the other elements, its whole is composed of individual particles. Like them, each particle occupies space, possesses the power of motion, requires time to move from one part of space to another, and can in no wise occupy two spaces at once. In all these respects it differs nothing from all other matter.

This substance is widely diffused among the elements of space. This Holy Spirit, under the control of the Great Eloheim, is the grand moving cause of all intelligences, and by which they act.

This is the great, positive, controlling element of all other elements. It is omnipresent by reason of the infinitude of its particles, and it comprehends all things.

It is the controlling agent or executive, which organizes and puts in motion all worlds, and which, by the mandate of the Almighty, or of any of His commissioned agents, performs all the mighty wonders, signs and miracles, ever manifested in the name of the Lord—the turning of the earth backward on its axis, the dividing of the sea, the removing of a mountain, the raising of the dead, or the healing of the sick.

It penetrates the pores of the most solid substances, pierces the human system to its most inward recesses, discerns the thoughts and intents of the heart. It has power to move through space with an inconceivable velocity, far exceeding the tardy motions of electricity, or of physical light.

It comprehends the past, present, and future, in all their fulness. Its inherent properties embrace all the attributes of intelligence
and affection.

It is endowed with knowledge, wisdom, truth, love, charity, justice, and mercy, in all their ramifications.

In short, it is the attributes of the eternal power and Godhead.

Those beings who receive of its fulness are called sons of God, because they are perfected in all its attributes and powers, and being in communication with it, can, by its use, perform all things.

Those beings who receive not a fulness, but a measure of it, can know and perform some things, but not all.

This is the true light, which in some measure illuminates all men. It is, in its less refined particles, the physical light which reflects from the sun, moon, and stars, and other substances; and by reflection on the eye, makes visible the truths of the outward world.

It is, also, in its higher degrees, the intellectual light of our inward and spiritual organs, by which we reason, discern, judge, compare, comprehend and remember the subjects within our reach.

Its inspiration constitutes instinct in animal life, reason in man, vision in the Prophets, and is continually flowing from the Godhead throughout all His creatures.

Such is the Godhead, as manifested in His words, and in His works. He dwells in His own eternal palaces of precious stones and gold, in the Royal City of the heavenly Jerusalem.

He sits enthroned in the midst of all His creations, and is filled and encircled with light unapproachable by those of the lower spheres.

He associates with myriads of His own begotten sons and daughters who, by translation or resurrection, have triumphed over death.

His ministers are sent forth from His presence to all parts of His dominions.

His Holy Spirit centres in His presence, and communicates with, and extends to the utmost verge of His dominions, comprehending and controlling all things under the immediate direction of His own will, and the will of all those in communication with Him, in worlds without end!

Chapter Six - Origin of the Universe

Boundless infinitude of time, and space,
And elements eternal! Who can trace
Earth with its treasures, Heaven with its spheres,
Time's revolutions, eternity's years?
But what are all these, when measured by thee,
But marks on thy dial, or motes on thy sea!

The idea of a God without "body, parts, or passions," is not more absurd or inconsistent than that modern popular doctrine, that all things were created from nonentity, or in other words, that something originated from nothing.

It is a self-evident truth, which will not admit of argument, that nothing remains nothing. Nonentity is the negative of all existence. This negative possesses no property or element upon which the energies of creative power can operate.

This mysticism must, therefore, share the fate of the other mysteries of false Theology and philosophy, which have for ages shrouded the world in the sable curtains of a long and dreary night. It must evaporate and disappear as a mere creation of fancy, while, in its place, are introduced the following self-evident and incontrovertible facts—

First. There has always existed a boundless infinitude of space.

Second. Intermingled with this space there exists all the varieties of the elements, properties, or things of which intelligence takes cognizance; which elements or things taken altogether compose what is called the Universe.

Third. The elements of all these properties or things are eternal, uncreated, self-existing. Not one particle can be added to them by creative power. Neither can one particle be diminished or annihilated.

Fourth. These eternal, self-existing elements possess in themselves certain inherent properties or attributes, in a greater or less degree; or, in other words, they possess intelligence, adapted to their several spheres.

These elements have been separated, by philosophers, into two grand divisions, viz.—

"PHYSICAL AND SPIRITUAL."

To a mind matured, or quickened with a fulness of intelligence, so as to be conversant with all the elements of nature, there is no use for the distinction implied in such terms.

To speak more philosophically, all the elements are spiritual, all are physical, all are material, tangible realities. Spirit is matter, and matter is full of spirit. Because all things which do exist are eternal realities, in their elementary existence.

Who then can define the precise point, in the scale of elementary existence, which divides between the physical and spiritual kingdoms? There are eyes which can discern the most refined particles of elementary existence. There are hands and fingers to whose refined touch all things are tangible.

In the capacity of mortals, however, some of the elements are tangible, or visible, and others invisible. Those which are tangible to our senses, we call physical; those which are more subtle and refined, we call spiritual.

Spirit is intelligence, or the light of truth, which filleth all things.

Its several emotions or affections, such as love, joy, &c., are but so many actions or motions of these elements, as they operate in their several spheres.

By these actions or emotions the elements manifest their eternal energies, attributes, or inherent powers.

In contemplating the works of creation, then, the student must not conceive the idea that space, or time, or element, or intelligence, was originated, but rather, that these are eternal, and that they constitute the energies which act, and the things acted upon, including the place and time of action.

The whole vast structure of universal organized existence, presents undeniable evidence of three facts, viz.—

First. The eternal existence of the elements of which it is composed.

Second. The eternal existence of the attributes of intelligence, and wisdom to design.

Third. The eternal existence of power, to operate upon and control these eternal elements, so as to carry out the plans of the designer.

It will be recollected that the last chapter recognizes a family of Gods, or, in other words, a species of beings, who have physical tabernacles of flesh and bones, in the form of man, but so constructed as to be capable of eternal life; that these tabernacles are quickened, or animated by a fulness of that holiest of all elements, which is called the Holy Spirit, which element or spirit, when organized, in individual form, and clothed upon with flesh and bones in the highest possible refinement, contains, in itself, a fulness of the attrib-

151

utes of light, intelligence, wisdom, love, and power; also that there are vast quantities of this spirit or element not organized in bodily forms, but widely diffused among the other elements of space.

A General Assembly, Quorum, or Grand Council of the Gods, with their President at their head, constitute the designing and creating power.

The motive power, which moves to action this grand creative power, is wisdom, which discovers a use for all these riches, and inspires the carrying out of all the designs in an infinite variety of utility and adaptation.

Wisdom inspires the Gods to multiply their species and to lay the foundation for all the forms of life, to increase in numbers, and for each to enjoy himself in the sphere to which he is adapted, and in the possession and use of that portion of the elements necessary to his existence and happiness.

In order to multiply organized bodies, composed of spiritual element, worlds and mansions composed of spiritual element would be necessary as a home, adapted to their existence and enjoyment. As these spiritual bodies increased in numbers, other spiritual worlds would be necessary, on which to transplant them.

Again. In order to enable these organized spirits to take upon them a fleshly tabernacle, physical worlds, with all their variety and fulness, would be necessary for their homes, food, clothing, &c., that they might be begotten, sustained, and born, that they might live, die, and rise again to receive their inheritances on their respective earths.

Hence the great work of regeneration of worlds, or the renovation and adaptation of the elements to the resurrection and eternal state of man, would also be endless, or eternally progressive.

Through every form of life, and birth, and change, and resurrection, and every form of progress in knowledge and experience, the candidates for eternal life must look upon the elements as their home; hence the elements, upon the principle of adaptation, must keep pace with the possessors who use them, in all the degrees of progressive refinement.

While room is found in infinite space:

While there are particles of unorganized element in Nature's storehouse:

While the trees of Paradise yield their fruits, or the Fountain of Life its river:

While the bosoms of the Gods glow with affection:

While eternal charity endures, or eternity itself rolls its successive ages, the heavens will multiply, and new worlds and more people be added to the kingdoms of the Fathers.

Thus, in the progress of events, unnumbered millions of worlds, and of systems of worlds, will necessarily be called into requisition, and be filled by man, and beast, and fowl, and tree, and all the vast varieties of beings, and things which ever budded and blossomed in Eden, or thronged the hills and valleys of the celestial Paradise.

When, in the endless progression of events, the full time had arrived for infinite wisdom to organize and people this globe which we inhabit, the chaotic elements were arranged in order. It appears at the commencement of this grand work, that the elements, which are now so beautifully arranged and adapted to vegetable and animal life, were found in a state of chaos, entirely unadapted to the uses they now serve.

There was one vast mixture of elements. Earth, water, soil, atmosphere— in short, the entire elements of which this mass was composed, seem to have been completely compounded, or mingled into one vast chaos, and the whole overwhelmed with a darkness so dense as to obscure the light of heaven.

Let us turn from the contemplation of scenes so sublimely fearful. Suffice it to say, the mandate came, darkness fled, the veil was lifted, light pierced the gloom, and chaos was made visible. Oh what a scene! A world without landscape, without vegetation, without animal life, without man, or animated beings. No sound broke on the stillness, save the voice of the moaning winds, and of dashing, foaming waters. Again, a voice comes booming over the abyss, and echoing amid the wastes, the mass of matter hears and trembles, and lo! the sea retires, the muddy shapeless mass lifts its head above the waters.

Molehills to mountains grow. Huge islands next appear, and continents at length expand to view, with hill and vale, in one wide dreary waste, unmeasured and untrodden.

The surface, warmed and dried by the cheering rays of the now resplendent sun, is prepared for the first seeds of vegetation.

A Royal Planter now descends from yonder world of older date, and bearing in his hand the choice seeds of the older Paradise, he plants them in the virgin soil of our new born earth. They grow and flourish there, and, bearing seed, replant themselves, and thus clothe the naked earth with scenes of beauty, and the air with fragrant incense. Ripening fruits and herbs at length abound. When, lo! from yonder world is transferred every species of animal life. Male and female, they come, with blessings on their heads; and a voice is heard again, "Be fruitful and multiply."

Earth—its mineral, vegetable and animal wealth—its Paradise, prepared, down comes from yonder world on high, a son of God, with his beloved spouse. And thus a colony from heaven, it may be from the sun, is transplanted on our soil. The blessings of their Father are upon them, and the first great law of heaven and earth is again repeated, "Be fruitful and multiply."

Hence, the nations which have swarmed our earth.

In after years, when Paradise was lost by sin; when man was driven from the face of his heavenly Father, to toil, and droop, and die; when heaven was veiled from view; and, with few exceptions, man was no longer counted worthy to retain the knowledge of his heavenly origin; then, darkness veiled the past and future from the heathen mind; man neither knew himself, from whence he came, nor whither he was bound. At length a Moses came, who knew his God, and would fain have led mankind to know Him too, and see Him face to face. But they could not receive His heavenly laws, or bide His presence.

Thus the holy man was forced again to veil the past in mystery, and, in the beginning of his history, assign to man an earthly origin.

Man, moulded from the earth, as a brick!

A Woman, manufactured from a rib!

Thus, parents still would fain conceal from budding manhood, the mysteries of procreation, or the sources of life's ever flowing river, by relating some childish tale of new born life, engendered in the hollow trunk of some old tree, or springing with spontaneous growth, like mushrooms, from out the heaps of rubbish. O man! When wilt thou cease to be a child in knowledge?

Man, as we have said, is the offspring of Deity. The entire mystery of the past and future, with regard to his existence, is not yet solved by mortals.

We first recognise him, as an organized individual or intelligence, dwelling with his Father in the eternal mansions. This organized spirit we call a body, because, although composed of the spiritual elements, it possesses every organ after the pattern, and in the likeness or similitude of the outward or fleshly tabernacle it is destined eventually to inhabit. Its organs of thought, speech, sight, hearing, tasting, smelling, feeling, &c., all exist in their order, as in the physical body; the one being the exact similitude of the other.

This individual, spiritual body, was begotten by the heavenly Father, in His own likeness and image, and by the laws of procreation.

154

It was born and matured in the heavenly mansions, trained in the school of love in the family circle, and amid the most tender embraces of parental and fraternal affection.

In this primeval probation, in its heavenly home, it lived and moved as a free and rational intelligence, acting upon its own agency, and, like all intelligence, independent in its own sphere. It was placed under certain laws, and was responsible to its great Patriarchal Head.

This has been called a "First Estate." And it is intimated that, of the spirits thus placed upon their agency, one-third failed to keep their first estate, and were thrust down, and reserved in chains of darkness, for future judgment. As these are not permitted to multiply their species, or to move forward in the scale of progressive being, while in this state of bondage and condemnation, we will trace them no further, as their final destiny is not revealed to mortals.

The spirits which kept their first estate, were permitted to descend below, and to obtain a tabernacle of flesh in the rudimental existence in which we find them in our present world, and which we will call a second estate.

In passing the veil which separates between the first and second estates, man becomes unconscious, and, on awakening in his second estate, a veil is wisely thrown over all the past.

In his mortal tabernacle he remembers not the scenes, the endearing associations, of his first, primeval childhood in the heavenly mansions. He therefore commences anew in the lessons of experience, in order to start on a level with the new born tabernacle, and to re-develope his intellectual faculties in a progressive series, which keep pace with the development of the organs and faculties of the outward tabernacle.

During his progress in the flesh, the Holy Spirit may gradually awaken his faculties; and in a dream, or vision, or by the spirit of prophecy, reveal, or rather awaken the memory to, a partial vision, or to a dim and half defined recollection of the intelligence of the past. He sees in part, and he knows in part; but never while tabernacled in mortal flesh will he fully awake to the intelligence of his former estate. It surpasses his comprehension, is unspeakable, and even unlawful to be uttered.

Having kept his second estate, and filled the measure of his responsibilities in the flesh, he passes the veil of death, and enters a third estate, or probationary sphere. This is called the world of spirits, and will be treated on more fully under its appropriate head.

Filling the measure of his responsibilities in the world of spirits, he passes, by means of the resurrection of the body, into his fourth estate, or sphere of human existence. In this sphere he finds himself clothed upon with an eternal body of flesh and bones, with every sense, and every organ, restored and adapted to their proper use.

He is thus prepared with organs and faculties adapted to the possession and enjoyment of every element of the physical or spiritual worlds, which can gratify the senses, or conduce to the happiness of intelligences. He associates, converses, loves, thinks, acts, moves, sees, hears, tastes, smells, eats, drinks and possesses.

In short, all the elements necessary to his happiness being purified, exalted, and adapted to the sphere in which he exists, are placed within his lawful reach, and made subservient to his use.

Chapter Seven - Destiny of the Universe

The mystic future, with its depths profound,
For ages counted as forbidden ground,
Now lifts its veil, that man may penetrate
The secret springs, the mysteries of fate;
Know whence he is, and whither he is bound,
And why the spheres perform their ample round.

The Grand Council having developed the vast structure of the heavens and the earth, with all their fulness, with the evident design of utility and adaptation to certain definite uses, it well becomes us to watch their progress, and to study with diligence their future and final destiny.

From a general traditional belief in an immaterial hereafter, many have concluded that the earth and all material things would be annihilated as mere temporary structures; that the material body, and the planets it occupies, make no part of eternal life and being; in short, that God, angels, and men, become at last so lost, dissolved, or merged in spirituality, or immateriality, as to lose all adaptation to the uses of the physical elements; that they will absolutely need no footstool, habitation, possession, mansion, home, furniture, food, or clothing; that the whole vast works and beautiful designs of the visible creation are a kind of necessary evil or clog on the spiritual life, and are of no possible use except to serve for the time being, for the home and sustenance of beings in their grosser, or rudimental state.

What a doleful picture! With what gloom and melancholy must intelligences contemplate the vast structure, as viewed in this light!

What a vastness of design!

What a display of wisdom!

What a field of labour in execution, do the works of creation present to the contemplative mind!

Yet all this wisdom of design, all this labour of execution, after serving a momentary purpose, to be thrown away as an incumbrance to real existence and happiness.

All these "spiritual," "immaterial" vagaries have no foundation in truth.

The earth and other systems are to undergo a variety of changes, in their progress towards perfection. Water, fire, and other elements are the agents of these changes. But it is an eternal, unchangeable fact, a fixed law of nature, easily demonstrated and illustrated by chemical experiment, that neither fire nor any other element can annihilate a particle of matter, to say nothing of a whole globe.

A new heaven and a new earth are promised by the sacred writers. Or, in other words, the planetary systems are to be changed, purified, refined, exalted and glorified, in the similitude of the resurrection, by which means all physical evil or imperfection will be done away.

In their present state they are adapted to the rudimental state of man. They are, as it were, the nurseries for man's physical embryo formation. Their elements afford the means of nourishing and sustaining the tabernacle, and of engendering and strengthening the organ of thought and mind, wherein are conceived and generated thoughts and affections which can only be matured and consummated in a higher sphere—thoughts pregnant with eternal life and love.

As the mind enlarges, the aspirations of an eternal being, once ennobled and honoured in the councils of heaven, among the sons of God, reach forth too high, and broad, and deep, to be longer adapted to the narrow sphere of mortal life. His body is imprisoned, chained to the earth, while his mind would soar aloft, and grasp the intelligence, wisdom and riches of the boundless infinite.

His rudimental body must therefore pass away, and be changed, so as to be adapted to a wider and more glorious sphere of locomotion, research, action and enjoyment.

When the planet on which he dwells has conceived, brought forth, and nourished the number of tabernacles assigned to it in its rudimental state, by infinite wisdom, it must needs be acted upon by a chemical process. The purifying elements; for instance, fire, must needs be employed to bring it through an ordeal, a refinement, a purification, a change commensurate with that which had before taken place in the physical tabernacle of its inhabitants. Thus renovated, it is adapted to resurrected man.

When man, and the planet on which he lives, with all its fulness, shall have completed all their series of progressive changes, so as to be adapted to the highest glories of which their several characters and species are capable, then, the whole will be annexed to, or numbered with the eternal heavens, and will there fulfil their eternal rounds, being another acquisition to the mansions, or eternally increasing dominions of the great Creator and Redeemer.

Worlds are mansions for the home of intelligences.

Intelligences exist in order to enjoy.

Joy, in its fulness, depends on certain principles, viz.—

Life Eternal. Love Eternal. Peace Eternal. Wealth Eternal. &c.

Without the first, enjoyment lacks durability.

Without the second, it can hardly be said to exist.

Without the third, it would not be secure.

Without the fourth, it must be limited, &c.

Eternal life, in its fulness, implies a spiritual intelligence, embodied in the likeness of its own species and clothed upon with an outward tabernacle of eternal, incorruptible flesh and bones. This state of existence can only be attained by the resurrection of the body, and its eternal re-union with the spirit.

Eternal life thus attained, and endowed with the eternal attributes of intelligence and love, could never exercise, or derive enjoyment from the affections of the latter, unless associated with other beings endowed with the same attributes.

Hence the object, or necessity of eternal kindred ties, associations, and affections, exercised as the attributes of that charity which never ends.

The third proposition, viz.—

Eternal Peace, could never be secured without the development of Eternal Law and government, which would possess in itself the attributes of infinite truth, goodness and power.

Any government short of this, could never guarantee Eternal Peace. It would be liable to be overthrown, by the lack of truth to discern, disposition to execute, or power to enforce, the measures necessary to insure peace.

The fourth proposition, viz.—

Eternal Wealth, must, of necessity, consist of an everlasting inheritance or title, defined and secured by this eternal government, to portions of the organized elements, in their pure, incorruptible and eternal state.

In order to be wealthy, eternal man must possess a certain portion of the surface of some eternal planet, adapted to his order or sphere of existence.

This inheritance, incorruptible, eternal in the heavens, must be sufficiently extensive for his accommodation, with all his family dependencies. It must also comprise a variety of elements, adapted to his use and convenience. Eternal gold, silver, precious stones, and other precious materials would be useful in the erection and furnishing of mansions, and of public and private dwellings or edifices.

These edifices combined, or arranged in wisdom, would constitute eternal cities. Gardens, groves, walks, rivulets, fountains, flowers and fruits, would beautify and adorn the landscape, please the eye, the taste, the smell; and thus contribute gladness to the heart of man.

Silks, linens, or other suitable materials would be necessary to adorn his person, and to furnish and beautify his mansions.

In short, eternal man, in possession of eternal worlds, in all their variety and fulness, will eat, drink, think, converse, associate, assemble, disperse, go, come, possess, improve, love and enjoy. He will increase in riches, knowledge, power, might, majesty and dominion, in worlds without end.

Every species of the animal creation ever organized by creative goodness, or that ever felt the pangs of death, or uttered a groan while subject to the king of terrors, or exulted in the joys of life and sympathy, and longed for the redemption of the body, will have part in the resurrection, and will live for ever in their own spheres, in the possession of peace, and a fulness of joy, adapted to their several capacities.

O Child of earth, conceived in corruption!
Brought forth in pain and sorrow! sojourning
In a world of mourning, mid sighs and tears,
And groans, and awaiting in sadness thy home
In the gloomy grave, as food for worms;
Lift up thy head, cast thine eyes around thee,

Behold yon countless hosts of shining orbs,
Yon worlds of light and life. Then turn to earth,
Survey the solid globe, its mineral wealth,
Its gems, its precious stones, its gold, its springs;
Its gardens, forests, fruits, and flowers;
Its countless myriads of breathing life,
From Mote to Man, through all the varied scale
Of animated being.
Visit the gloomy caverns of the dead,
The ancient sepulchre, where e'en the worm
Of death himself, has died for want of food,
And bones disjointed are crumbled fine, and
Mingled with the dust.
Nay, deeper still, descend the fathomless
Abyss of souls condemned, in darkness chained,
Or thrust in gloomy dungeons of despair—
Where the very names of Mercy, of Hope,
And of death's conqueror remain unknown.
Observe with care the whole, indulge in tears,
But hope, believe, and clothed with charity
Which never fails, thine eyes enlightened,
Thy person clad in light ethereal.
Time fades, and opens on eternity.
Again review the scene beheld before.
You startle, seem surprised! confused! o'erwhelmed!
Death is conquered, corruption is no more,
All is life, and the word ETERNITY
Is inscribed in characters indelible,
On every particle and form of life.

Socrates, Plato, Confucius, and many other philosophers and divines have written largely on the immortality of the soul or spirit of man.

Some of these have suffered, with joy and cheerfulness, imprisonment, torture, and even death, with only this limited view of eternal existence.

Could these martyrs to a portion of truth so limited, and yet so full of hope and consolation, have handled immortal flesh and bones in the persons of Enoch or Elijah translated, or of Jesus raised from the dead; could they have learned from their sacred lips, and realized the full import of that joyful sentence—

"Behold! I make all things new;"

...could they have contemplated eternal worlds, of matter in all its elements and forms of animal life, indissoluble and everlasting; could they have beheld eternal man, moving in the majesty of a God, amid the planetary systems, grasping the knowledge of universal nature, and with an intellect enlightened by the experience and observations of thousands and even millions of years; could they have had a glimpse of all this, and heard the promise—

"There shall be no more death,"

...issuing from the fountain of truth, prompted by infinite benevolence and charity, re-echoing amid the starry worlds, reaching down to earth, vibrating, with a thrill of joy, all the myriads of animated nature, penetrating the gloomy vaults of death, and the prisons of the spirit world, with a ray of hope, and causing to spring afresh, the well-springs of life, and joy, and love, even in the lonely dungeons of despair! O! how would their bosoms have reverberated with unutterable joy and triumph, in view of changing worlds.

Could the rulers of this world have beheld, or even formed a conception of, such riches, such nobility, such an eternal and exceeding weight of glory, they would have accounted the wealth, pleasures, honours, titles, dignities, glories, thrones, principalities and crowns of this world as mere toys—the playthings of a day, dross, not worth the strife and toil of acquiring, or the trouble of maintaining, except as a duty, or troublesome responsibility.

With this view of the subject, what man so base, so grovelling, so blind to his own interests, as to neglect those duties, self-denials, sacrifices, which are necessary in order to secure a part in the first resurrection, and a far more exceeding and eternal weight of glory in that life which never ends?

Chapter Eight - Key of Knowledge, Power, and Government

Heaven's Nobility, whom worlds obey,
Clad in the brightness of eternal day,
Enthroned in majesty, as "Priests and Kings,"
To whom the universe its incense brings!
Angels, its ministers! Heaven is its throne!
The stores of infinitude are all its own!

Having given a general view of the powers, operations and effects of Theology, as developed amongst the nations of antiquity, the mysteries of the Godhead, the law of nature, and the origin and destiny of the universe, the subject next in order is the KEY of knowledge, power and government, as developed in the heavens and on the earth, for the organization, order, peace, happiness, education, improvement, and exaltation of intelligences in the image of God—His sons and daughters.

The great family of man, comprising the inhabitants of unnumbered millions of worlds, in every variety and degree of progress, consists of five principal spheres, or grand divisions, in the scale of progressive being, viz.—

First. The Gods, composed of embodied spirits, who inhabit tabernacles of immortal flesh and bones in their most refined state, and who are perfected in all the attributes of intelligence and power.

Second. The Angels, who are also composed of spirits and immortal flesh and bones, less refined, and endowed with vast intelligence and power, but not a fulness.

Third. Embodied Spirits, without a tabernacle of flesh and bones. These are they who hate passed the veil of death, and are awaiting a resurrection.

Fourth. Embodied Spirits, with mortal tabernacles, as in the present world.

Fifth. Embodied Spirits, who have not yet descended to be clothed upon with mortality, but who are candidates for the same.

There is also a sixth division, but of those we need not speak, as they are not, as yet, included in the scale of progressive being, not having kept their first estate.

The spirits of all men in their primeval states, were intelligent. But among these intelligences some were more noble, that is to say, more intelligent than others.

And God said, these will I make rulers in my kingdoms.[A] Upon this principle was manifested the election, before the foundation of the world, of certain individuals to certain offices, as written in the Scriptures.

In other words, certain individuals, more intelligent than the others, were chosen by the Head, to teach, instruct, edify, improve, govern, and minister truth and salvation to others; and to hold the delegated powers or keys of government, in the several spheres of progressive being.

These were not only chosen, but set apart, by a holy ordinance in the eternal worlds, as Embassadors, Foreign Ministers, Priests, Kings, Apostles, &c., to fill the various stations in the vast empire of the Sovereign of all.

Jesus Christ, being the first Apostle thus commissioned, and the President of all the powers thus delegated, is Lord of lords, and King of kings, in the heavens and on the earth. Hence this Priesthood is called the Priesthood after the order of the Son of God. It holds the keys of all the true principles of government in all worlds, being without beginning of days or end of life. It was held by Adam, Seth, Enoch, Noah, Shem, Melchisedec, and others. Abraham obtained this Priesthood, and an election of the same in his seed after him to all generations. The decree went forth in an everlasting covenant, that in Abraham and his seed, all the nations and kindreds of the earth should be blessed.

Of this lineage according to the flesh were the Prophets, John the Baptist, Jesus Christ, and the Jewish Apostles. Since the covenant and election thus manifested, the keys of revelation, government and miraculous powers on earth have been held exclusively by the literal descendants of this noble and royal house.

The Gentiles could partake of a portion of the same blessings, but this could only be done through their ministry, and by adoption into the same family.

This election or covenant with the house of Israel will continue for ever. In the great restoration of all things, this lineage will hold the keys of Priesthood, salvation and government, for all nations. As saith the Prophet Isaiah— "The nation and kingdom that will not serve thee shall perish; yea, those nations shall be utterly wasted."

And again—"Ye shall be the priests of the Lord; men shall call you the ministers of our God: but strangers shall build your walls, and the sons of the alien shall be your ploughmen and your vine dressers."

This Priesthood, including that of the Aaronic, holds the keys of revelation of the oracles of God to man upon the earth; the power and right to give laws and commandments to individuals, churches, rulers, nations and the world; to appoint, ordain, and establish constitutions and kingdoms; to appoint kings, presidents, governors or judges, and to ordain or anoint them to their several holy callings, also to instruct, warn, or reprove them by the word of the Lord.

It also holds the keys of the administration of ordinances for the remission of sins, and for the gift of the Holy Spirit; to heal the sick, cast out demons, or work miracles in the name of the Lord; in fine, to bind or loose on earth and in heaven. For the exercise of all which powers the student of Theology will find abundant precedents in the sacred Scriptures.

Man holding the keys of the Priesthood and Apostleship after the order of the Son of God, are his representatives, or embassadors, to mankind. To receive them, to obey their instructions, to feed, clothe, or aid them, is counted the same, in the final judgment, as if all had been done to the Son of God in person. On the other hand, to reject them, or their testimony or message, or the word of God through them, in any matter, is counted the same as if done to Jesus Christ, in his own person. Indeed, such embassadors will be the final judges of the persons, rulers, cities or nations to whom they are sent.

Although the chosen instruments to hold the keys of this Priesthood must be the literal lineage of Israel, yet that lineage are not all thus commissioned, nor indeed are any of them Priests merely because they are of the chosen seed. Such an instrument must be revealed, and his ordination which he had before the world began, be renewed and confirmed upon his fleshly tabernacle, or he cannot be a Priest on earth.

One who already holds the authority, or keys of Priesthood, can reveal, by the word of the Lord, and ordain and anoint others to similar callings, and through these ordinances fill them with the Holy Spirit, as a qualification for their holy calling. By this means Joshua succeeded Moses, Elisha succeeded Elijah, &c. And by this means the great Apostle of the Father chose and ordained the Twelve Apostles of the Jews, and gave the keys or presidency of the kingdom to Peter.

There have, however, been times when, by a general martyrdom or apostacy, the keys of this power have been taken from the earth, (see chapters 2, 3, 4.) In such case there would be no longer visions, revelations or miraculous gifts from the Lord, manifested among men, because the Priesthood is the channel, and the ordinances are the means, through which such blessings are enjoyed by man. In the absence of these offices and powers, darkness, ignorance, superstition, priestcraft and kingcraft, idolatry, and every species of abuse, would fill the earth, and usurp the place of the true government of the kingdom of God.

The most remarkable and long continued instance of this kind, which perhaps ever transpired in our world, commenced with the destruction of the Apostles and Saints who immediately succeeded the Lord Jesus Christ, and continued until the present century, producing in its consequences all the human butcheries, wars, oppressions, misrule, ignorance, superstitions, kingcraft, priestcraft, and misery, which have visited the world in the false name of Christianity.

On the Western Hemisphere, the Apostleship, oracles, miracles, and gifts of the Spirit, ceased from among the people in the fourth century.

The precise time of the discontinuance of these powers on the eastern continents, or in the Roman world, is not known. Suffice it to say, the last of the Twelve Apostles predicted, in his vision on the Isle of Patmos, the reign of a certain power which should make war with the Saints, overcome them, be drunken with their blood, and hear rule over all nations. "And by thy sorceries," said he, "were all nations deceived." If these predictions have had their fulfilment, then it is the height of inconsistency for any one to contend, that Rome or any nation has perpetuated the Priesthood, Apostleship, or Church. This would be the same as to say, the Saints were destroyed, and yet perpetuated; all nations were deceived, and yet had the truth.

Could a universal or catholic power at once destroy the Saints, and perpetuate them? Could the same power, at the same time, be the conservator and promulgator of a system of universal salvation, and of universal deception?

But leaving the prediction, and the reasoning on this subject, what are the facts which present themselves for our own inspection, clearly visible to all men?

Do we not find the world, for many ages, and up to the present time, destitute of those manifestations, visions, powers, and keys of knowledge and government, which would enlighten, purify and exalt the race, and establish permanent righteousness and peace? In short, have the powers of the eternal Priesthood, as described and exemplified in the Holy Scriptures, and in this work, been manifested for the government of the Catholic, or Protestant world, or any nation thereof, since the destruction of the ancient Saints and Apostles?

If we answer this last question in the negative, then, we verify the truth of the prediction by the last of the Twelve; if in the affirmative, we deny both the truth of the prediction, and the facts which clearly present themselves in the past history and present circumstances of the world called "Christian."

When there is no longer a commissioned Priesthood perpetuated on the earth, it becomes necessary, in order to restore the government of God, for the man or men last holding the keys of such power, to return to the earth as ministering angels, and to select, by the word of the Lord, and ordain, certain individuals of the royal lineage of Israel, to hold the keys of such Priesthood, and to ordain others, and thus restore and re-organize the government of God, or His kingdom upon the earth.

After the destruction of the Apostles and Saints, who succeeded Jesus Christ, there is but one dispensation or restoration predicted by the Prophets.

That dispensation will fulfil the times of the Gentiles, complete their fulness, restore the kingdom to Israel, gather home their twelve tribes, organize them into a theocratic government, that is, a government founded and guided by Prophets, Priesthood, visions and revelations. It will, in fact, not only restore to them the ministration of angels, but receive its final consummation, by the resurrection of the ancient Saints, and their return to the earth, accompanied by the Son of God, in his own proper person. To this dispensation, all nations must submit.

All merely human religious or political institutions, all republics, states, kingdoms, empires, must be dissolved, the dross of ignorance and falsehood be separated, and the golden principles of unalloyed truth be preserved, and blended for ever in the one consolidated, universal, eternal government of the Saints of the Most High, and all nations shall serve and obey Him.

*[**Note A:** See Book of Abraham, translated from Papyrus, lately taken from the Catacombs of Thebes in Egypt.]*

Chapter Nine - Revival or Restoration of the Science of Theology Is the Present Age

A modern Prophet! Yes, a mighty Seer!
From Israel's royal line, must next appear;
Clad in the spirit of Elijah's power,
To prune the vineyard in th' eleventh hour;
To light the dawn of that effulgent day,
When King Messiah shall his sceptre sway.

The nineteenth century opened upon the world with far more favourable auspices than any other age since the destruction of the people of the Saints, and the reign of universal mystery. That spirit of freedom, and independence of thought, of speech, and of action, which a few centuries before had germinated in Europe, and which, after a stunted growth amid the thorns and thistles of kingcraft, the tares of priestcraft, and the weeds of superstition, in the old world, transplanted itself, and obtained a more vigorous growth in the new world, had now grown to a degree of maturity, and become consolidated, opening resources for all nations, under the inestimable guarantee of constitutional liberty.

To this standard the most enterprising, intelligent, and thinking of every nation in Europe, had commenced to gather like a flowing stream. Here, far separated from the practical influence, the false glare, the empty show, or even the senseless name and titles of a self-styled or imaginary nobility, their minds enlarged, their energies had full scope, and their intellectual faculties, unfettered and free, and surrounded with inexhaustible stores of unoccupied elementary riches, soon opened and developed new channels of thought, of action, of enterprise and improvement, the results of which have revolutionized the world in regard to geographical knowledge, commerce, intercommunication, transportation, travel, transmission of news, and mutual acquaintance and interchange of thought.

The triumphs of steam over earth and sea, the extension of railroads, and, above all, the lightning powers of the telegraph, are already, gradually but rapidly, developing, concentrating and consolidating the energies and interests of all nations, preparatory to the universal development of knowledge, neighbourly kindness, and mutual brotherhood.

Physically speaking, there seems to need but the consummation of two great enterprises more, in order to complete the preparations necessary for the fulfilment of Isaiah and other Prophets, in regard to the restoration of Israel to Palestine, from the four quarters of the earth, and the annual re-union of all nations to the new standards, holy shrines and temples of Zion and Jerusalem, under the auspices of that great, universal and permanent theocracy which is to succeed the long reign of mystery.

One of these is the Great Eastern Railway from Europe to India and China, with its branches, and accompanying telegraphic wires, centering at Jerusa-lem.

The other is the Great Western Railway, with its branches and accompany-ing telegraphic lines, from the Atlantic to the Pacific.

Politically speaking, some barriers yet remain to be removed, and some conquests to be achieved, such as the subjugation of Japan, and the triumph of constitutional liberty among certain nations where mind, and thought, and religion are still prescribed by law.

These things achieved, even the most incredulous in regard to the truth of Scripture Prophecy will be constrained to acknowledge, that, physically and politically speaking, there is nothing impossible, or even improbable, in the belief, that the twelve tribes of Israel will be concentrated from all nations in their own land, that Jerusalem will become the capitol of political govern-ment, the seat of knowledge, and the shrine of worship, for the yearly resort of all the nations and countries included in the world known to the Prophets of old; while the Western Hemisphere, separated as it is, by two great oceans, from the Old World, will naturally form its own central capitol, its Zion, or New Jerusalem, to which all its tribes and nations may perform their annual visits for instruction, devotion, and mutual interchange of thought, of fellow-ship and affection.

Can the student of prophecy contemplate all these preparations, clearly predicted thousands of years ago, and now bursting upon the world with seemingly preconcerted connexion and exactness, revolutionizing all things in a single age, and not be struck with the reflection, that the hand of God must be in all this, and that moral energy and spiritual light must be forth-coming from the heavens commensurate with the physical and political preparations for a new Era?

The same Prophets who have contemplated and described the develop-ment of national freedom, universal intercourse, mutual peace, knowledge, union of worship, reunion of the tribes of Israel; that have described highways, trains of cars flying as it were with a cloud, ocean steamers, ships, litters and swift beasts, as the instruments of restoration, have also predicted that, in connexion with all these preparations, a new dispensation should be manifested, a new covenant established, "A Standard" for the nation, "An Ensign" for the people. In short, "Swift Messengers," "Teachers," Prophets would be commissioned, revelations be manifested, and a new organization be developed, fitted to the times, and with principles and laws adapted to the reorganization, order, and government of a renovated world.

Where and when should we look for the "grain of mustard seed," the germ, the nucleus of such organization? Of course in a land of free institutions, where such organization could be legally developed, and claim constitutional protection, until sufficiently matured to defend itself against the convulsions, the death struggles, the agonizing throes, which precede the dissolution of the long reign of mystic tyranny; and at a time when modern freedom had been consolidated, nationalized, and its standard recognized among the nations.

Such an organization should also be looked for, in its first development, as cotemporary with the first dawn or development of the physical and political means provided for the same result.

The beginning of the present century gave birth to those chosen instruments who were destined to hold the keys of restoration for the renovation of the world.

The United States of America was the favoured nation raised up, with institutions adapted to the protection and free development of the necessary truths, and their practical results. And that Great Prophet, Apostle, and Martyr—

JOSEPH SMITH,

...was the Elias, the Restorer, the presiding Messenger, holding the keys of the "Dispensation of the fulness of times."

Yes, that extraordinary man, whose innocent blood is now dripping fresh, as it were, from the hands of assassins and their accessories, in the United States, was the chosen vessel honoured of God, and ordained by angels, to ordain other Apostles and Elders, to restore the Church and kingdom of God, the gifts of the Holy Spirit, and to be a messenger in the spirit and power of Elijah, to prepare the way of the Lord. "For, behold, he will suddenly come to his temple!"

Like John, who filled a similar mission preparatory to the first advent of the Son of God, he baptized with water unto repentance, for the remission of sins; like him, he was imprisoned; and like him, his life was taken from the earth; and finally, like all other true messengers, his message is being demonstrated by its progressive fulfilment—the powers, gifts, and signs following the administration of his message in all the world, and every minute particular of his predictions fulfilling in the order of events, as the wheels of time bring them due.

But in one important point his message differs from all former messages. The science of Theology revived by him will never decline, nor its keys be taken from the earth. They are committed to man for the last time. Their consummation will restore the tribes of Israel and Judah; overthrow all corrupt institutions; usher in the reign of universal peace and knowledge; introduce to the earth her lawful and eternal King, the crucified Nazarene, the resurrected Messiah; banish darkness and death, sorrow, mourning and tears, from the face of our globe; and crown our race with the laurels of victory and eternal life.

Ages yet unborn will rise up and call him blessed. A thousand generations of countless myriads will laud his praise and recount his deeds, while unnumbered nations bask in the light and enjoy the benefits of the institution founded by his instrumentality.

His kindred, the nation that gave him birth, and exulted at his death, nay, his very murderers and their posterity, will yet come bending unto him, and seek his forgiveness, and the benefits of his labours.

But, Oh! the pain! the dark despair! the torments of a guilty conscience! the blackness of darkness, in the lower hell, which the guilty wretches will experience before that happy day of deliverance!

Oh! the countless myriads of the offspring of innocent and honourable men who will walk the earth, tread on the ashes, or plow and reap over the bones and dust of those miserable murderers and their accomplices who have consented to the shedding of innocent blood! ere the final trump shall sound, which calls up their sleeping dust from its long slumbers in the tomb, and their spirits from the prison of the damned.

And even when this, to them almost interminable, period has rolled away, and they rise from the dead, instead of a welcome exaltation to the presence and society of the sons of God, an eternal banishment awaits them. They never can come where God and Christ dwell, but will be servants in the dominions of the Saints, their former victims.

This extraordinary personage was born in Sharon, Windsor County, Vermont, United States, December 23rd, 1805.

He removed with his father, during childhood, and settled near Palmyra, in Wayne County, New York. Amid these forest wilds he was reared a farmer, and inured to all the hardships, toils, and privations of a newly settled country. His education was therefore very limited. When about seventeen years of age, he had several open visions, in which a holy angel ministered to him, admonished him for his sins, taught him repentance, and faith in the crucified and risen Messiah, opened to him the Scriptures of the Prophets, unfolding the field of prophecy pertaining to the latter-day glory, and the doctrines of Christ and his ancient Apostles.

On the 22nd Sept., 1827, the angel directed him to a hill a few miles distant, called anciently Cumorah. Around this hill, in the fifth century of the Christian era, had rallied the last remnant of a once powerful and highly polished nation called the Nephites.

Here, two hundred and thirty thousand men, women and children, marshalled themselves for a last defence, in legions of ten thousand each, under their respective commanders, at whose head was the renowned Mormon, the General of a hundred battles. And here they received the enemy in untold numbers, and melted away before them, till none remained except a few that fled to the southward, and a few that fell wounded, and were left by the enemy among the unburied dead.

Among these latter were General Mormon, and his son, and second in command—General Moroni.

These were the last Prophets of a nation, now no more. They held the sacred records, compiled and transmitted from their fathers, from the remotest antiquity. They held the Urim and Thummim, and the compass of Lehi, which had been prepared by Providence, to guide a colony from Jerusalem to America.

In the hill Cumorah, they deposited all these things. Here they lay concealed for fourteen hundred years. And here did the angel Moroni direct the young Joseph to behold these sacred things, in their sacred deposit, and to receive, from these long-silent and gloomy archives, an abridged record of the whole, and with it the Urim and Thummim.

The abridged record, thus obtained, was engraved in Egyptian characters, on gold plates, by the hands of the two Prophets and Generals—Mormon and Moroni. By the instructions of the angel, and the use of the Urim and Thummim, the youthful Joseph, now a Prophet and Seer, was enabled to translate the abridgment, or rather the unsealed portion which was destined for the present age.

This done, the angel of the Lord appeared to three other persons, called Martin Harris, Oliver Cowdery, and David Whitmer; showed them the golden plates, and the engravings thereon; bore testimony of their correct translation by the Prophet Joseph, and commanded them to bear a faithful testimony of the same. Two of these were respectable farmers, and the other was a school-master.

Early in 1830, this translation with the accompanying testimony, was published in English, in the United States, under the title of the Book Of Mormon.

It is now, 1853, translated and published in nearly all European languages.

This book more deeply interests the world, and every intelligent, accountable being therein, than any other book, save the Jewish Scriptures, which is now extant. Its history penetrates the otherwise dark oblivion of the past, as it regards America, through the remote ages of antiquity; follows up the stream of the generations of man, till arriving at the great fountain, the distributor of nations, tribes and tongues—the Tower of Babel, it ceases, or is lost in, and sweetly blended with, that one great undivided Adamic river, whose source is in Paradise, the cradle of man; whose springs issue from beneath the throne of the Eternal; and whose secret fountains comprise the infinite expanse, the boundless ocean of intellect, fact, and historic truth, as recorded in the archives of eternity. Its prophetic vision opens the events of unborn time. The fate of nations; the restoration of Judah and Israel; the downfall of corrupt churches and institutions; the end of superstition and misrule; the universal prevalence of peace, truth, light and knowledge; the awful wars which precede those happy times; the glorious coming of Jesus Christ as King; the resurrection of the Saints, to reign upon the earth; the great, grand rest of a thousand years; the jubilee of universal nature upon our planet, are all predicted in that book. The time and means of their fulfilment are pointed out with clearness, showing the present age more pregnant with events than all the ages of Adam's race which have gone before it. Its doctrines are developed in such plainness and simplicity, and with such clearness and precision, that no man can mistake them. They are there as they flowed from the mouth of a risen Redeemer, in the liquid eloquence of love, mingled with immortal tears of joy and compassion, and were written by men whose tears of overwhelming affection and gratitude bathed his immortal feet.

It was ascertained by revelation, by means of the Urim and Thummim, that the youthful Prophet Joseph was of the house of Israel, of the tribe of Joseph.

He continued to receive visions, revelations, and the ministry of angels, by whom he was at length ordained to the Apostleship, or High Priesthood after the order of Melchizedec, to hold the keys of the kingdom of God, the dispensation of the fulness of times.

Thus qualified, he proceeded, on the 6th of April, A.D. 1830, to organize the Church of the Saints, which then consisted of six members. The gifts of healing, of prophecy, of visions and miracles, began to be manifested among the believers, thus confirming his testimony with signs following.

In this same year, the principles restored by him were proclaimed, and Branches of the Church were organized in various parts of his own State, in Pennsylvania, Ohio, and elsewhere; and the number of his disciples increased from six members, to upwards of one thousand.

During the three following years, hundreds of ministers, ordained by him, were sent out in all directions through the country, and Branches of the Church were organized in most of the States of the American Union.

In eighteen hundred and thirty five, he ordained by commandment of the Lord, a quorum of Twelve Apostles, and several quorums of seventy, as a traveling ministry.

In 'thirty-six, a temple was completed and dedicated, in Kirtland, Ohio; in which these quorums, and the Priesthood in general were assembled in a school of the Prophets, and were instructed, and anointed to their holy calling. In this same year, some of the Apostles visited Upper Canada, and spread the fulness of the Gospel in Toronto and all the region round, gathering several Branches of the Church.

In 'thirty-seven, a mission was sent to England, which was attended with the same powers, and with remarkable success.

In 'thirty-eight, the State of Missouri undertook the extermination of the Church from its borders, murdered many men, women and children, and finally succeeded in the forcible expulsion of about ten thousand people, and the seizure of their lands and property.

In eighteen hundred and forty, the quorum of the Twelve Apostles visited England, gathered great numbers into the Church, and published the Book of Mormon, and several other works, among which was a periodical called the Millennial Star, which now, in 1853, has a circulation of nearly eighteen thousand copies weekly.

Between the years 'forty, and 'forty-four, our youthful Prophet gathered about him many thousands of his disciples; erected the great city of Nauvoo, on the banks of the Mississippi; commenced the erection of one of the most splendid temples in the world; and organized a legion of citizen soldiers for its defence. This legion comprised nearly six thousand men, and was commanded by the young Prophet Joseph, who held a government commission, as Lieutenant-General.

From this centre of science and heavenly light, there emanated rays, by the aid of a foreign ministry, penetrating afar, and lighting up the dawn of that effulgent day which is destined to break over all the earth, and shine for ever.

Apostles, High Priests, Elders, Counsellors and Ministers of every degree, here thronged our youthful Prophet and hero, and were taught in this great school of Theology and spiritual philosophy; while a hundred thousand disciples in the nation and beyond the seas, looked to this centre for light and instruction.

Such was the progress of the science of Theology, revived in the present age; such the result of fourteen years of the ministry of an unlettered youth, crying in the wilderness the proclamation of repentance, baptizing for the remission of sins, and holding the keys of this divine, eternal power.

His unparalleled success, and still increasing influence, now alarmed his former persecutors, and raised their jealousy and envy to the highest pitch of frenzy and madness.

Several counties of Illinois combined with the former enemies, who had robbed and destroyed the Saints in Missouri, and, calling public meetings, passed resolutions to destroy the city of Nauvoo, and to force the Saints, once more, to abandon their homes and farms to the possession of the land pirates. They also entered into covenant, to take the life of the young Joseph.

To resist this overwhelming storm, our hero and Prophet marshalled his legion of six thousand men, in his beloved city of Nauvoo, prepared for the most vigorous defence, and awaited the onset. The cowardly enemy soon discovered the impropriety of an open attack, and resolved on stratagem. They caused a magistrate of their own number to issue a writ; and sent a constable to bring the person of Joseph into the midst of those who had sworn to kill him. To yield to this mockery would be to lose his life. To resist it would be construed into treason and would bring on him the whole forces of the State. This stratagem succeeded—Nauvoo, its legion and its general, were declared in rebellion. His Excellency, Thomas Ford, Governor of the State of Illinois, mustered an army, marched to the scene of conflict, took sides with the enemy, and in fact incorporated their entire forces with his own troops.

With this formidable force he marched to Carthage, a small town eighteen miles from Nauvoo. He then sent a captain, named Singleton, to take command of the Nauvoo legion, and demanded its Lieutenant-General to repair to Carthage, and place himself in the hands of those who had publicly combined to take his life. Sooner than have submitted to these insults and humiliating demands, the legion would have joyfully marched to Carthage, and cut to pieces this cowardly band of rebels against American institutions and all the rights of man.

But the Saints were located between two powerful States, who were now combined against the laws, constitutions and liberties of their country. To destroy one army, or even resist its most extravagant demands, would be to draw upon themselves and families, the overwhelming forces of the ferocious, ignorant, and worse than savage beings, who had long thirsted for their plunder and their blood.

The young Prophet had no confidence in the Governor's pledge to protect his person. He felt the hour had come, when his own blood alone could appease the enemy, and preserve the lives of his flock. He restrained the ardour of the legion; called upon them, by the love they had ever borne to him as a Prophet and Apostle; and conjured them, by the respect and confidence they had shown him as their General, to submit to the extravagant demands of his Excellency, and leave the event with God. He now took an affectionate leave of his beloved legion, who were dissolved in tears; tore himself from the embraces of his aged and widowed mother, and frantic wife and children, and repaired to Carthage. He was accompanied by his brother Hyrum, and the two of the Twelve, that were not abroad on foreign missions, who would not forsake him. On the way he was cheerful but solemn. He spoke little, but observed to those about him, "I am going like a lamb to the slaughter; but I am calm as a summer's morning; I have a conscience void of offence towards God, and towards all men. I shall die innocent: and it shall yet be said of me— He was murdered in cold blood."

Arriving at Carthage, he delivered himself to his enemies; answered to the charge in the original writ, to enforce which all the Governor's forces had been mustered, and was then committed to prison to answer the charge of treason.

In this dungeon he was still accompanied by the two Apostles and his brother Hyrum, who were determined to die with him.

Here as the four friends sat in the upper room, singing hymns, on the afternoon of the 27th day of June, 1844, the prison was suddenly surrounded with demons in the flesh, armed with muskets and bayonets, and their faces as black as Cain—the original murderer. These commenced firing through the doors and windows of the prison, while a portion assaulted and broke open the door. Hyrum suddenly fell, and died without a groan, being pierced with four balls. Taylor fled, wounded and bleeding, to the window, and was about to throw himself out, when a ball aimed at his heart, hit his watch in his vest pocket, and threw him back into the room. The other Apostle, Willard Richards, stood and parried the guns with his hand staff, receiving slight injury.

In the midst of all this scene, the Prophet's presence of mind did not forsake him. He saw his brother Hyrum fall, stiffen and die. He then exclaimed, in the anguish of his soul—"O my brother!" and sprang for the window, amid showers of ball as thick as hail. He instantly threw himself from the upper story into the midst of the bristling bayonets of the enemy, and, on alighting, was pierced with a shower of balls, and instantly died without a struggle or a groan.

His presence of mind, and prompt action, in thus throwing himself among the enemy, drew them from the prison in time to save the lives of the two Apostles, which was, no doubt, the object of this, the last glorious act of his life.

Thus ended the mortal career of a youth who had revealed the ancient history of a continent; restored to man the keys and powers of the divine science of Theology; organized the Church and kingdom of God, and revealed, and re-established those principles, which will eventually prevail, and govern the sons of earth, in countless ages yet unborn. "The good shepherd," said Jesus, "layeth down his life for the sheep."

When the news of this horrid tragedy spread abroad, the fear of vengeance from the Nauvoo legion seized the Governor, his troops, and the whole gang of pirates; all fled, and even the inhabitants of the guilty villages in the vicinity, vacated their habitations, and fled in terror and dismay.

As the news reached Nauvoo, a thrill of horror and of anguish unutterable ran, as with electricity, through every pulse. The legion sprang to arms, and would have desolated the whole rebel counties, now left unprotected, had not their judgments balanced the burning attribute of justice which swelled their bosoms.

As it was, they smothered their resentment, and prepared for the burial of the illustrious dead. The bodies of the two martyrs were borne to the city; being met by the entire populace, bowed with sorrow, bathed in tears, and their bosoms upheaved with a sense of sorrow and outraged humanity, such as, perhaps, an entire populace at once never felt, since man was doomed to mourn.

The Twelve, who were abroad, soon returned, soothed and comforted the sheep, and exhorted them to union and perseverance. The work on the temple was resumed, and finally completed, at an expense of many hundred thousand dollars. In this holy edifice, after its dedication to the Lord, a portion of the Priesthood received those holy washings, anointings, keys, ordinances, oracles and instructions, which were yet wanting to perfect them in the fulness of the Priesthood.

In the autumn of 1845, the enemy again rallied, and commenced to desolate the borders of the Nauvoo settlements by fire and sword.

Wearied with long continued vexation and persecution, the council of the Apostles now determined to seek peace for the Saints, amid the far-off and almost unexplored deserts and mountains of the interior. In February, 1846, this emigration was commenced, headed by the Apostles and their families.

On the 24th of July, 1847, the first pioneers of this vast emigration, headed by the President of the whole Church, Brigham Young, entered the Valley of Great Salt Lake.

In the meantime, the beautiful Nauvoo, and its surrounding farms and villas fell a prey to the enemy, after a vigorous defence. Its temple, the pride and glory of America, was laid in ashes. Its last remnant plundered, robbed of their all, sick, destitute, wounded, bleeding, dying, at length disappeared beyond the horizon of the illimitable plains of the west, and, for a moment, the curtain of oblivion closed over this strange drama, and the kingdom of God seemed lost to mortal view.

Again it rises, and what do we behold!

The banner of freedom unfurled a thousand miles from the frontiers of the persecuting foe; its waving folds, amid the snow-clad peaks of the Rocky mountains, inviting to liberty and light, the oppressed of every clime; and a free and sovereign State rising, in majesty and smiling splendour, amid the fastnesses of nature's eternal ramparts; while the exhaustless treasures of the golden mountains of California, revealed by the providence-guiding keys of modern Theology, are poured like a flowing stream into the treasury of the Lord, to aid in the gathering and subsistence of the Saints.

Can the student of Theology contemplate all these grand events and their results, all verging to one focus, all combining to prepare the way for the consummation of the entire volume of unfulfilled prophecy, and still be so much at a loss as to query, like one of old, "Art thou he that should come; or, look we for another?" If so, we can only recommend, to one so slow of heart, to search the Scriptures, and all good books extant on the subject. And, while he searches, let him turn from his sins, and live in newness of life, and call upon God, the Father of all, in the name of Messiah, that his understanding may be enlightened, and his stubborn heart subdued, and constrained to yield to the force of Truth.

Chapter Ten - Keys of Initiation in Practical Theology

Is't possible! A sinful man like me,
A candidate for heaven's mystery!
May I approach the gate and enter in,
Be wash'd and cleans'd from all my former sin,
Renew'd in spirit, and partake the power
Of bless'd Theology from this good hour.

The student of this deeply interesting science, who has traced, with us, the thrilling incidents of its history on earth, till he finds it restored in all its beauties, and its powers taking root in the earth, to bear eternal fruit, will, doubtless, feel a desire to be instructed in the first principles—the ordinances or means by which he may personally partake of its benefits, and exercise its gifts.

There are certain qualifications, or personal preparations indispensably necessary, without which, no person can be a proper candidate for blessings so divine.

First. He must believe in Jesus Christ, and in the testimony of the Apostle, or commissioned officer, to whom he looks for the administration of these blessings.

Secondly. He must forsake a sinful course of life; must deny himself of every impure or unlawful indulgence; must do right with his fellow creatures, and determine to keep the commandments of Jesus Christ.

With these qualifications he comes to the Apostle, Elder, or Priest of the Church of the Saints, who, after a covenant on the part of the candidate to forsake his sins, and keep the commandments of Jesus Christ, goes down into the water with him, and there buries him, in the name of the Father, Son and Holy Spirit, for remission of sins, and then raises him from his watery grave.

This ordinance is to represent the death, burial and resurrection of Jesus Christ, and is called Baptism.

Having passed through this ordinance, the hands of some one, or more, of the authorised Priesthood, are next laid upon the head of the candidate, in the same sacred names, and the gift of the Holy Spirit is confirmed upon him. This baptism of water and of the Spirit is called a new birth; and it is in reality a repetition of the natural birth, or entrance into the elements of a new existence.

To realise this, the student must be indoctrinated in the philosophy of his natural birth, which involves three principles; viz.—"The spirit, the water and the blood."

The embryo formation of the human body, is commenced and sustained by blood and spirit, in the womb of nature, where, until the period of birth, it floats in the element of water. At birth, then, it is literally born of water, that is, it emerges from that element in which it has been so long immersed, into a different element, called the atmosphere, which then becomes a necessary element of existence.

To be born again, then, is to enter into the same element, suspend the breath in the watery womb, and emerge from that element into the atmosphere, and again gasp the first breath in the new creation; while, at the same time, the blood of Atonement is applied to the individual, for remission of sins, and is followed by the outpouring of the Holy Spirit of promise. As it is written—"There are three that bear record on the earth; the spirit, the water, and the blood."

The things of this visible creation, are the patterns of things in the invisible world; and are so arranged as to exactly correspond—the one answering to the other, as face to face in a mirror.

The immersion in water, in the name of the Father, Son, and Holy Spirit, for remission of sins; and the baptism of the Holy Spirit, which follows according to promise, by the laying on of the hands of the holy Priesthood; were instituted from before the foundation of the world, as a pattern of the birth, death, resurrection and new life of man.

The candidate is now initiated into the first principles of the science of Divine Theology. His mind is quickened, his intellectual faculties are aroused to intense activity. He is, as it were, illuminated. He learns more of divine truth in a few days, than he could have learned in a life time in the best merely human institutions in the world.

His affections are also purified, exalted, and increased in proportion. He loves his heavenly Father, and Jesus Christ, with a perfect love. He also loves the members of the Church, or the body of Christ, as he loves his own soul; while his bosom swells with the tenderest sympathies, and emotions of good will and benevolence, for all mankind. He would make any sacrifice which might be expedient, to do good. He would lay down his life most cheerfully, without one moment's hesitation, or regret, if required of him by the cause of truth.

He also feels the spirit of prayer and watchfulness continually, and pours out his soul in the same, and finds he is answered in all things which are expedient. He is now in a fit capacity to exercise some one or more of the spiritual gifts.

He may perhaps speak in power, in the word of wisdom, in the word of knowledge, in prophecy, or in other tongues. He may see a vision, dream an inspired dream, or possess the gift to be healed, or to heal others, by the laying on of hands in the name of Jesus Christ.

To impart a portion of the Holy Spirit by the touch, or by the laying on of hands; or to impart a portion of the element of life, from one animal body to another, by an authorized agent who acts in the name of God, and who is filled therewith, is as much in accordance with the laws of nature, as for water to seek its own level; air, its equilibrium; or heat, and electricity, their own mediums of conveyance.

This law of spiritual fluid, its communicative properties, and the channel by which it is imparted from one person to another, bear some resemblance, or analogy, to the laws and operations of electricity. Like electricity, it is imparted by the contact of two bodies, through the channel of the nerves.

But the two fluids differ very widely. The one is a property nearly allied to the grosser elements of matter; not extensively endowed with the attributes of intelligence, wisdom, affection, or moral discrimination. It can therefore be imparted from one animal body to another, irrespective of the intellectual or moral qualities of the subject or recipient. The other is a substance endowed with the attributes of intelligence, affection, moral discrimination, love, charity, and benevolence pure as the emotions which swell the bosom, thrill the nerves, or vibrate the pulse of the Father of all.

An agent filled with this heavenly fluid cannot impart of the same to another, unless that other is justified, washed, cleansed from all his impurities of heart, affections, habits or practices, by the blood of atonement, which is generally applied in connexion with the baptism of remission.

A man who continues in his sins, and who has no living faith in the Son of God, cannot receive the gift of the Holy Spirit through the ministration of any agent, however holy he may be. The impure spirit of such a one will repulse the pure element, upon the natural laws of sympathetic affinity, or of attraction and repulsion.

An intelligent being, in the image of God, possesses every organ, attribute, sense, sympathy, affection, of will, wisdom, love, power and gift, which is possessed by God Himself.

But these are possessed by man, in his rudimental state, in a subordinate sense of the word. Or, in other words, these attributes are in embryo; and are to be gradually developed. They resemble a bud—a germ, which gradually developes into bloom, and then, by progress, produces the mature fruit, after its own kind.

The gift of the Holy Spirit adapts itself to all these organs or attributes. It quickens all the intellectual faculties, increases, enlarges, expands and purifies all the natural passions and affections; and adapts them, by the gift of wisdom, to their lawful use. It inspires, developes, cultivates and matures all the fine toned sympathies, joys, tastes, kindred feelings and affections of our nature. It inspires virtue, kindness, goodness, tenderness, gentleness and charity. It developes beauty of person, form and features. It tends to health, vigour, animation and social feeling. It developes and invigorates all the faculties of the physical and intellectual man. It strengthens, invigorates, and gives tone to the nerves. In short, it is, as it were, marrow to the bone, joy to the heart, light to the eyes, music to the ears, and life to the whole being.

In the presence of such persons, one feels to enjoy the light of their countenances, as the genial rays of a sunbeam. Their very atmosphere diffuses a thrill, a warm glow of pure gladness and sympathy, to the heart and nerves of others who have kindred feelings, er sympathy of spirit. No matter if the parties are strangers, entirely unknown to each other in person or character; no matter if they have never spoken to each other, each will be apt to remark in his own mind, and perhaps exclaim, when referring to the interview—"O what an atmosphere encircles that stranger! How my heart thrilled with pure and holy feelings in his presence! What confidence and sympathy he inspired! His countenance and spirit gave me more assurance, than a thousand written recommendations, or introductory letters." Such is the gift of the Holy Spirit, and such are its operations, when received through the lawful channel—the divine, eternal Priesthood.

Chapter Eleven - Philosophy of Miracles

Trembling with awe and fear, the mind inquires—
"What master spirit, now, the bard inspires;
What bold philosophy shall dare assign
A law to govern miracles divine—
Tell how effects transpire without a cause,
And how kind nature breaks kind nature's laws?"

Among the popular errors of modern times, an opinion prevails that miracles are events which transpire contrary to the laws of nature, that they are effects without a cause.

If such is the fact, then, there never has been a miracle, and there never will be one. The laws of nature are the laws of truth. Truth is unchangeable, and independent in its own sphere. A law of nature never has been broken. And it is an absolute impossibility that such law ever should be broken.

That which, at first sight, appears to be contrary to the known laws of nature, will always be found, on investigation, to be in perfect accordance with those laws. For instance, had a sailor of the last century been running before the wind, and met with a vessel running at a good rate of speed, directly in opposition to the wind and current, this sight would have presented, to his understanding, a miracle in the highest possible sense of the term, that is, an event entirely contrary to the laws of nature, as known to him. Or if a train of cars, loaded with hundreds of passengers, or scores of tons of freight, had been seen passing over the surface of the earth, at the rate of sixty miles per hour, and propelled, seemingly, by its own inherent powers of locomotion, our fathers would have beheld a miracle—an event which would have appeared, to them, to break those very laws of nature with which they were the most familiar.

If the last generation had witnessed the conveyance of news from London to Paris, in an instant, while they knew nothing of the late invention of the electric telegraph, they would have testified, in all candour, and with the utmost assurance, that a miracle had been performed, in open violation of the well known laws of nature, and contrary to all human knowledge of cause and effect.

But, once familiar with the arts of the living age, all those miracles cease to be such, and the laws of nature, and of cause and effect, are found to be still moving, unimpaired, in all the harmony of primeval existence and operation.

The same views will apply, with equal force, to all the spiritual phenomena of the universe.

The terms miracle and mystery must become obsolete, and finally disappear from the vocabulary of intelligences, as they advance in the higher spheres of intellectual consistency. Even now they should be used only in a relative or limited sense, as applicable to those things which are not yet within reach of our powers, or means of comprehension.

We will here remind the student of two principles, or laws of existence, developed in a former chapter of this work, which will account for all the miraculous powers of the universe—all the mighty works ever manifested by God, or by His servants.

First. All the elements of the material universe are eternal.

Second. There is a divine substance, fluid or essence, called Spirit, widely diffused among these eternal elements.

This spiritual substance is the most refined, subtle, and powerful element in the universe. It is endowed with all wisdom, all knowledge, all intelligence and power. In short, it is the light, life, power and principle of all things, by which they move; and of all intelligences, by which they think.

This divine element, or Spirit, is the immediate, active, or controlling agent, in all holy, miraculous powers.

Angels, and all holy men, perform all their miracles, simply, to use a modern magnetic term, by being in "communication" with this divine substance. Two beings, or two millions—any number thus placed in "communication"—all possess one mind. The mind of the one is the mind of the other, the will of the one is the will of the other, the word of the one is the word of the other. And the holy fluid, or Spirit, being in communication with them all, goes forth to control the elements, and to execute all their mandates which are legally issued, and in accordance with the mind and wisdom of the Great Eloheim.

God the Father is the Head. The mandates of Jesus Christ must be in the name of the Father.

The mandates of angels, or of holy men, in order to be legal, or of due force and power, must be issued in the name of Jesus Christ, or of the three who compose the Head Council; and must be in accordance with their united mind and will. The Holy Spirit then goes forth and executes their mandates. This agency being invisible, and the effect visible, the act performed appears to those who are unacquainted with spiritual agency, as a miracle, or an effect without a cause.

When Jesus Christ was clothed upon with a mortal tabernacle, he had not the fulness of this divine substance at the first, but grew and increased in the same, till, being raised from the dead, he received a fulness and, therefore, had all power, in heaven and on earth.

His Apostles received a portion of this Spirit, but not a fulness, while they were mortal; therefore, they could know and perform some things, but not all.

The members of the Church also partook of this Spirit, through the ministry of the Apostles, by which miraculous gifts were imparted unto them, some to one, and some to another: some to speak in tongues; some to interpret, or translate from one language into another; some to prophesy, see visions, or converse with angels; and others to control, or cast out devils, or heal the sick; and others, again, to teach and edify the Church, or the world, by the word of wisdom, and by the word of knowledge.

All these gifts and miracles were the workings of that one, and the self same Spirit given to the members of the Church of the Saints, while the world did not partake of a sufficient measure of the Spirit to possess these gifts. The reason of this is, that they did not repent, and believe in Jesus Christ, and be baptized in his name, and receive the gift of the Holy Spirit, by the laying on of the hands of the Priesthood—these duties and ordinances, being the legal or appointed channel by which the gift of the Holy Spirit was imparted. The reason why these gifts of the Spirit have not been enjoyed in all ages of the so called "Christian Church" is because it is not the true Church; nor, is the true ministry or Apostleship to be found among the Church, or Churches, where these gifts are denied. Every minister and member of such institutions have need to repent, and be baptized, in the name of Jesus Christ, for remission of sins; and to receive the gift of the Holy Spirit, by the laying on of hands of those who have authority, in order to enter into the kingdom of God.

These ordinances, ministered by a legal Priesthood, being divinely appointed, are the only legitimate means by which man may receive and exercise these divine powers; or, in other words, they are the means ordained of God, by which one being may communicate or impart a portion of this divine substance to another, so as to place that other in communication with the Father, Son, and Holy Spirit, and with angels, and the spirits of just men in the world of spirits, and with the members of the true Church on the earth.

To heal a person by the touch, or by the laying on of hands in the name of Jesus Christ, or to impart the Holy Spirit by the laying on of hands, is as much in accordance with the laws of nature, as for water to seek its own level, an apple to fall to the ground when loosened from the tree where it grew, quicksilver to attract its own affinities, or the magnet to obey its own laws.

As the electric fluid obeys its own laws upon the wire, so, also, does the spiritual or holy fluid convey itself, through certain channels, from one body to another, in accordance with certain legitimate laws.

The usual channel for all spiritual fluids, whether holy or impure, in their operations upon the human system, or in their passage from one animal body to another, is the nerves.

A person commissioned of Jesus Christ, and filled with this spiritual substance, can impart of the same to another, provided there is a preparation of heart, and faith on the part of the receiver. Or if, as in cases of healing, casting out devils, &c., it happens that the receiver has no command of his own mind—as in cases of little children, persons swooned, fainted, deranged, or dead, then the faith of the administrator alone, or in connexion with other friends and agents, in his behalf, is sufficient, in many cases, to perform the work.

However, the touch, or laying on of hands, is not the only means of communicating the gift of healing. A word spoken, a mandate issued, or even a handkerchief, apron, or other garment, worn or touched by a person full of this Spirit, and conveyed to another, has, according to sacred history, and also the experience of the present age, proved sufficient to communicate the spiritual fluid, between minds of strong and mutual faith. So well acquainted was the Prophet Elisha with this principle, that he sent his servant to lay his staff upon a dead child, in order to raise it from the dead; but, in this instance, the undertaking failed. The Prophet could only resuscitate the child by placing face on face, eye to eye, mouth to mouth, hand to hand, &c., so as to give the greatest possible effect to the imparting of the spirit of life.

For the holy and divine fluid, or spiritual element, to control all other elements, agreeable to its own will, and the will of others, who are in communication or in perfect unison with itself, is just as natural as for the greater to control the less, or the strong the weak. It is upon the same principle that a higher intelligence is able to comprehend, circumscribe, and instruct that which is less.

Hence, when the worlds were framed, God spake, and this divine fluid went forth and executed the mandate, by controlling the elements, in accordance with the will, pattern, or design, formed in the mind of Him that spake, and it that executed. Wisdom pondered the pattern of all created things, weighed their properties, attributes and uses in the balance of mature intellect. Every minute portion and member of the several departments of life and being, every adaptation to their natural use, was clearly conceived, formed in the mind, and matured, ere the mandate was issued. And the whole was executed in exact accordance with the pattern matured in the Divine Mind.

By this divine Spirit all things were designed and formed. By this divine Substance all things live, move, and have a being. By this agency Moses controlled the sea; Joshua, the motions of the earth; Daniel, the mouths of the lions; and his brethren, the flames. By this, the heavens were opened, and were shut; the rain or the dearth prevailed; armies were subdued; the sick healed, or the dead raised; and all in accordance with the laws of nature, it being perfectly natural for the subordinate elements to obey the supreme, all controlling, all pervading element, which contains in itself the innate, and inalienable, controlling power.

The modern world, called "Christian" claims to have perpetuated the system called "Christianity," while, at the same time, it declares, that the miraculous gifts of the Spirit have ceased.

With as much propriety it might be contended, that the magnet had been perpetuated, but had lost its magnetic properties; that water was perpetuated with all its virtues, but had lost its power to quench thirst, or seek its own level; that fire was still fire, but had lost its heat.

How, we inquire, can Christianity have been perpetuated, while its virtues, its legitimate powers, its distinguishing features, its very life and essence have ceased from among men? Or, of what possible use is it if it does exist? Is a compass of use when its needle has lost its magnetic attraction? Is water of use when it no longer seeks its level, or quenches thirst? Is fire of use when it loses its heat? Is a sun dial of use in a dark and cloudy day; or, a watch without a mainspring?

Or, are the mere forms and ceremonies of any system of use, when the divine, or legitimate powers, for which such forms were instituted, are withdrawn?

O man! be no longer deceived by solemn mockeries of things sacred, or by great and holy names applied to corrupt and degenerate systems.

When the miracles and gifts of the divine Spirit ceased from among men, Christianity ceased, the Christian ministry ceased, the Church of Christ ceased.

That ministry which sets aside modern inspiration, revelation, prophecy, angels, visions, healings, &c., is not ordained of God; but is Anti-Christian in spirit. In short, it is that spirit of priestcraft and kingcraft, by which the world, for many ages, has been ruled as with a rod of iron.

The sooner the present generation lose all reverence and respect for modern "Christianity," with all its powerless forms and solemn mockeries, the sooner they will be prepared to receive the kingdom of God. The sooner the treasuries of nations, and the purses of individuals, are relieved from the support of priestcraft and superstitions, so much sooner will they be able and willing to devote their means and influence to print and publish the glad tidings of the fulness of the Gospel, restored in this age, to assist in the gathering of the house of Israel, and in the building of the cities and temples of Zion and Jerusalem.

Chapter Twelve - Angels and Spirits

Boast not your lightning wires to bear the news,
Such tardy means the Saints would never choose;
Too slow your fluid, and too short your wires
For heavenly converse, such as love inspires.
If man would fain commune with worlds above,
Angels transport the news on wings of love.

"Are they not all ministering spirits, sent forth to minister for them who shall be heirs of salvation?" - **Heb. i. 14.**

Angels are of the same race as men. They are, in fact, men who have passed from the rudimental state to the higher spheres of progressive being. They have died and risen again to life, and are consequently possessed of a divine, human body of flesh and bones, immortal and eternal. They eat, drink, sing and converse like other men. Some of them hold the keys of Apostleship and Priesthood, by which they teach, instruct, bless, and perform miracles and many mighty works. Translated men, like Enoch, Elijah, John the Apostle, and three of the Apostles of the Western Hemisphere, are also like the angels.

Angels are ministers, both to men upon the earth, and to the world of spirits. They pass from one world to another with more ease, and in less time than we pass from one city to another. They have not a single attribute which man has not. But their attributes are more matured, or more developed, than the attributes of men in this present sphere of existence.

Whenever the keys of Priesthood, or, in other words, the keys of the science of Theology, are enjoyed by man on the earth, the people thus privileged, are entitled to the ministering of angels, whose business with men on the earth, is to restore the keys of the Apostleship, when lost; to ordain men to the Apostleship, when there has been no Apostolic succession; to commit the keys of a new dispensation; to reveal the mysteries of history; the facts of present or past times; and to unfold the events of a future time. They are, sometimes, commissioned also to execute judgments upon individuals, cities or nations. They can be present in their glory, or, they can come in the form and appearance of other men. They can also be present without being visible to mortals.

When they come as other men, they will perhaps eat and drink, and wash their feet; and lodge with their friends. Hence, it is written—"Be not forgetful to entertain strangers: for thereby some have entertained angels unawares."

Their business is, also, to comfort and instruct individual members of the Church of the Saints; to heal them by the laying on of hands in the name of Jesus Christ, or to tell them what means to use in order to get well; to teach them good things, to sing them a good song, to warn them of approaching danger, or, to deliver them from prison, or from death.

These blessings have always been enjoyed by the people, or Church of the Saints, whenever such Church has existed on our planet. They are not peculiar to one dispensation more than another.

They were busy in the Patriarchal dispensation, in the Mosaic, and in the Gospel dispensations. They delivered Lot and destroyed Sodom.

They were busy with Moses and the Prophets. They foretold to Zechariah the birth of John. They predicted to Mary her conception, and the birth of Jesus Christ. They informed Joseph, her husband, of her situation. They announced the birth of Jesus to the shepherds of Judea, and sang an anthem of peace on earth and good will to man, to hail him welcome. They attended on his footsteps, in all his sojourn on the earth. In fact, an angel was the instrument to open the gloomy prison of the sepulchre, and to call forth the sleeping body of the Messiah, the first to exclaim, "He is not here, but is risen." Two angels in white raiment, were the first to announce his second advent, while he ascended up in the presence of his disciples. Thus, being delivered from the personal attendance on their Master on the earth, they turned their attention to the Apostles, opened the way for their ministry among Jew and

Gentile, delivering them from prison and from danger, and revealing the mysteries which God saw fit to make known to the Saints of that age. And when all the other Apostles had fallen asleep, and the Apostle John had been banished, to dig in the coal mines of the lone isle of Patmos, they still were faithful to their charge. They followed him there, and there unfolded to him the events of all ages and generations.

The darkness of the middle ages; the corruptions of Anti-Christ, under the name of Christianity; the rivers of blood, and the oceans of tears, which would flow during eighteen centuries of error; the mighty angel who should again commit the Gospel to the earth, for every nation, kindred, tongue, and people; the judgments of God, in the downfall of error and mystery; the restitution or restoration of the Church of the Saints; their final triumph and dominion over the earth; the descent of Jesus Christ to reign over all kingdoms; the resurrection of the Saints, and their reign over the earth; the end of death, and sorrow, and tears, and weeping; were all, all foretold by the angel to the last of the Twelve.

Again, in the present age, have angels restored the Gospel. Again have they committed the keys of Apostleship. Again have they opened some of the events of the past, present, and future.

Again have they attended upon the footsteps of Apostles, Prophets, and holy Martyrs, from the cradle to the grave. Again have they aided in the ministry, and assisted to deliver from prisons, and from persecutions and death, the Saints of the Most High. And again are they about to execute vengeance on great and notable cities and nations of the earth.

O what an unspeakable blessing is the ministry of angels to mortal man! What a pleasing thought, that many who minister to us, and watch over us, are our near kindred—our fathers who have died and risen again in former ages, and who watch over their descendants with all the parental care and solicitude which characterize affectionate fathers and mothers on the earth.

Thrice happy are they who have lawful claim on their guardianship, and whose conduct does not grieve them, and constrain them to depart from their precious charge.

SPIRITS are those who have departed this life, and have not yet been raised from the dead.

These are of two kinds, viz.—Good and evil.

These two kinds also include many grades of good and evil.

The good spirits, in the superlative sense of the word, are they who, in this life, partook of the Holy Priesthood, and of the fulness of the Gospel.

This class of spirits minister to the heirs of salvation, both in this world and in the world of spirits. They can appear unto men, when permitted; but not having a fleshly tabernacle, they cannot hide their glory. Hence, an unembodied spirit, if it be a holy personage, will be surrounded with a halo of resplendent glory, or brightness, above the brightness of the sun.

Whereas, spirits not worthy to be glorified will appear without this brilliant halo; and, although they often attempt to pass as angels of light, there is more or less of darkness about them.

Many spirits of the departed, who are unhappy, linger in lonely wretchedness about the earth, and in the air, and especially about their ancient homesteads, and the places rendered dear to them by the memory of former scenes. The more wicked of these are the kind spoken of in Scripture, as "foul spirits," "unclean spirits," spirits who afflict persons in the flesh, and engender various diseases in the human system. They will sometimes enter human bodies, and will distract them, throw them into fits, cast them into the water, into the fire, &c. They will trouble them with dreams, nightmare, hysterics, fever, &c. They will also deform them in body and in features, by convulsions, cramps, contortions, &c., and will sometimes compel them to utter blasphemies, horrible curses, and even words of other languages. If permitted, they will often cause death. Some of these spirits are adulterous, and suggest to the mind all manner of lasciviousness, all kinds of evil thoughts and temptations.

A person, on looking another in the eye, who is possessed of an evil spirit, will feel a shock—a nervous feeling, which will, as it were, make his hair stand on end; in short, a shock resembling that produced in a nervous system by the sight of a serpent.

Some of these foul spirits, when possessing a person, will cause a disagreeable smell about the person thus possessed, which will be plainly manifest to the senses of those about him, even though the person thus afflicted should be washed and change his clothes every few minutes.

There are, in fact, most awful instances of the spirit of lust, and of bawdy and abominable words and actions, inspired and uttered by persons possessed of such spirits, even though the persons were virtuous and modest so long as they possessed their own agency.

Some of these spirits cause deafness, others dumbness, &c.

We can suggest no remedy for these multiplied evils, to which poor human nature is subject, except a good life, while we are in possession of our faculties, prayers and fastings of good and holy men, and the ministry of those who have power given them to rebuke evil spirits, and cast out devils, in the name of Jesus Christ.

Among the diversified spirits abroad in the world here are many religious spirits, which are not of God, but which deceive those who have not the keys of Apostleship and Priesthood, or, in other words, the keys of the science of Theology to guide them. Some of these spirits are manifested in the camp-meetings of certain sects, and in nearly all the excitements and confusions in religious meetings falsely called "revivals." All the strange extacies, swoon-ings, screamings, shoutings, dancings, jumpings, and a thousand other ridicu-lous and unseemly manifestations, which neither edify nor instruct, are the fruits of these deceptive spirits.

We must, however, pity, rather than ridicule, or despise, the subjects or advocates of these deceptions. Many of them are honest, but they have no Apostles, nor other officers, nor gifts to detect evil, or to keep them from be-ing led by every delusive spirit.

Real visions, or inspirations which would edify and instruct, they are taught to deny. Should Peter or Paul, or an angel from heaven, come among them, they would denounce him as an impostor, with the assertion that Apostles and angels were no longer needed.

There is still another class of unholy spirits at work in the world—spirits diverse from all these, far more intelligent, and, if possible, still more dan-gerous. These are, the spirit of divination, vision, foretelling, familiar spirits, "Animal Magnetism," "Mesmerism," &c., which reveal many and great truths mixed with the greatest errors, and also display much intelligence, but have not the keys of the science of Theology—the Holy Priesthood.

These spirits, generally, deny the divinity of Christ, and the great truths of the atonement, and of the resurrection of the body. Of such are the Shakers of the United States, and their revelations. They deny the resurrection of the body. From this source are the revelations of Emmanuel Swedenborg, which also deny the resurrection. From this source, also, are the revelations of An-drew Jackson Davis, of Poughkeepsie, New York, which deny the resurrection and the atonement. From this source are all the revelations which deny the ordinances of the Gospel, and the keys and gifts of the Holy Apostleship.

Last of all, these are they who climb up in some other way, besides the door, into the sheepfold; and who prophesy or work in their own name, and not in the name of Jesus Christ.

No man can do a miracle in the name and by the authority of Jesus Christ, except he be a good man, and authorized by him.

Chapter Thirteen – Dreams

Mysterious power, whence hope ethereal springs!
Sweet heavenly relic of eternal things!
Inspiring oft deep thoughts of things divine:
The past, the present, and the future thine.
Thy reminiscences transport the soul
To memory's Paradise—its future goal.

"For God speaketh once, yea twice, yet man perceiveth it not. In a dream, in a vision of the night, when deep sleep falleth upon men, in slumberings upon the bed: then he openeth the ears of men, and sealeth their instruction." - **Job xxxiii. 14, 15, 16.**

In all ages and dispensations God has revealed many important instructions and warnings to men by means of dreams.

When the outward organs of thought and perception are released from their activity, the nerves unstrung, and the whole of mortal humanity lies hushed in quiet slumbers, in order to renew its strength and vigour, it is then that the spiritual organs are at liberty, in a certain degree, to assume their wonted functions, to recall some faint outlines, some confused and half defined recollections, of that heavenly world, and those endearing scenes of their former estate, from which they have descended in order to obtain and mature a tabernacle of flesh. Their kindred spirits, their guardian angels then hover about them with the fondest affection, the most anxious solicitude. Spirit communes with spirit, thought meets thought, soul blends with soul, in all the raptures of mutual, pure, and eternal love.

In this situation, the spiritual organs are susceptible of converse with Deity, or of communion with angels, and the spirits of just men made perfect.

In this situation, we frequently hold communication with our departed father, mother, brother, sister, son or daughter; or with the former husband or wife of our bosom, whose affection for us, being rooted and grounded in the eternal elements, or issuing from under the sanctuary of Love's eternal fountain, can never be lessened or diminished by death, distance of space, or length of years.

We may, perhaps, have had a friend of the other sex, whose pulse beat in unison with our own; whose every thought was big with the aspirations, the hopes of a bright future in union with our own; whose happiness in time or in eternity, would never be fully consummated without that union. Such a one, snatched from time in the very bloom of youth, lives in the other sphere, with the same bright hope, watching our every footstep, in our meanderings through the rugged path of life, with longing desires for our eternal happiness, and eager for our safe arrival in the same sphere.

With what tenderness of love, with what solicitude of affection will they watch over our slumbers, hang about our pillow, and seek, by means of the spiritual fluid, to communicate with our spirits, to warn us of dangers or temptation, to comfort and soothe our sorrow, or to ward off the ills which might befall us, or perchance to give us some kind token of remembrance or undying love!

It is the pure in heart, the lovers of truth and virtue, that will appreciate these remarks, for they know, by at least a small degree of experience, that these things are so.

Those who are habitually given to vice, immorality and abomination; those who walk in the daily indulgence of unlawful lust; those who neither believe in Jesus Christ, nor seek to pray to him, and keep his commandments; those who do not cultivate the pure, refined and holy joys of innocent and heavenly affection, but who would sacrifice every finer feeling at the shrine of lawless pleasure and brutal desires—those persons will not understand and appreciate these views, because their good angels, their kindred spirits have long since departed, and ceased to attend them, being grieved and disgusted with their conduct.

The Spirit of the Lord has also been grieved, and has left them to themselves, to struggle alone amid the dangers and sorrows of life; or to be the associates of demons and impure spirits. Such persons dream of adultery, gluttony, debauchery, and crimes of every kind. Such persons have the foreshadowings of a doleful death, and of darkness, and the buffetings of fiends and malicious spirits.

But, blessed are they who forfeit not their claims to the watchful care and protection of, and communion with, the heavenly powers, and pure and lovely spirits.

We can only advise the other classes of mankind, and entreat them, by the joys of love, by all the desires of life, by all the dread of death, darkness, and a dreary hereafter, yea, by the blood of Him who died, by the victory of him who rose in triumph from the grave, by their regard for those kindred spirits which would gladly love them in worlds without end, to turn from their sinful course of life, to obey the ordinances and commandments of Jesus Christ, that the Spirit of God may return to them, and their good angels and spirits again return to their sacred charge.

O what a comfort it is, in this dreary world, to be loved and cared for by all-powerful, warm-hearted, and lovely friends!

A Dream!

What have not dreams accomplished?

Dreams and their interpretation brought the beloved son of Jacob from his dungeon, made him prime minister of Egypt, and the saviour of a nation, and of his father's house.

Dreams, and the interpretation of dreams, raised a Daniel from slavery or degrading captivity in Babylon, to wear a royal chain of gold, and to teach royalty how to rule, whilst himself presided over the governors and presidents of more than a hundred provinces.

Dreams, and the interpretation of dreams, have opened the future, pointed out the course of empire through all the troublous times of successive ages, till Saints alone shall rule, and immortality alone endure.

Oh, what a doleful situation was Saul the king of Israel placed in, when the army of the Philistines stood in battle array against him, and the Lord answered him not, either by dream, by Prophet, by vision, or by Urim and Thummim!

He sought the unlawful gift of familiar spirits, or "Magnetism." He there learned his doom, and rushed to battle with the desperation of hopeless despair.

Himself, his sons, and the hosts of Israel, fell in battle in that awful day; while David, to whom these gifts had been transferred by the ordination and holy anointing of Samuel, arose by their use to the throne of Israel.

A dream announced to Joseph that his virgin wife should have a son. A dream forewarned him to flee into Egypt with the young child and his mother. A dream announced to him in Egypt the death of Herod, and warned him to return to his native land.

A dream warned the wise men from the east to return home another way, and not return to Herod to betray the young child.

Dreams and visions warned Paul, and the Apostles, and the Saints of his day, of various dangers, shipwrecks, persecutions and deaths, and pointed out the means of escape.

Dreams and visions attended and guided them, more or less, in their whole ministry and sojourn on the earth.

Chapter Fourteen - The World of Spirits

Ye worlds of light and life, beyond our sphere;
Mysterious country! let your light appear.
Ye angels, lift the vail, the truth unfold,
And give our Seers a glimpse of that bright world;
Tell where ye live, and what are your employ,
Your present blessing, and your future joy.
Say, have you learn'd the name, and tun'd the lyre,
And hymn'd the praise of him—the great Messiah?
Have love's emotions kindl'd in your breast,
And hope enraptur'd seiz'd the promis'd rest?
Or wait ye still the resurrection day,
That higher promise of Millennial sway?
When Saints and angels come to earth again,
And in the Mesh with King Messiah reign?
The spirits answer'd as they soar'd away—
"We're happy now, but wait a greater day,
When sin and death, and hell, shall conquer'd be,
And earth, with heaven, enjoy the victory."

The spirit of man consists of an organization, or embodiment of the elements of spiritual matter, in the likeness and after the pattern of the fleshly tabernacle. It possesses, in fact, all the organs and parts exactly corresponding to the outward tabernacle.

The entrance of this spirit into its embryo tabernacle of flesh, is called quickening. The infallible evidence of its presence is voluntary motion, which implies a degree of independent agency, or inherent will, which individual identity alone possesses.

When this spirit departs, the outward tabernacle is said to be dead, that is, the individual who quickened and imparted voluntary motion to the said tabernacle is no longer there. This individual, on departing from its earthly house, repasses the dark vale of forgetfulness, and awakes in the spirit world.

The spirit world is not the heaven where Jesus Christ, his Father, and other beings dwell, who have, by resurrection or translation, ascended to eternal mansions, and been crowned and seated on thrones of power; but it is an intermediate state, a probation, a place of preparation, improvement, instruction, or education, where spirits are chastened and improved, and where, if found worthy, they may be taught a knowledge of the Gospel. In short, it is a place where the Gospel is preached, and where faith, repentance, hope and charity may be exercised; a place of waiting for the resurrection or redemption of the body; while, to those who deserve it, it is a place of punishment, a purgatory or hell, where spirits are buffetted till the day of redemption.

As to its location, it is here on the very planet where we were born; or, in other words, the earth and other planets of a like sphere, have their inward or spiritual spheres, as well as their outward, or temporal. The one is peopled by temporal tabernacles, and the other by spirits. A vail is drawn between the one sphere and the other, whereby all the objects in the spiritual sphere are rendered invisible to those in the temporal.

To discern beings or things in the spirit world, a person in the flesh must be quickened by spiritual element, the vail must be withdrawn, or the organs of sight, or of hearing, must be transformed, so as to be adapted to the spiritual sphere. This state is called vision, trance, second sight, clairvoyance, &c.

The elements and beings in the spirit world are as real and tangible to spiritual organs, as things and beings of the temporal world are to beings of a temporal state.

In this spirit world there are all the varieties and grades of intellectual being, which exist in the present world. For instance, Jesus Christ and the thief on the cross, both went to the same place, and found themselves associated in the spirit world.

But the one was there in all the intelligence, happiness, benevolence, and charity, which characterized a teacher, a messenger, anointed to preach glad tidings to the meek, to bind up the broken-hearted, to comfort those who mourned, to preach deliverance to the captive, and open the prison to those who were bound; or, in other words, To preach the Gospel to the spirits in prison, that they might he judged according to men in the flesh; while the other was there as a thief, who had expired on the cross for crime, and who was guilty, ignorant, uncultivated, and unprepared for resurrection, having need of remission of sins, and to be instructed in the science of salvation.

The former bid farewell to the world of spirits on the third day, and returned to his tabernacle of flesh, in which he ascended to thrones, principalities, and powers, while the latter is, no doubt, improving in the spirit world, and waiting, believing, hoping for the redemption of the body.

In the world of spirits there are Apostles, Prophets, Elders, and members of the Church of the Saints, holding keys of Priesthood, and power to teach, comfort, instruct, and proclaim the Gospel to, their fellow-spirits, after the pattern of Jesus Christ.

In the same world there are also the spirits of Catholics, and Protestants of every sect, who have all need to be taught, and to come to the knowledge of the true, unchangeable Gospel, in its fulness and simplicity, that they may be judged the same as if they had been privileged with the same in the flesh.

There is also the Jew, the Mahometan, the infidel, who did not believe in Christ while in the flesh. All these must be taught, must come to the knowledge of the crucified and risen Redeemer, and hear the glad tidings of the Gospel.

There are also all the varieties of the heathen spirits; the noble and refined philosopher, poet, patriot, or statesman of Rome or Greece; the enlightened Socrates, Plato, and their like; together with every grade of spirits, down to the most uncultivated of the savage world.

All these must be taught, enlightened, and must bow the knee to the eternal king, for the decree hath gone forth, that unto him every knee shall bow and every tongue confess.

O what a field of labour, of benevolence, of missionary enterprise now opens to the Apostles and Elders of the Church of the Saints! As this field opens they will begin to realize more fully the extent of their divine mission, and the meaning of the great command to "Preach the Gospel to every creature."

In this vast field of labour, the Priesthood are, in a great measure, occupied, during their sojourn in the world of spirits while awaiting the resurrection of the body; and at the same time they themselves are edified, improved, and greatly advanced and matured in the science of divine Theology.

In the use of the keys of this science, by them administered, and in connexion with the ministration of certain ordinances, by the Priesthood in this mortal life, for, and in behalf of, those who are dead, the doors of the prisons of the spirit world are opened, and their gloomy dungeons made radiant with light. Hope then springs afresh. Joy and gladness swell the bosom accustomed to anguish, and smiles assume the place of tears, while songs of triumph, and the voice of melody and thanksgiving occupy the hearts, and flow from the lips, of those who have long dwelt in darkness, and in the region and shadow of death.

The times of sojourn of a spirit in the world of spirits, and also its privileges and degrees of enjoyment, or of suffering, while there, depend much on its preparations while in the flesh.

For instance, the people swept off by the flood of Noah, were imprisoned in the world of spirits, in a kind of hell; without justification, without Priesthood or Gospel, without the true knowledge of God, or a hope of resurrection, during those long ages which intervened between the flood and the death of Christ. It was only by the personal ministry of the spirit of Jesus Christ, during his sojourn in the spirit world, that they were at length privileged to hear the Gospel, and to act upon their own agency, the same as men in the flesh; whereas, if they had repented at the preaching of Noah, they might have been justified, and filled with the hope and knowledge of the resurrection while in the flesh.

When Jesus Christ had returned from his mission in the spirit world, had triumphed over the grave, and re-entered his fleshly tabernacle, then the Saints who had obeyed the Gospel while in the flesh, and had slept in death, or finished their sojourn in the spirit world, were called forth to re-enter their bodies, and to ascend with him to mansions and thrones of eternal power, while the residue of the spirits remained in the world of spirits to await another call.

Those who obeyed the Gospel on the earth, after this first resurrection, will also be called from their sojourn in the spirit world, and re-united with their tabernacles of flesh, at the sounding of the next trump, and will reign on the earth in the flesh, one thousand years, while those who rejected the Gospel will remain in the spirit world without a resurrection, till after the thousand years.

Again, those who obey the Gospel in the present age will rise from the spirit world, and from the grave, and reign on the earth during the great thousand years; while those who reject it will remain in condemnation in the spirit world, without a resurrection, till the last trump shall sound, and death and hell deliver up their dead.

Chapter Fifteen - Resurrection, Its Times and Degrees—First, Second and Third Heavens, Or the Telestial, Terrestrial and Celestial Kingdoms

The grave and death and hell no more retain
Their lawful captives. Earth yields its slain.
The raging ocean, from its lowly bed,
At Michael's call, delivers up its dead.
Then comes the judgment, and the final doom
Of man—his destiny beyond the tomb.

There are three general resurrections revealed to man on the earth; one of these is past, and the other two are future.

The first general resurrection took place in connexion with the resurrection of Jesus Christ. This included the Saints and Prophets of both hemispheres, from Adam down to John the Baptist; or, in other words, all those who died in Christ before his resurrection.

The second will take place in a few years from the present time, and will be immediately succeeded by the coming of Jesus Christ, in power and great glory, with all his Saints and Angels. This resurrection will include the Former and Latter-day Saints—all those who have received the Gospel since the former resurrection.

The third and last resurrection will take place more than a thousand years afterwards, and will embrace all the human family not included in the former resurrections or translations.

After man is raised from the dead he will be judged according to his works, and will receive the reward, and be consigned to the sphere, exactly corresponding to his former deeds, and the preparations or qualifications which he possesses.

In the former resurrection, those raised left the earth and ascended, or, were transplanted far on high, with the risen Jesus, to the glorified mansions of his Father, or to some planetary system already redeemed and glorified. The reasons for thus leaving the earth are obvious. Our planet was still in its rudimental state, and therefore subject to the rule of sin and death. It was necessary that it should continue thus, until the full time of redemption should arrive; it was, therefore, entirely unfitted for the residence of immortal man.

But in the resurrection which now approaches, and in connexion with the glorious coming of Jesus Christ, the earth will undergo a change in its physical features, climate, soil, productions; and in its political, moral, and spiritual government.

Its mountains will be levelled, its valleys exalted, its swamps and sickly places will be drained and become healthy, while its burning deserts, and its frigid polar regions, will be redeemed and become temperate and fruitful.

Kingcraft and priestcraft, tyranny, oppression and idolatry will be at an end, darkness and ignorance will pass away, war will cease, and the rule of sin, and sorrow, and death will give place to the reign of peace, and truth, and righteousness.

For this reason, and to fulfil certain promises made to the Fathers, the Former and Latter-day Saints included in the two resurrections, and all those translated, will then receive an inheritance on the earth, and will build upon and improve the same for a thousand years.

The heathen nations, also, will then be redeemed, and will be exalted to the privilege of serving the Saints of the Most High. They will be the ploughmen, the vine-dressers, the gardeners, builders, etc. But the Saints will be the owners of the soil, the proprietors of all real estate, and other precious things; and the kings, governors, and judges of the earth.

As the children of man multiply in those peaceful times, a careful and wise system of agriculture will be rapidly developed, and extended over the face of the whole earth; its entire surface will at length become like the garden of Eden, the trees of life being cultivated, and their fruits enjoyed.

Science, and the useful and ornamental arts, will also be greatly extended and cultivated. The fine toned instrument of many strings, the melodious organs of the human voice, will then be tuned to poetry and sentiments equally pure and refined, and will pour forth melodies and strains of holy joy, calculated to purify and melt every heart in love, and fill every soul with mutual sympathy and extasy of heavenly union.

Geographical knowledge, history, astronomy, mathematics and navigation, will be greatly extended and matured. Railroads and telegraphic lines of communication, will be universally extended, and the powers of steam, or other means of locomotion brought to the highest state of perfection.

Thus all nations will be associated in one great brotherhood. A universal Theocracy will cement the whole body politic. One king will rule. One holy city will compose the capitol. One temple will be the centre of worship. In short, there will be one Lord, one Faith, one Baptism, and one Spirit.

One equable, just and useful commercial interest, founded on the necessity and convenience of mutual exchange of products, will also form another important bond of union.

Mineralogy will also be greatly improved, and its knowledge extended. Its hidden treasures will be developed, and gold, silver and the most precious and beautiful stones will be the building materials in most common use, and will compose the utensils and furniture of the habitations of man.

The earth and man thus restored and exalted, will not yet be perfect in the celestial sense of the word, but will be considered, in the light of eternity, as occupying an intermediate and still progressive position amid the varieties of nature.

The flesh, bones, sinews, nerves—all the organs—all the particles of the celestial body, must be quickened, filled, surrounded with that divine and holy element, which is purer, more intelligent, more refined and active, fuller of light and life, than any other substance in the universe.

Every organ must be restored, and adapted to its natural and perfect use in the celestial body.

> *The Greek Philosopher's immortal mind,*
> *Again with flesh and bone and nerve combined;*
> *Immortal brain and heart—immortal whole,*
> *Will make, as at the first, a living soul.*

Man, thus adapted to all the enjoyments of life and love, will possess the means of gratifying his organs of sight, hearing, taste, &c., and will possess, improve and enjoy the riches of the eternal elements. The palace, the city, the garden, the vineyard, the fruits of the earth, the gold, the silver, the precious stones, the servants, the chariots, horses and horsemen are for his use; also thrones and dominions, principalities and powers, might, majesty, and an eternal increase of riches, honours, immortality and eternal life are his. He is, in a subordinate sense, a god; or, in other words, one of the sons of God. All things are his, and he is Christ's, and Christ is God's.

Such is the great Millennium.

And such is celestial man, in his progress towards perfection.

Besides the peculiar glory of the celestial, there are in the resurrection and final reward of man, many subordinate spheres, many degrees of reward adapted to an almost infinite variety of circumstances, conditions, degrees of improvement, knowledge, accountability and conduct.

The final state of man, though varying in almost infinite gradations and rewards, adapted to his qualifications and deserts, and meted out in the scale of exact justice and mercy, may be conceived or expressed under three grand heads, or principal spheres, viz.—

First. The Telestial, or least heaven, typified by the stars of the firmament.

Secondly. The Terrestrial, or intermediate heaven, typified by the moon.

Thirdly. The Celestial, or third heaven, of which the sun of the firmament is typical.

The qualifications which fit and prepare intelligences, for these different spheres or rewards, are an all important consideration, and well worthy of the sincere attention of all people.

These several kingdoms or degrees, and their comparative happiness, and what characters are candidates for each degree, are revealed in a most concise, clear, lucid and beautiful manner, in one of the visions of our great Prophet and founder. We will therefore complete this chapter by the insertion of said

"VISION.

"Hear, O ye heavens, and give ear, O earth, and rejoice, ye inhabitants thereof, for the Lord is God, and beside him there is no Saviour: great is His wisdom, marvellous are His ways, and the extent of His doings none can find out; His purposes fail not, neither are there any who can stay His hand; from eternity to eternity He is the same, and His years never fail.

"For thus saith the Lord, I, the Lord, am merciful and gracious unto those who fear me, and delight to honour those who serve me in righteousness and in truth unto the end. Great shall be their reward and eternal shall be their glory; and to them will I reveal all mysteries, yea, all the hidden mysteries of my kingdom from days of old, and for ages to come will I make known unto them the good pleasure of my will concerning all things pertaining to my kingdom; yea, even the wonders of eternity shall they know, and things to come will I show them, even the things of many generations; and their wisdom shall be great, and their understanding reach to heaven: and before them the wisdom of the wise shall perish, and the understanding of the prudent shall come to naught, for by my Spirit will I enlighten them, and by my power will I make known unto them the secrets of my will; yea, even those things which eye has not seen, nor ear heard, nor yet entered into the heart of man.

"We, Joseph Smith, jun., and Sidney Rigdon, being in the Spirit on the sixteenth of February, in the year of our Lord, one thousand eight hundred and thirty-two, by the power of the Spirit our eyes were opened and our understandings were enlightened, so as to see and understand the things of God—even those things which were from the beginning, before the world was, which were ordained of the Father, through His only begotten Son, who was in the bosom of the Father, even from the beginning, of whom we bear record, and the record which we bear is the fulness of the Gospel of Jesus Christ, who is the Son, whom we saw and with whom we conversed in the heavenly vision; for while we were doing the work of translation, which the Lord had appointed unto us, we came to the twenty-ninth verse of the fifth chapter of John, which was given unto us as follows. Speaking of the resurrection of the dead, concerning those who shall hear the voice of the Son of man, and shall come forth; they who have done good in the resurrection of the just, and they who have done evil in the resurrection of the unjust. Now this caused us to marvel, for it was given unto us of the Spirit; and while we meditated upon these things, the Lord touched the eyes of our understandings and they were opened, and the glory of the Lord shone round about; and we beheld the glory of the Son, on the right hand of the Father, and received of his fulness; and saw the holy angels, and they who are sanctified before His throne, worshipping God and the Lamb, who worship Him for ever and ever. And now, after the many testimonies which have been given of him, this is the testimony last of all, which we give of him, that he lives; for we saw him, even on the right hand of God, and we heard the voice bearing record that he is the only begotten of the Father—that by him and through him, and of him the worlds are and were created, and the inhabitants thereof are begotten sons and daughters unto God. And this we saw also, and bear record, that an angel of God who was in authority in the presence of God, who rebelled against the only begotten Son, whom the Father loved, and who was in the bosom of the Father, was thrust down from the presence of God and the Son, and was called Perdition, for the heavens wept over him—he was Lucifer, a son of the morning. And we beheld, and lo, he is fallen! is fallen! even a son of the morning. And while we were yet in the Spirit, the Lord commanded us that we should write the vision, for we beheld Satan, that old serpent—even the devil, who rebelled against God, and sought to take the kingdom of our God, and His Christ, wherefore he maketh war with the Saints of God, and encompasses them round about. And we saw a vision of the sufferings of those with whom he made war and overcame, for thus came the voice of the Lord unto us.

"Thus saith the Lord, concerning all those who know my power, and have been made partakers thereof, and suffered themselves, through the power of the devil, to be overcome, and to deny the truth and defy my power—they are they who are the sons of perdition, of whom I say that it had been better for them never to have been born, for they are vessels of wrath, doomed to suffer the wrath of God, with the devil and his angels in eternity; concerning whom I have said there is no forgiveness in this world nor in the world to come, having denied the Holy Spirit after having received it, and having denied the only begotten Son of the Father—having crucified him unto themselves, and put him to an open shame. These are they who shall go away into the lake of fire and brimstone, with the devil and his angels, and the only ones on whom the second death shall have any power; yea, verily, the only ones who shall not be redeemed in the due time of the Lord, after the sufferings of his wrath; for all the rest shall be brought forth by the resurrection of the dead, through the triumph and the glory of the Lamb, who was slain, who was in the bosom of the Father before the worlds were made. And this is the Gospel, the glad tidings which the voice out of the heavens bore record unto us, that he came into the world, even Jesus, to be crucified for the world, and to bear the sins of the world, and to sanctify the world, and to cleanse it from all unrighteousness; that through him all might be saved whom the Father had put into his power and made by him, who glorifies the Father, and saves all the works of his hands, except those sons of perdition, who deny the Son after the Father has revealed him; wherefore, he saves all except them; they shall go away into everlasting punishment, which is endless punishment, which is eternal punishment, to reign with the devil and his angels in eternity, where their worm dieth not, and the fire is not quenched, which is their torment; and the end thereof, neither the place thereof, nor their torment, no man knows, neither was it revealed, neither is, neither will be revealed unto man, except to them who are made partakers thereof: nevertheless I, the Lord, show it by vision unto many, but straightway shut it up again; wherefore the end, the width, the height, the depth, and the misery thereof, they understand not, neither any man except them who are ordained unto this condemnation. And we heard the voice, saying, Write the vision, for lo! this is the end of the vision of the sufferings of the ungodly!

"And again we bear record, for we saw and heard, and this is the testimony of the Gospel of Christ, concerning them who come forth in the resurrection of the just; they are they who received the testimony of Jesus, and believed on his name and were baptized after the manner of his burial, being buried in the water in his name, and this according to the commandment, which he has given, that by keeping the commandments they might be washed and cleansed from all their sins, and receive the Holy Spirit by the laying on of the hands of him who is ordained and sealed unto this power, and who overcome by faith, and are sealed by the Holy Spirit of promise, which the Father sheds forth upon all those who are just and true. They are they who are the Church of the first born. They are they into whose hands the Father has given all things. They are they who are priests and kings, who have received of His fulness, and of His glory, and are priests of the Most High, after the order of Melchisedek, which was after the order of Enoch, which was after the order of the only begotten Son; wherefore, as it is written, they are gods, even the sons of God; wherefore all things are theirs, whether life or death, or things present, or things to come, all are theirs and they are Christ's and Christ is God's; and they shall overcome all things; wherefore let no man glory in man, but rather let him glory in God, who shall subdue all enemies under His feet—these shall dwell in the presence of God and His Christ for ever and ever. These are they whom he shall bring with him, when he shall come in the clouds of heaven, to reign on the earth over his people. These are they who shall have part in the first resurrection. These are they who shall come forth in the resurrection of the just. These are they who are come unto Mount Zion, and unto the city of the living God, the heavenly place, the holiest of all. These are they who have come to an innumerable company of angels, to the general assembly and Church of Enoch, and of the first born. These are they whose names are written in heaven, where God and Christ are the judge of all. These are they who are just men made perfect through Jesus the mediator of the new covenant, who wrought out this perfect atonement through the shedding of his own blood. These are they whose bodies are celestial whose glory is that of the sun, even the glory of God, the highest of all, whose glory the sun of the firmament is written of as being typical.

"And again, we saw the terrestrial world, and behold and lo, these are they who are of the terrestrial, whose glory differs from that of the Church of the first-born, who have received the fulness of the Father, even as that of the moon differs from the sun in the firmament— behold, these are they who died without law, and also they who are the spirits of men kept in prison, whom the Son visited, and preached the Gospel unto, that they might be judged according to men in the flesh, who received not the testimony of Jesus in the flesh, but afterwards received it. These are they who are honourable men of the earth, who were blinded by the craftiness of men. These are they who receive of his glory, but not of his fulness. These are they who receive of the presence of the Son, but not of the fulness of the Father; wherefore, they are bodies terrestrial, and not bodies celestial, and differ in glory as the moon differs from the sun. These are they who are not valiant in the testimony of Jesus; wherefore they obtained not the crown over the kingdom of our God. And now this is the end of the vision which we saw of the terrestrial, that the Lord commanded us to write while we were yet in the Spirit.

"And again, we saw the glory of the telestial, which glory is that of the lesser, even as the glory of the stars differs from that of the moon in the firmament. These are they who received not the Gospel of Christ, neither the testimony of Jesus. These are they who deny not the Holy Spirit. These are they who are thrust down to hell. These are they who shall not be redeemed from the devil, until the last resurrection, until the Lord, even Christ the Lamb, shall have finished his work. These are they who receive not of his fulness in the eternal world, but of the Holy Spirit, through the ministration of the terrestrial; and the terrestrial through the ministration of the celestial; and also the telestial receive it of the administering of angels who are appointed to minister for them, or who are appointed to be ministering spirits for them, for they shall be heirs of salvation. And thus we saw in the heavenly vision, the glory of the telestial, which surpasses all understanding, and no man knows it except him to whom God has revealed it. And thus we saw the glory of the terrestrial, which excels in all things the glory of the telestial, even in glory, and in power, and in might, and in dominion. And thus we saw the glory of the celestial which excels in all things—where God, even the Father, reigns upon His throne for ever and ever; before whose throne all things bow in humble reverence and give Him glory for ever and ever. They who dwell in His presence are the Church of the first-born, and they see as they are seen, and know as they are known, having received of His fulness and of His grace; and He makes them equal in power, and in might, and in dominion. And the glory of the celestial is one, even as the glory of the sun is one. And the glory of the terrestrial is one, even as the glory of the moon is one. And the glory of the telestial is one, even as the glory of the stars is one, for as one star differs from another star in glory, even so differs one from another in glory in the telestial world; for these are they who are of Paul, and of Apollos, and of Cephas. These are they who say they are some of one and some of another—some of Christ, and some of John, and some of Moses, and some of Elias, and some of Esaias, and some of Isaiah, and some of Enoch; but received not the Gospel, neither the testimony of Jesus, neither the Prophets, neither the Everlasting Covenant. Last of all, these all are they who will not be gathered with the Saints, to be caught up unto the Church of the firstborn, and received into the cloud. These are they who are liars, and sorcerers, and adulterers, and whoremongers, and whosoever loves and makes a lie. These are they who suffer the wrath of God on the earth. These are they who suffer the vengeance of eternal fire. These are they who are cast down to hell and suffer the wrath of Almighty God, until the fulness of times when Christ shall have subdued all enemies under his feet, and shall have perfected his work, when he shall deliver up the Kingdom, and present it unto the Father spotless, saying—I have overcome and have trodden the wine-press alone, even the wine-press of the fierceness of the wrath of Almighty God. Then shall he be crowned with the crown of His glory, to sit on the throne of his power to reign for ever and ever. But behold, and lo, we saw the glory and the inhabitants of the telestial world, that they were as innumerable as the stars in the firmament of heaven, or as the sand upon the sea shore, and heard the voice of the Lord saying—these all shall bow the knee, and every tongue shall confess to him who sits upon the throne for ever and ever; for they shall be judged according to their works, and every man shall receive according to his own works, his own dominion, in the mansions which are prepared, and they shall be servants of the Most High, but where God and Christ dwell they cannot come, worlds without end. This is the end of the vision which we saw, which we were commanded to write while we were yet in the Spirit.

"But great and marvellous are the works of the Lord, and the mysteries of His kingdom which He showed unto us, which surpasses all understanding in glory, and in might, and in dominion, which He commanded us we should not write while we were yet in the Spirit, and are not lawful for man to utter; neither is man capable to make them known, for they are only to be seen and understood by the power of the Holy Spirit, which God bestows on those who love Him, and purify themselves before Him; to whom He grants this privilege of seeing and knowing for themselves; that through the power and manifestation of the Spirit, while in the flesh, they may be able to bear His presence in the world of glory. And to God and the Lamb be glory, and honour, and dominion for ever and ever. Amen."

Chapter Sixteen - Further Remarks on Man's Physical and Intellectual Progress

PHILOSOPHY OF WILL, AS ORIGINATING, DIRECTING, AND CONTROLLING ALL VOLUNTARY ANIMAL MOTION—ASTOUNDING FACTS IN RELATION TO THE SPEED, OR VELOCITY OF MOTION, AS ATTAINABLE BY PHYSICAL MAN—INTERCOMMUNICATION OF THE INHABITANTS OF DIFFERENT AND DISTANT PLANETS.

Wide, and more wide, the kindling bosom swells,
As love inspires, and truth its wonders tells.
The soul enraptured tunes the sacred lyre.
And bids a worm of earth to heaven aspire,
Mid solar systems numberless, to soar,
The depths of love and science to explore.

As I have before remarked, man is a candidate for a series of progressive changes, all tending to develop his intellectual and physical faculties, to expand his mind, and to enlarge his sphere of action, and consequent usefulness and happiness.

He begins his physical, or rudimental, fleshly career by descending below all things. He has at his birth less power of locomotion, or even instinct, than other animals.

His powers of motion are so very limited, that for several months he is entirely unable to change his locality. Wherever he is placed, there he must remain until removed by the agency of others. He can hardly be said to have a will, or, at least, it is so undeveloped, as scarcely to manifest itself by any effort beyond the movement of some portion of his members. While he remains in this state of mental inability and physical helplessness, a casual observer, entirely unacquainted with his progress and destiny, might very naturally conclude that this was the climax of his maturity, the natural sphere of his eternal existence.

A few months, however, develop a marked change—he begins to learn the use, and put forth the powers of his will. The body, developed in a commensurate degree, is able to obey that will. Thus commences locomotion. The child crawls or creeps about the floor; explores the little world—that is to say, the room where he resides, or the adjoining apartment—becomes familiar with its dimensions, bearings and contents, and recognizes his associates or fellow citizens of the same little world. Then he becomes familiar with the science of geography and of history, if I may so call it, in his little world.

Prompted by curiosity, he may, perhaps, cast an occasional glance beyond the limits of his own abode. He may contemplate a building or landscape on the other side of the street or field, but with much of the same feeling as a man, more matured, casts his eyes to the distant planets. He concludes that these distant objects are entirely beyond the reach of his powers of locomotion.

In a short time, however, his faculties, still expanding, develop new and increasing energies. He conceives "big thoughts." He even thinks of dispensing with his plodding, creeping manner of locomotion, and of trying to stand upright, and even make a first step towards walking. It is a great undertaking. He hesitates, doubts, fears, hopes, till finally, being cheered onward in his career by his parents or his nurse, he makes the attempt. After several falls, failures, and disappointments, he at length succeeds in walking two or three steps. O what a triumph in his powers of locomotion! He is cheered, embraced, overwhelmed, by those who have been watching his progress and encouraging him, until, overcome and carried away by an extasy of transport, he falls, blushing, smiling and exulting into the arms held out for his reception. He dreams not of a higher attainment. He is now, in his own estimation, at the very highest pinnacle of human development.

Improving in his new mode of locomotion, he soon runs about the yard, along the street, through the field, makes new discoveries, sees new habitations, enlarges his geographical knowledge, and begins to conceive the probability that his views have been too narrow, and that there may be a bigger world, more people, and more buildings than were dreamed of in his philosophy.

In a few years he may become familiar with the geography and history of the island or continent on which he lives. He may even begin to aspire after the knowledge of other climes, and to conceive or conjecture that beyond the limits of the almost infinite expanse of waters, things and beings may exist after the similitude of his own sphere. He longs to overcome the physical barriers, which confine him in so limited a sphere, and thus enlarge his acquaintance, his social feelings, his friendship, his affections and his scientific knowledge.

So boundless and varied is the field, so complicated are the obstacles to be surmounted, so vast the preparations, improvements and inventions to be brought into requisition, that, after ages and generations have exhausted their energies, much is still left to be done—much which can only be done by the progress and extension of those modern triumphs of art, by which the elements—the fire, the wind, the water, the lightning, submit to the control of man, and become his chariot, his bearer of despatches. By these means the globe we occupy will soon be explored, the limits, boundaries and resources of every dark corner be clearly defined and understood.

Man already moves over the surface of the earth at the rate of fifty, sixty, and even ninety miles per hour, and still he aspires. He contemplates making the air his chariot, and wafting himself through the open firmament at the rate of, perhaps, a thousand miles per hour. Suppose he attains to this, what then? Will the great, the infinite principle within him be satisfied? No. He lifts his eyes to the contemplation of those myriads of shining orbs on high. He knows by actual admeasurement that some of them are much larger than the planet he occupies. He also knows by analogy that eternal riches are there; that a boundless store of element and resources is there; that they are treasured there for the use, comfort, convenience, and enjoyment, of intellectual and physical beings—beings, for aught he knows, of his own species, and connected with him by kindred ties, or by the law of universal sympathy and affection. He has reason to believe that there is gold and silver, that there are precious stones, and houses, and cities, and gardens. That there are walks of pleasure, and fountains, forests, brooks, and rivers of delight; that there are bosoms fraught with life and joy, and swelling with all the tender sensibilities of a pure, holy and never-ending affection.

Why, then, should his aspirations not reach forth, his mind expand, his bosom swell with love, and his heart beat with the boundless, fathomless infinitude of thought, of feeling, and of love? Why not be noble and boundless in charity, like the God whom he calls his father? Why does he not rise from his groveling sphere in this small island, which floats in the ocean of space, as a small black speck, amid the numberless shining orbs? The reason is obvious; it is not for the want of noble aspirations; it is not for the want of grand conceptions; it is not for the lack of will. It is because the body is chained, imprisoned, confined here, by the operation or attraction of surrounding elements, which man has not yet discovered the means to control. It may be said that the powers of earth enslave him, and chain him down, beyond the possibility or hope of escape.

Reader, in order to illustrate this subject try an experiment on your own physical and mental powers. For instance; will your arm to move, and it will instantly obey you. Will your body to go three miles, and it will obey you as fast as it can; perhaps in one hour it will have accomplished the journey assigned to it by your will.

But tie your hand behind you, and then will it to move up and down, forward and backward, and it will make the effort to obey you, but cannot, because it is confined. Chain your body in a dungeon, bolt and bar the door, and will it to go to a certain place, and it will not obey you, because it is physically incapable.

Unchain this body, provide the means of conveyance at the rate of a mile per minute, the body, at the bidding of the will, will then go the three miles in three minutes.

Now, if it were possible to overcome the resisting elements, so as to increase the speed of conveyance for your body—that is, if there were no resisting element to be overcome, your will might dictate, and your body would move through actual space with the speed of light, or electricity. There is no apparent limit to the speed attainable by the body when unchained, set free from the elements which now enslave it, and dictated by the will.

> "The lightning on its wiry way would lag behind.
> The sun-ray drag its slow length along."

This immense velocity of locomotion, as applied to a body of flesh and bones, or of material elements, may at first thought, strike the mind as being contrary to the known laws of physical motion.

But let it be recollected that the vast earth on which we dwell, with all its weight and bulk, its cities, animals and intelligences, moves through actual space, at the astonishing velocity of eighteen miles per second, one thousand and eighty miles per minute, or sixty-four thousand eight hundred miles per hour.

If so vast a bulk of gross, and in a great measure inanimate matter, can move through space, at a rate of speed so inconceivably great, how easily we can conceive the probability of vastly increased powers of locomotion on the part of animate bodies released from their earthly prison, quickened by superior and celestial element, dictated by an independent, inherent principle called the will, and urged onward by the promptings of the eternal, infinite mind and affections, in their aspirations for knowledge and enjoyment.

A corporeal, human body, raised from the dead, and quickened by elements so refined, so full of life and motion, so pure, and so free from the influences control, or attractions of more gross elements, will, like the risen Jesus, ascend and descend at will, and with a speed nearly instantaneous.

Let us pause, and contemplate, for a moment, such a being taking leave of the confines of the earth, and sea, and clouds, and air, with all their dark and gloomy shadows. Behold him as he speeds his way on the upper deep, and launches forth in the clear and boundless expanse bespangled with millions of resplendent orbs.

He calculates his distance, and regulates his course by observing the relative position of those most familiar to him, and soaring upwards still, his bosom swells with an unutterable and overwhelming sensation of the infinitude of his own eternal being, and of all around, above, below him, till unable to contain his gratitude, and joy, and exultation, he breaks forth in the language of a celebrated British poet, and sings as he flies—

> "Heavens broad day hath o'er me broken,
> Far above earth's span of sky!
> Am I dead? Nay, by this token,
> Know that I have ceased to die!"

Planets will be visited, messages communicated, acquaintances and friendships formed, and the sciences vastly extended and cultivated.

The science of geography will then be extended to millions of worlds, and will embrace a knowledge of their physical features and boundaries, their resources, mineral and vegetable; their rivers, lakes, seas, continents and islands; the attainments of their inhabitants in the science of government; their progress in revealed religion; their employments, dress, manners, customs, &c. The science of astronomy will also be enlarged in proportion to the means of knowledge. System after system will rise to view in the vast field of research and exploration! Vast systems of suns and their attendant worlds, on which the eyes of Adam's race, in their rudimental sphere, have never gazed, will then be contemplated, circumscribed, weighed in the balance of human thought, their circumference and diameter be ascertained, their relative distances understood. Their motions and revolutions, their times and laws, their hours, days, weeks, sabbaths, months, years, jubilees, centuries, millenniums and eternities, will all be told in the volumes of science.

The science of history will embrace the vast "univercoelum" of the past and present. It will in its vast compilations, embrace and include all nations, all ages, and all generations; all the planetary systems in all their varied progress and changes, in all their productions and attributes.

It will trace our race in all its successive emigrations, colonies, states, kingdoms and empires; from their first existence on the great, central, governing planet, or sun, called Kolob, until they are increased without number, and widely dispersed and transplanted from one planet to another, until, occupying the very confines of infinitude, the mind of immortal, eternal man, is absorbed, overwhelmed, wearied with the vastness, the boundless expanse of historic fact, and compelled to return and retire within itself for refreshment, rest and renewed vigour.

Next in order, will be the field of prophetic science. The spirit of prophecy will be poured upon the immortal mind, till, from seeing in part, and knowing in part, man will be able to gaze upon a boundless prospective, a future of still increasing glory, knowledge, light, love, might, majesty, power and dominion, in which the sons of God-the kings and priests of heaven and earth, and of the heaven of heavens, and all their retinue of kingdoms and subjects, will find ample room for boundless increase and improvement, worlds without end. Amen.

Chapter Seventeen - Laws of Marriage and Procreation

Ye kindred spirits, filled with mutual love,
Pure as the dews descending from above,
All hail! for you the sacred Keys are given,
To make you one on earth, and one in heaven.
Be fruitful then, and let your race extend;
Fill Earth, the stars, and worlds that never end.

The great science of life consists in the knowledge of ourselves, the laws of our existence, the relations we sustain to each other, to things and beings around us, to our ancestry, to our posterity, to time, to eternity, to our heavenly Father, and to the universe.

To understand these laws, and regulate our actions by them, is the whole duty of intelligences. It should therefore comprise our whole study.

This science comprises the fountain of wisdom, the well-springs of life, the boundless ocean of knowledge, the infinitude of light, and truth, and love. It penetrates the depths, soars to the heights, and circumscribes the broad expanse of eternity.

Its pursuit leads to exaltation, glory, immortality, and to an eternity of life, light, purity, and unity of fellowship with kindred spirits.

To contemplate man in his true light, we must, as it were, forget that death is in his path; we must look upon him as an eternal, ever living being, possessing spirit, flesh and bones, with all the mental and physical organs, and all the affections and sympathies which characterise him in this world. Or rather, all his natural affections and sympathies will be purified, exalted, and immeasurably increased.

Let the candidate for celestial glory forget, for a moment, the groveling sphere of his present existence, and make the effort to contemplate himself in the light of eternity, in the higher spheres of his progressive existence, beyond the grave—a pure spirit, free from sin and guile, enlightened in the school of heaven, by observation and experience, and association with the highest order of intelligences, for thousands of years; and clothed with immortal flesh, in all the vigour, freshness and beauty of eternal youth; alike free from pain, disease, death, and the corroding effects of time; looking back through the vista of far distant years, and contemplating his former sojourn amid the sorrows and pains of mortal life, his passage through the dark valley of death, and his sojourn in the spirit world, as we now contemplate a transient dream, or a night of sleep, from which we have awakened, renewed and refreshed, to enter again upon the realities of life.

Let us contemplate, for a moment, such a being, clothed in the finest robes of linen, pure and white, adorned with precious stones and gold; a countenance radiant with the effulgence of light, intelligence and love; a bosom glowing with all the confidence of conscious innocence dwelling in palaces of precious stones and gold; bathing in the crystal waters of life; promenading or sitting 'neath the evergreen bowers and trees of Eden; inhaling the healthful breezes, perfumed with odours, wafted from the roses and pinks of paradise, or assembled with the countless myriads of heaven's nobility, to join in songs of praise and adoration to the Great Parent of every good, to tune the immortal lyre in strains celestial; or move with grace immortal to the soul-inspiring measure of music flowing from a thousand instruments, blending, in harmonious numbers, with celestial voices, in heavenly song, or mingling in graceful circles with joyous thousands, immersed in the same spirit, and moving in unison and harmony of motion, as if one heart, one pulse, one thrill of heavenly melody inspired the whole.

O candidates for celestial glory! Would your joys be full in the countless years of eternity without forming the connexions, the relationship, the kindred ties which concentrate in the domestic circle, and branch forth, and bud and blossom, and bear the fruits of eternal increase?

Would that eternal emotion of charity and benevolence which swells your bosoms be satisfied to enjoy in, "single blessedness," without an increase of

215

posterity, those exhaustless stores of never-ending riches and enjoyments? Or, would you, like your heavenly Father, prompted by eternal benevolence and charity, wish to fill countless millions of worlds, with your begotten sons and daughters, and to bring them through all the gradations of progressive being, to inherit immortal bodies, and eternal mansions in your several dominions?

If such be your aspirations, remember that this present probation is the world of preparation for joys eternal. This is the place where family organization is first formed for eternity; and where the kindred sympathies, relationships, and affections take root, spring forth, shoot upward, bud, blossom, and bear fruit to ripen and mature in eternal ages.

Here, in the holy temples and sanctuaries of our God, must the everlasting covenants be revealed, ratified, sealed, bound and recorded in the holy records, and guarded and preserved in the archives of God's kingdom, by those who hold the keys of eternal Apostleship, who have power to bind on earth that which shall be bound in heaven, and to record on earth that which shall be recorded in the archives of heaven, in the Lamb's book of life.

Here, in the holy sanctuary, must be revealed, ordained and anointed the kings and queens of eternity.

All vows, covenants, contracts, marriages, of unions, not formed by revelation, and sealed for time and all eternity, and recorded in the holy archives of earth and heaven, by the ministration of the holy and eternal Priesthood, will be dissolved by death, and will not be recognised by the eternal authorities, after the parties have entered through the vail into the eternal world.

This is heaven's eternal law, as revealed to the ancients of all ages, who held the keys of eternal priesthood, after the order of the Son of God; and, as restored with the priesthood of the Saints of this age.

Again, it was a law of the ancient Priesthood, and is again restored, that a man who is faithful in all things, may, by the word of the Lord, through the administration of one holding the keys to bind on earth and heaven, receive and secure to himself, for time and all eternity, MORE THAN ONE WIFE.

Thus did Abraham, Isaac, Jacob, Moses, the Patriarchs and Prophets of old.

The principal object contemplated by this law, is the multiplication of the children of good and worthy fathers, who will teach them the truth, and train them in the holy principles of salvation. This is far preferable to sending them into the world in the lineage of an unworthy or ignorant parentage, to be educated in error, folly, ignorance and crime.

The peculiar characteristics of the blessings included in the Everlasting Covenant made with Abraham, Isaac, Jacob and their lineage, was the multiplicity of their seed; and the perpetuity of the royal, priestly and kingly power in their lineage.

To assist in carrying out and fulfilling this covenant, good and virtuous women were given to their faithful Prophets, rulers, and wise and virtuous men; and, as it was said of the four wives of Jacob, "These did build the house of Israel."

While peculiar blessings and encouragements were given to a good and faithful man, and to his wives and children; while they were honoured of God, and respected by all who knew them; while the father of a hundred children was had in greater honour than the hero of a hundred battles, adultery, fornication, and all unlawful intercourse was strictly prohibited, and even punished by the strictest laws—the penalty of which was death.

A daughter of Israel, who, by prostitution, was rendered unworthy, or unqualified for the duties of a virtuous wife and mother, was considered unfit to live. While the male who would thus trifle with the fountain of life, and contribute to render a female unworthy to answer the end of her creation, was also condemned to death.

Strict laws were also given and diligently taught to both sexes, regulating the intercourse between husband and wife. All intercourse peculiar to the sexes was strictly prohibited at certain seasons which were untimely. Nor were the bonds of wedlock and shield from condemnation, where the parties, by untimely union, excess, or voluntary act, prevented propagation, or injured the life or health of themselves or their offspring.

The object of the union of the sexes is the propagation of their species, or procreation; also for mutual affection, and the cultivation of those eternal principles of never-ending charity and benevolence, which are inspired by the Eternal Spirit; also for mutual comfort and assistance in this world of toil and sorrow, and for mutual duties towards their offspring.

Marriage, and its duties, are therefore, not a mere matter of choice, or of convenience, or of pleasure to the parties; but to marry and multiply is a positive command of Almighty God, binding on all persons of both sexes, who are circumstanced and conditioned to fulfil the same. To marry, propagate our species, do our duty to them, and to educate them in the light of truth, are among the chief objects of our existence on the earth. To neglect these duties, is to fail to answer the end of our creation, and is a a very great sin.

While to pervert our natures, and to prostitute ourselves, and our strength to mere pleasures, or to unlawful communion of the sexes, is alike subversive of health, of pure, holy and lasting affection; of moral and social order; and of the laws of God and nature.

If we except murder, there is scarcely a more damning sin on the earth than the prostitution of female virtue or chastity at the shrine of pleasure, or brutal lust; or that promiscuous and lawless intercourse which chills and corrodes the heart, perverts and destroys the pure affections, cankers and destroys, as it were, the well-springs, the fountains, or issues of life.

A man who obeys the ordinances of God, and is without blemish or deformity, who has sound health and mature age, and enjoys liberty and access to the elements of life; is designed to be the head of a woman, a father, and a guide of the weaker sex, and of those of tender age, to mansions of eternal life and salvation.

A woman, under similar circumstances, is designed to be the glory of some man in the Lord; to be led and governed by him, as her head in all things, even as Christ is the head of the man; to honour, obey, love, serve, comfort and help him in all things; to be a happy wife, and if blessed with offspring, a faithful and affectionate mother, devoting her life to the joys, cares and duties of her domestic sphere.

It frequently happens, in the course of human events, that there is, in a community, a majority of females. In such cases, human laws have no right to interfere with the divine eternal laws of nature, or of nature's God, by suffering females to be prostituted to minister to the wanton pleasures of the lawless, to become the unlawful, dishonoured mistress, the illegitimate mother, or the wretched outcast of shame, disease and crime. Nor yet, on the other hand, have human laws the right to doom a portion of heaven's fair daughters, to single wretchedness, loneliness and gloom, without the lawful privilege of becoming honoured wives and mothers.

A wise legislation, or the law of God, would punish, with just severity, the crimes of adultery or fornication, and would not suffer the idiot, the confirmed, irreclaimable drunkard, the man of hereditary disease, or of vicious habits, to possess or retain a wife; while, at the same time, it would provide for a good and capable man, to honourably receive and maintain more wives than one. Indeed, it should be the privilege of every virtuous female, who has the requisite capacity and qualifications for matrimony; to demand either of individuals or government, the privilege of becoming an honoured and legal wife and mother; even if it were necessary for her to be married to a man who has several wives; or, as Jesus said in the parable, to take the one talent from the place where it remains neglected or unimproved, and give it to him who has ten talents.

The false and corrupt institutions, and still more corrupt practices of "Christendom" have had a downward tendency in the generations of man for many centuries. Our physical organization, health, vigour, strength of body, intellectual faculties, inclinations, &c., are influenced very much by parentage. Hereditary disease, idiocy, weakness of mind, or of constitution, deformity, tendency to violent and ungovernable passions, vicious appetites and desires, are engendered by parents; and are bequeathed as a heritage from generation to generation. Man becomes a murderer, a thief, an adulterer, a drunkard, a lover of tobacco, opium, or other nauseous or poisonous drugs, by means of the predisposition, and inclinations engendered by parentage.

The people before the flood, and also the Sodomites and Canaanites, had carried these corruptions and degeneracies so far, that God, in mercy, destroyed them, and thus put an end to the procreation of races so degenerate and abominable; while Noah, Abraham, Melchesidech, and others, who were taught in the true laws of procreation, "were perfect in their generation," and trained their children in the same laws.

The overthrow of those ancient degenerate races is a type of that which now awaits the nations called "Christian," or in other words, The great whore of all the earth, for her sins have reached unto heaven, and God hath remembered her iniquities.

Where is the nation called "Christian," that does not uphold or permit prostitution, fornication and adultery with all their debasing, demoralizing, degenerating and corroding effects, with all their tendencies to disease and crime, to operate unchecked, and to leaven and corrode all classes of society?

Where is the "Christian nation" that does not prohibit the law of God, as given to Abraham and the ancients in relation to marriage?

Where is the "Christian nation" that punishes the crime of adultery and fornication with death, or other heavy penalties?

Where are the institutions which prohibit the marriage of all persons disqualified by nature, or by vicious habits and practices, to answer the ends of an institution so holy and pure?

Where are the institutions which would protect, encourage, and honour the patriarch Jacob, with his four wives and their children?

Where is the community who would feel themselves honoured in associating with such a family—although, all corrupt practices would be frowned down, and all persons discountenanced, who, under the name of gentility, nobility, or royalty, glory in their conquests and victories over the principles and practices of virtue and innocence?

Echo answers, Where?—unless we look to the far off mountains and distant vales of Deseret, a land peopled by the Latter-day Saints, and governed by the law of God, the keys of the eternal Priesthood, and organized in the New and Everlasting Covenant.

Amid these eternal mountains shall be reared the holy temple of our God, and all nations shall flow unto it, in order to be taught in His ways, and to walk in His paths, for out of Zion has gone forth the law, as predicted by the Prophet Isaiah. [A]

By this law those distant communities live. There the patriarch of a hundred children is had in reverence and honour. His virtuous and honourable wives are considered as mothers in Israel, the daughters of Abraham and Sarah, and worthy to be numbered with the holy women of old. And there the daughters of Israel are not prostituted with impunity. There, the crimes of adultery and fornication are seldom mentioned, or known to exist. There, no virtuous female is doomed by law, or custom, to drag out a useless life in the loneliness of the cloister; the monotonous and sinful pleasures of the Harem; the haunts of vice and crime; or in the lonely and heartrending gloom and solitude of a single life.

There, in the holy chambers of the sanctuary, are revealed and ministered those sacred ordinances, covenants, and sealings, which lay the foundation of kindred sympathies, associations, and family ties, indissoluble and eternal. Ties which are stronger than death, more durable than the ramparts of their snow-clad mountains, and which will never be dissolved—

"While life, or thought, or being lasts;
Or immortality endures."

The restoration of these pure laws and practices has commenced to improve or regenerate a race. A holy and temperate life; pure morals and manners; faith, hope, charity; cheerfulness, gentleness, integrity; intellectual development, pure truth, and knowledge; and above all, the operations of the Divine Spirit, will produce a race more beautiful in form and features, stronger, and more vigorous in constitution, happier in temperament and disposition, more intellectual, less vicious, and better prepared for long life and good days in their mortal sojourn.

Each succeeding generation, governed by the same principles, will still improve, till male and female may live and multiply for a hundred years upon the earth—-

"And after death in distant spheres,
The union still renew."

The eternal union of the sexes, in and after the resurrection, is mainly for the purpose of renewing and continuing the work of procreation. In our present or rudimental state, our offspring are in our own image, and partake of our natures, in which are the seeds of death. In like manner, will the offspring of immortal and celestial beings, be in the likeness and partake of the nature of their divine parentage. Hence, such offspring will be pure, holy, incorruptible and eternal. They will in no wise be subject unto death, except by descending to partake of the grosser elements, in which are the inherent properties of dissolution or death.

To descend thus, and to be made subject to sorrow, pain and death, is the only road to the resurrection, and to the higher degrees of immortality and eternal life. It is by contrast that intelligences appreciate and enjoy. How shall the sweet be known without the bitter? How shall joy be appreciated without sorrow? Or, how shall life be valued, or its eternal duration appreciated without a contact with its mortal antagonist—death?

Hence, the highest degrees of eternal felicity are approached by the straight gate, and the narrow path which leads through the dark valley of death, to eternal mansions in the realms of endless life. This path has been trodden by the eternal Father, by His son Jesus Christ,—and by all the sons and daughters of God, who are exalted to a fulness of joys celestial.

As has been before remarked, the union of the sexes, in the eternal world, in the holy covenant of celestial matrimony, is peculiar to the ordinances and ministrations of the Apostleship, or Priesthood after the order of the Son of God, or after the order of Melchisedec. The Aaronic Priesthood, or the institutions peculiar to the law of Moses, seemed to have recognized no such ordinances or eternal covenants, hence, the Jewish ordinances of matrimony come to end by death.

Nor did the sects of the Pharisees, Sadducees, or others of that nation, conceive of anything more lasting than this life, in the covenants of matrimony. Hence, the Son of God, in answer to the Sadducees, referred to the order of the angels, in the resurrection, instead of the order of the gods.

But, the Apostles, holding the keys of the eternal mysteries of God's kingdom, to seal both on earth and in heaven, understood and testified, that, "The man is not without the woman, nor the woman without the man in the Lord."

All persons who attain to the resurrection, and to salvation, without these eternal ordinances, or sealing covenants, will remain in a single state, in their saved condition, to all eternity, without the joys of eternal union with the other sex, and consequently without a crown, without a kingdom, without the power to increase.

Hence, they are angels, and are not gods; and are ministering spirits, or servants, in the employ and under the direction of THE ROYAL FAMILY OF HEAVEN—THE PRINCES, KINGS, AND PRIESTS OF ETERNITY.

[**Note A:** *See the law of God on Marriage, revealed for the government of the Saints. First published at Great Salt City, Deseret, 1852.]*